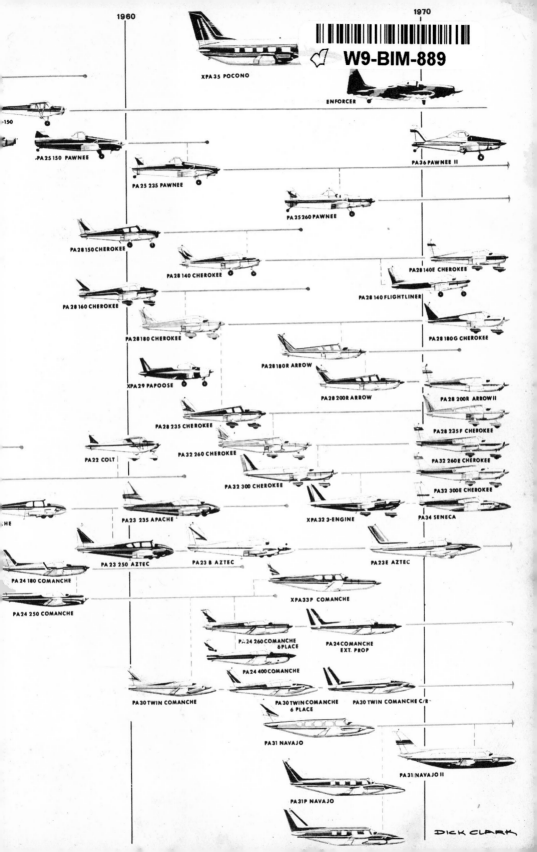

1960 1970

XPA 35 POCONO

W9-BIM-889

ENFORCER

-150

XPA 25 150 PAWNEE

PA 36 PAWNEE II

PA 25 235 PAWNEE

PA 25 260 PAWNEE

PA 28 150 CHEROKEE

PA 28 140 CHEROKEE

PA 28 140E CHEROKEE

PA 28 140 FLIGHTLINER

PA 28 160 CHEROKEE

PA 28 180 CHEROKEE

PA 28 180G CHEROKEE

PA 28 180R ARROW

XPA 29 PAPOOSE

PA 28 200R ARROW

PA 28 200R ARROW II

PA 28 235 CHEROKEE

PA 28 235F CHEROKEE

PA 22 COLT

PA 32 260 CHEROKEE

PA 32 260E CHEROKEE

PA 32 300 CHEROKEE

PA 32 300E CHEROKEE

XPA 32 3-ENGINE

PA 34 SENECA

HE

PA 23 235 APACHE

PA 23 B AZTEC

PA 23E AZTEC

PA 23 250 AZTEC

PA 24 180 COMANCHE

XPA 33P COMANCHE

PA 24 250 COMANCHE

P. 24 260 COMANCHE
6 PLACE

PA 24 COMANCHE
EXT. PROP

PA 24 400 COMANCHE

PA 30 TWIN COMANCHE

PA 30 TWIN COMANCHE
6 PLACE

PA 30 TWIN COMANCHE C/R

PA 31 NAVAJO

PA 31 NAVAJO II

PA 31P NAVAJO

DICK CLARK

Mr. Piper and His Cubs

MR. PIPER AND HIS CUBS

DEVON FRANCIS

The Iowa State University Press, Ames, Iowa
1973

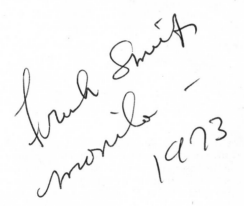

DEVON FRANCIS is a Hoosier by birth, a Kansan by education (University of Kansas, 1924), a New York suburbanite by adoption. A journalist for forty-eight years, he has authored four aviation books and won two national awards for aviation writing. He was the founding president of the Aviation (now Aviation/Space) Writers Association and the first general aviation editor of the Associated Press. For twenty-four years he was a magazine staff writer. He learned to fly in 1940. A son, Devon Alan, is an airline pilot and a stepson, Robert Ball, a newspaperman.

Mr. Francis' writings are products of a partnership with his wife Rosemary in "The Wordsmithery," White Plains, New York.

© 1973 The Iowa State University Press
Ames, Iowa 50010. All rights reserved
Composed and printed by
The Iowa State University Press
First edition, 1973

Library of Congress Cataloging in Publication Data

Francis, Devon Earl, 1901–
  Mr. Piper and his Cubs.

  Bibliography: p.
  1. Piper, William Thomas, 1881–1970. 2. Piper Aircraft Corporation, Lock Haven, Pa.
3. Lock Haven, Pa.—Industries—History. I. Title.
TL724.5.P5F7   338.7′62′91300924   [B]   72–1890
ISBN 0–8138–1250–X

TO
THE HUNDREDS OF THOUSANDS
WHO LEARNED TO FLY
IN PIPER CUBS,
AND FOR ROSEMARY,
WHO DID TOO

Contents

viii

Foreword

NONE OF US WHO ONCE PILOTED or have flown as passengers in the other seat of a Piper Cub have ever forgotten the experience or the little craft, whether it bore the traditional civilian canary yellow paint job, or the army "drab" so familiar to me during my active duty years, and especially during World War II and the Korean conflict, when the Cub type was indeed ubiquitous in the war zones, and often indispensable to the commander requiring firsthand knowledge of the battlefield. I don't know what I would have done without my "puddle jumper," for often the prepared airstrips which might have accommodated larger aircraft were cratered beyond use and we landed instead on the nearest road. Also, outfitted with pontoons, the Cub gave me greater operational flexibility, particularly in the Anzio landings.

Indeed, the versatility of the plane, when combined with the hand of a dexterous pilot, gave rise to numerous anecdotes about the Cub, especially in military circles, where pilot and aircraft rivalries are traditional. For example, when I was the Commanding General of the Field Forces at Fort Monroe, I built a small strip which would take lightplanes. I named it after Jack Walker, the pilot who was with me most of the war and who was killed in the late months of the war. One day I had to fly to Washington and it was before I had dedicated this "Walker Field." I kept the Cub at Langley Field. I got in it and we were taxiing to a position for a takeoff when a B–17 seemed to cut into our path, likewise preparing for takeoff. My pilot, not to be outdone, taxied under the wing of the B–17, much to the surprise of its pilot, whom I heard radio the tower requesting: "Get that army doodlebug out of my way." John Oswalt, a major who had flown me after Jack Walker's death in Italy, was my pilot. He promptly radioed the tower announcing "The army doodlebug referred to has General Mark Clark as a passenger and requests permission for immediate takeoff." The B–17 pilot was listening in and promptly radioed the tower, saying: "Please express my apologies to General Clark; I saw no insignia of rank on the plane," to which John Oswalt replied: "The apologies of the truck driver are accepted."

To the lay public, the name Piper has been synonymous with the word Cub while, to the aviation buff, civilian and military, the word Cub was, and is, synonymous with the name Piper, as was the lightplane segment of the general aviation industry. This book quite naturally reinforces these impressions. But it does more in focusing on the name and extraordinary man behind the machine.

As much as I have enjoyed reading of the airplane's development and service and appreciated the generous relation of my own wartime experiences with it, fond memories rekindled, I am more grateful for the moral, so to speak, of the story—it seeming to me a convincing confirmation of the American entrepreneurial ideal, if not of the Horatio Alger dream.

Today, when large numbers of the populace are doubtful or forgetful of their heritage, are confused as to whither they go, and, to me, seem valueless in that they disclaim established values, upholding instead little or naught, we need to be reminded of what made this nation the greatest on earth in this century. Over and above the abundance of natural and material resources, I submit, has been the human product of a free enterprise society.

Although there might be greater, more successful examples of the entrepreneur in industrial history, none seem more simply noble than W. T. Piper. It is to the great credit of the author that he has shown us the character of the man and men behind the machine, leading us to the heart of the matter: intelligence, imagination, faith, drive, and perseverance are the essence of the American way to progress. Unfettered by doubt and mod convention, men like Piper dared to do. Such confidence made Piper great, as it did his product. In turn, his product, both conceptual and material, contributed greatly to his industry and ultimately as greatly to his nation.

A popular soap commercial of today begins with a personal expression of use and concludes with the suggestion, "Don't you wish everybody did?" I feel that way about this book; having personal knowledge of its contents and worth, I wish everybody did. The nation would be the better for it.

Mark W. Clark

Charleston, S.C.
June 1972

General Mark Wayne Clark is a distinguished soldier and a statesman, having served in both world wars. In World War II he commanded the U.S. Fifth Army in the Anglo-American invasion of Italy and the investment of Rome. Subsequently he was commanding general of the Fifteenth Army Group and commander in chief of U.S. Ground Forces in Europe. After the war he was, successively, U.S. high commissioner and commanding general of U.S. Forces in Austria, deputy secretary of state, commanding general of the Sixth Army, chief of the Army Field Forces, commander in chief of the United Nations Command, commanding general of the Army Forces in the Far East, governor of the Ryukyu Islands, and for eleven years president of The Citadel, the Military College of South Carolina. He now serves the institution as president emeritus. In 1945 the U.S. House of Representatives voted him its appreciation for his services to the nation. His awards include the army's Distinguished Service Cross and the Distinguished Service Medal with three Oak Leaf Clusters, and the navy's Distinguished Service Medal. He is a Knight Commander, Order of the British Empire, and a Knight Commander of the Bath. He holds an honorary doctorate of civil law from Oxford University. General Clark is the author of two books: Calculated Risk, *and* From the Danube to the Yalu.

Mr. Piper and His Cubs

BRADFORD, PA., 1937
Before and after the fire.

The Fire

SAINT PATRICK'S DAY, 1937, WAS nothing for weather conscious Californians to boast about. In San Francisco, the slim, pixie-faced Amelia Earhart and her navigator, Fred Noonan, finally found a hole in the clouds to take off on a world flight that would be aborted, resumed in June, and climaxed by one of aviation's biggest disappearance mysteries. In Los Angeles a chill wind blew. Rain-laden clouds scudded over the city, yet to be transformed by war and its aftermath of immigrants drawn from the featureless flatlands of the midwest into one of the world's great metropolises. The words "smog" and "freeway" had not become fixtures in the language. Brick-red streetcars whined their way north and west from downtown to Hollywood Boulevard, passing the Temple of the Foursquare Gospel where an evangelist named Aimee Semple McPherson, attired in robes of alabaster, had preached in the past to overflow crowds. By now Sister Aimee had lost some of her luster. Eleven years before, she had dived into the ocean at Santa Monica and surfaced in the Sonora Desert south of Douglas, Arizona, and bilious-eyed legal authorities asked her endless questions about her tale that she had been kidnapped by a brace of Mexican brigands. The authorities had reason. Men had died diving for her remains in the azure sea.

Under the brow of the Hollywood Hills, the junction of Hollywood and Vine was as famous in Bordeaux and Beirut as it was in Boston. Hollywood was at the height of its glory, the epicenter of celluloid romance manufacture. Television was still in the laboratory.

So was commercial aviation. Powered flight had been born at Kitty Hawk, North Carolina, thirty-four years before. Yet a decade after Lindbergh, the Atlantic Ocean remained virgin to scheduled commercial airplane service. A world war had done little to advance the cause of peacetime flying. Airlines, true, were in being. Their aircraft hummed around carrying, at best, less than two dozen passengers each, their pace an electrifying three miles a minute.

Personal—private—flying was for the affluent, the country club types. Wings for the ordinary citizen, who wanted only to gaze upon

3

the topography of the land from a perch in the sky under his own command, were either prohibitively expensive or annoyingly slow. Seventy miles an hour in an airplane within reach of the average purse was par for the times. Such machines were playthings. A man could take off and he could land. Most neophytes kept the airport—usually a grassy plot of a few acres—in sight. Only hardy souls essayed flights cross-country, landing frequently to refuel and watching anxiously to see that white, fluffy, cumulus clouds did not metamorphose into blue-black cumulonimbus.

In the early morning hours of this gray Wednesday in Los Angeles, crowds were still streaming through the second annual National Pacific Aircraft and Boat Show at the Pan Pacific Auditorium on Beverly Boulevard near Fairfax Avenue. The list of persons in attendance sparkled with big names in aviation: Vincent Bendix, the manufacturer; Louise Thaden, internationally known aviatrix whose children were so used to flying that they considered a ride on a streetcar a treat; Delos C. Emmons, commander of the first wing of the General Headquarters Air Force; Waldo Waterman, inventor of a roadable airplane; and Jimmy Doolittle and Benny Howard, speed merchants. A "giant," twenty-one-passenger Douglas airliner, so described by the *Los Angeles Times,* was the biggest aircraft in the show. It was flanked by dozens of others, including a cabin job of 550 horsepower, reputed to be the fastest nonmilitary machine in the world.

Other exhibits were more modest. One had been brought in by trailer behind a beaten-up, secondhand car by a man named W. T. Piper. His entries were two simple—aye, primitive—little airplanes, each with a tiny engine of thirty-seven horsepower. With a tailwind, Mr. Piper's airplanes could almost keep up with a Ford V–8. William Piper had a homespun look. Stocky, big boned, he had a long upper lip, a full, straight mouth, and a rather long face embossed with a jutting jaw. His movements were those of a methodical man. Nine years before, he had gone into the aircraft business, but hardly by choice. He had backed into it; worse, he had been pushed. He was manufacturing these slow, tiny airplanes that were flown by men who otherwise would be on the links reaching for a wedge to blast out of a sand trap. Making airplanes was rather incidental to his principal purpose. What William Piper really wanted to make was money. Despite the limited utility of his product, he was not doing badly.

No one outside his immediate family and a few intimate friends addressed William Thomas Piper by any other name than his surname preceded by "Mr." Nobody knew why or, indeed, questioned the practice. It certainly was not inspired by any posture of dignity on his part. He was the prototype of the unprepossessing man. His battered felt hats were his trademark. He clung to them tenaciously, even militantly, far past the time when the bleariest derelict would have scorned them. His suits looked tired. In crowds he was quiet to the point of self-effacement. Possibly he was always addressed as "Mr. Piper" because he was an older man in what essentially was a young man's game, but the salutation was not of his own choosing. "No one," he remarked in mild complaint one day to a business associate, Gordon Curtis, "ever calls me Bill."

One day during the initial years of W. T. Piper's aircraft manufacture a distributor flew onto the factory airstrip after hours. He brought with him another pilot, a young man, to ferry away a new airplane that the distributor was buying. A fellow well past middle age met them at the door. Courteous to a fault, he showed them through the plant before turning over the new machine.

"The nicest guy," related the youngster to friends later, "let us see how they made the airplanes. He was the night watchman." The "night watchman" had been W. T. Piper.

Some of William Piper's personal habits were the despair of his family.

"We can talk in my car," he suggested to one customer. It was a hot day, and the automobile would be a haven from the sun.

The customer opened the right-hand door. On the floor was a bed of peanut shells three inches deep.

"Oh," said W. T. Piper, recognizing the puzzlement on the other man's face, "those. Great nutrition, peanuts, when you're driving."

At this point in his life Mr. Piper had addressed himself to the problem of survival in a competitive world and made peace with himself and his environment, and between each dawn and sunset tried to turn a dollar without cutting off his fellow men at the pockets. He made mistakes. He would make others in the coming years. One would be a dandy—it would almost wreck his company. In this instance he would not be alone. Other men would make the identical mistake at the same time, like lemmings bent on mass suicide, and the banking community remorselessly would behead most of them. William Piper would escape by an eyelash.

He had a phobia about credit. He borrowed freely, if cautiously, from banks for his business enterprises.

"Dad," asked one of his three sons one day in the course of a family council, "how many banks have you borrowed from?"

"Hmm," said his father, and began to tot them up. Presently he said, "I'm afraid I've lost count."

His credit standing was as good as gold. In the depths of the Great Depression he approached a grocer, a personal friend, with a proposition.

"I can't pay my employes," he said. "I want to keep going, and they've got to eat. I'd like to give them food chits redeemable by you. The company will give you a note to guarantee the chits."

"I won't take your company's note," replied his friend, "but I'll take your personal word."

Yet W. T. Piper refused to buy an automobile on time. It was wicked to use credit that way.

Now he wandered around the Los Angeles exhibition hall amid the potted palms, running a critical eye over the display of his own aircraft and those of his competition. "Taylor CUB" read the legend on his airplanes.

"Mr. Piper?" asked an attendant. "You're wanted on the telephone."

"Yes," he said, picking up the receiver in a booth.

"This is Ted Weld," said the instrument. Theodore Vance Weld was general manager of W. T. Piper's factory in far-off Bradford, Pennsylvania.

"Yes, Ted."

"Mr. Piper, I hate to be the one to tell you this, but you haven't got an airplane factory anymore. It burned down last night."

"I can't hear you so well, Ted," said Mr. Piper into the transmitter. "Speak up. Sounds like you said we haven't got an airplane factory anymore."

"That's right, it burned down."

The loss, with the building, construction materials, and equipment, amounted to $200,000. In the devalued currency of later years it was a pittance. In 1937, with the country only then reaching the tag end of the depression, it was a small fortune. A mere 5 percent was covered by insurance. Mr. Piper did not shock easily. Crises were a way of life.

"Anyway," he ruminated philosophically as he hung up, "we'll get some publicity out of it."

In 1937 William Thomas Piper was hardly yet on the threshold of one of the outstanding success stories of American business. For all his open-handed honesty, he was shrewd. It was not the shrewdness of the Yankee trader. It was the shrewdness of a farm community boy, which he had been, who had to be clipped only once in the shell game at the circus to learn his lesson. He had made some money in the oil business and in airplane manufacture. It wasn't a lot, but then he didn't demand a lot. He would get along. He would recover from the fire.

He was the last man in the world at that moment to suspect

that the name Piper in the next ten years would become a household word. "Piper" was to become synonymous with an industry that was just aborning. Piper history in a large sense would be the history of so-called "lightplane" manufacture not only in the United States but around the world. His flying machines would be the nursery for four of five American pilots in World War II and would give peacetime wings to men in ninety nations. They would fly explorers up the Amazon and missionaries up the Congo. They would grow robust in size and power. They would island-hop routinely on delivery from California to Manila across the wastes of the Pacific. One, setting a record in its class, would fly nonstop from Capetown, South Africa, to Saint Petersburg, Florida, a distance of 7,787 miles.

W. T. Piper, in these early hours of Saint Patrick's Day in Los Angeles, unknowingly was approaching the flood tide of his affairs. He was fifty-six years old and had had a career. Most men, over the hill, would have been fretting at the prospect of sixty. Not W. T. Piper. He was ageless. His original investment in an airplane factory that he had known nothing and cared less about, had been made by a partner without his consent. That had been $400. In the next three decades he would parlay that into a family fortune of $30 million.

Britches without a Fly

THE MAN WHO WAS TO EARN THE sobriquet, "the Henry Ford of aviation," was both merchant and mystic. William Piper was an anachronism, the gambler and the archconservative. He took risks, but they were calculated; he kept his options open. Politically he was as far right of center as the spectrum went; he had no truck with the newfangled socioeconomic theories that were coming into vogue. He was a romantic and a missionary zealot in the world of small business. Near the half-century mark in age when he was inducted into aircraft manufacture, he had visions that puddle-jumper airplanes might—just might—one day become important. He was a salesman. The daily ritual of shuffling papers on an office desk bored him. He wanted to be out recruiting customers and let someone else mind the store. He loathed statistics; he insisted that intricate figures be reduced to simple mathematics for ready digestion. He felt that when a man reached for a slide rule, it was a defensive gesture. He was a showman with a tincture of Phineas T. Barnum: thirty years before gasoline filling stations began bonus game gimmickry, he was passing out tickets to customers at his pumps in the center of Bradford, entitling them to a free ride in his airplanes. He was small-town, distrusting the money men of the big cities, specifically New York.

His paternal grandfather, Jennings Piper, emigrated to Massachusetts from Robertsbridge, Sussex, England, eleven miles from Hastings, scene of the battle in 1066 between King Harold and Duke William of Normandy.

William's parents were Thomas (no middle initial), one of ten children, and Sarah Maltby Piper. Thomas too had gambling instincts. Consigned to a farmer's role on 100 acres of land twenty miles west of Buffalo near Lake Erie he early displayed a restlessness to go adventuring. The oil business in the Bradford area, where wells began producing in 1879, was just his dish. Forsaking the soil, he moved to Knapp Creek, New York (pop. 390), near Bradford, a community of 19 thousand almost within spitting distance of the western New York State line. There, on January 8, 1881, William

Piper, one of six children, was born squalling on the kitchen table.

Eight years would elapse before the first horseless carriage would go on exhibit. William Piper lived to see men land on the moon.

Tom Piper did dabble at dairy farming between forays into the oil business. Several of his Jersey cows produced enough milk to be sold locally. William Thomas learned to milk when he was eight, and his father sold the milk whole. He had no cream separator. When Sarah Piper needed butter she put the milk out to rise on the back porch and poured the cream into a hand-operated churn. The Pipers did enjoy one convenience not common to households outside the oil fields—natural gas. A product of oil exploration, it was piped throughout the area.

"But the plumbing," remembered W. T. Piper, "wasn't inside." He carried water from a spring.

Knapp Creek had two religious sects, Catholic and Methodist, both poor. Services for the Methodists, who were even poorer than the Catholics, were held in the schoolhouse. The Pipers lived at one end of town and the schoolhouse was at the other. Six saloons, all on one side of the street, intervened. By parental edict, the little Pipers looked straight ahead as they walked past the saloons to church. Tom Piper was a religious fundamentalist and a militant member of the Prohibition Party. He never drank or smoked, nor did he curse. Growing up, William Thomas was exposed to the mores of a period in U.S. history that in severity outdid those of Victoria. Evangelists stalked up and down the land preaching hellfire and damnation. God and the devil were real persons and heaven and hell real places. Heaven was reachable only by the pure of heart, and the one-armed brother at the rear of the sanctuary would please pass the collection plate. Some of the preachers were charlatans, selftrained in theatrics. One, especially gifted at fleecing his sheep, came storming through the countryside during William's boyhood.

"The ushers," he shouted from the pulpit of his tabernacle during a revival meeting, "will go up and down the aisles and see that every woman in the audience has her legs crossed!"

The ushers complied.

"And now," thundered the evangelist, "now that the gates of hell are closed, we will proceed with the services!"

William retained few of the scars of these encounters, but he came to manhood staunchly opposed to liquor and tobacco. Drinking in particular was evil. He remained a teetotaler for all his days, and for years the salesmen in his employ entered a prodigious number of undecipherable hieroglyphics on their expense accounts.

A brother, Arthur, was even more faithful to the stern parental precepts. He grew up to become a missionary in the Congo.

William's childhood was abnormal in that the family knew on-

and-off poverty as his father pursued a dream of riches in oil. At one point, currently in money, Tom Piper moved his brood into a rather nice house in Bradford. It had the luxury of faucets, and William saw a bathtub for the first time in his life. In Knapp Creek a washtub in the kitchen had served the purpose. The Bradford residency lasted for only the year that Tom Piper had signed for. Oil was selling at one dollar a barrel. Then a big, new field blew in near Pittsburgh, and the price plummeted to sixty and then fifty cents, not enough to meet Tom's bank loans at 8 percent. He packed up, moved the family to an oil lease, and built a little house, again without plumbing.

At the age of nine William got a dirty-fingered introduction to the oil business. Steam-operated pumps had suction cups at the well bottoms. These got worn. To replace them a series of "sucker rods" to which they were attached had to be pulled to the surface. Tom had no money to hire help. William toted the twenty-five-foot rod segments—sometimes as many as sixty—from the wellhead down a hill to a shack for inspection and repair. To keep his clothes from getting filthy, he wore one of his father's old shirts as an overall. It came to his ankles.

Store clothes were out of the question, and when William needed a suit to play sandlot baseball, his mother made it for him. In place of a buttoned fly, like that on the pants of his playmates, she provided a small hole. He was mortified.

"I don't know of anything," he recalled, "that hurt me so much."

Oil climbed to $2.60 a barrel. The family's fortunes improved. They moved off the lease, back into Bradford. William played fullback on the high school football team. He had begun to show his independence, and in his final year deliberately flunked Latin; he had no practical use for a dead language.

In 1898, when he was seventeen, war hysteria fanned by the Hearst press swept the country. With parental consent, he fibbed about his age and joined up. In a tattered column of recruits he marched up Bradford's main street lugging a bag of canned goods an anxious uncle had given him. The citizenry lined the sidewalks. At an intersection one of the women spectators gave the embryo soldiers the back of her hand.

"That's Bullhead McClure," she announced to a woman standing beside her, "and the biggest bunch of bums in town. This is the best thing that ever happened to Bradford. There's not a decent man in the bunch."

Her hearer was Sarah Maltby Piper.

William's outfit engaged in one skirmish with a ragtag platoon of the enemy that had no deep philosophical convictions about dying

DOING LAUNDRY IN SPANISH-AMERICAN WAR
The enemy had no convictions about dying for the Crown.

for the crown. The war over, William was mustered out in October.

Now, said Tom Piper, conscious of his own educational short-comings, William would go to college. William liked Yale, but Yale it would not be.

"There are no saloons in Cambridge," said Tom Piper. "You'll go to Harvard."

Young William Piper had been an indifferent student in high school. Now he decided that if ever he was going to amount to anything, he had best address himself seriously to books. He read avariciously. He made good marks in his chosen major, engineering. He was still interested in athletics.

In high school, helping now and then on the oil leases, he had practiced throwing a sledgehammer, to the consternation of workmen who were not accustomed to dodging unguided missiles. At Harvard his aim with the sixteen-pound hammer was better. He made the track team. He became, in fact, a star, and won his event in the "big" meet with Yale in his junior year on May 24, 1902. Under the tutelage of Coach John Graham, he threw the hammer 128 feet, 10 inches.

In 1903 he was graduated with a bachelor of science degree in mechanical engineering, cum laude. His class was one year ahead of that of a man named Franklin Delano Roosevelt. He began a dozen years of construction work. Assigned to throwing up buildings at the U.S. Steel Corporation plant in Portsmouth, Ohio, he witnessed for the first time the ravages of a river on the rampage.

"The Ohio carried away railway coal cars," he said, "as though they were so much kindling."

W. T. Piper's heart was not in engineering. He dabbled, building among other things the first stressed concrete garage in New York City. For a time he leavened the dullness of his chores by singing in a theatrical troupe touring the Southeast. In a church choir where he also sang he met a comely girl from Buffalo, Marie van de Water, and in 1910 she and William T. Piper were married. By 1915 the Pipers were reconnoitering his father's old love, the oil business, in Bradford. This was his metier. It was business and it meant selling. Tom Piper had died in 1907. His son would take up where he had left off. With a partner, Ralph Lloyd, he founded the Dallas Oil Company. "Secondary recovery," first with steam under high pressure and later with water, was just coming into vogue in the Bradford field. Business was good. If the two men didn't make a fortune in crude, they made out.

AT HARVARD
He won his event in the big meet with Yale.

MR. PIPER AND HIS CUBS
Thomas F., William, Sr., Howard, Bill, Jr.

In 1917 America entered World War I. W. T. Piper was now thirty-six years old. Wars were for young men, yet he decided to enlist. Marie Piper, essentially a nest-maker, was no one to gainsay her husband. A neighborhood friend was more outspoken.

"You're an engineer," said he. "Why don't you get a commission, for heaven's sake?

On August 9 W. T. Piper was endowed with a captaincy in the Corps of Engineers. He never got overseas. In January 1919, two months after the Armistice, he was back in mufti.

Of W. T. Piper's five children, three more diverse personalities than those of the boys could hardly have come from the same womb. Bill, Jr., the eldest, was the closest to his father in temperament. Unflappable even as a child, he made decisions without fret. Tall, blond, and handsome as he matured, he was tailored to the social graces. He could look impeccably dressed in an open shirt. On the testimony of his father, he also was lazy in his formative years. He had too good a time in his junior and senior years in high school, playing basketball and quarterbacking the football team, to apply himself to his studies.

"You're going to college," said W. T. Piper, laying down the law, "and you'll have to make up your credits to get in." College, of course, meant Harvard.

William, Jr., had to spend a year in prep school in penance to earn his credits toward a higher education. Like his father he enjoyed a business climate and majored in economics and business administration. Like his father he was quiet but gregarious. He flavored his book education with minor athletics—dormitory football, basketball, and track. He shared his father's distaste for big cities.

"It's a good thing we got out of the New York banks," he remarked after one bruising experience with the money changers. "The smaller banks may not be charitable institutions, but they're not brutal."

Thomas Francis Piper—nicknamed "Tony"—the second son, was taut of nerve and inclined to moodiness. Of Tony, his younger brother Howard once remarked, "He's not as flexible as the rest of us." An excellent student, Tony liked the practical sciences, something he could touch. Courses in psychology were, as he put it, "off dreaming somewhere." He could grasp the reasons for algebra and geometry, but the poetic overtones of integral calculus left him cold. Mechanically, he worked out solutions to problems propounded in class, but invariably asked, "Now that I've done it, what's it good for?" But draw him into a conversation on the geology of Pennsylvania, and he could expound for an hour on the origin of the "folded mountains" that were laid down as sedimentary rock in the vast seas that covered the area 200 million years before. Ask him about company finances, and he could reel off figures from memory. Cost accounting was at his fingertips. Thirty years after he and a company official made a flying trip to New England, he could tick off the registration number of the airplane they used. Tony had one pronounced soft spot—he could not bring himself to put a worm on a fishing line, much less draw a bead on a deer. With a sister, Mary, he had his mother's brunette coloration, and from this, as a toddler, he got his nickname. He was in the habit of wandering away from home, and the Bradford police were alerted. The cops were predominantly Italian. They would telephone the house, "We've found Tony."

In high school, where he was president of his class in his senior year, Tony played football and basketball and in track did a commendable pole vault.

A geneticist could have had a field day with Tony and his father.

While he was wholly unlike William, Sr., Tony nonetheless from the beginning had more rapport with the head of the household than the other two boys. In his retirement years, still maintaining an office in the aircraft plant to which he went daily with religious dedication, William, Sr., would say, "They don't give me anything to do," and it was into Tony's office that he would wander for companionship. It was perhaps inevitable that two such dissimilar personalities would have conflicts.

"Tony," W. T. Piper would remark uncomplainingly, "gives me hell."

Howard Piper, named for an uncle on his mother's side and, like his paternal grandfather shortchanged on a middle name, shared few attributes with his brothers. He was the only son with Mr. Piper's facial structure. A nickname of "Pug" was bestowed by his mother, possibly as a contraction of "Pugnacious." Even as a baby, he showed bulldog tendencies. Learning to walk, he fell and got up without blubbering to try again. At five he decided to ride a horse. Its back was broad and he kept parting company with the animal. All day long he kept at it and by nightfall had learned how to hang on. At ten he pedaled an ungeared bicycle, roundtrip, over hill and dale to the home of some relatives thirty miles away.

As he matured Pug began displaying other personality traits—impatience, impulsiveness, and often a painful frankness. He also became the true romantic of the clan. He fell hopelessly in love with flying. Within the aircraft corporation he was the idea man, and he left his indelible marks on the design of its products. He wanted corporate growth and plant expansion, and he and the conservative Tony frequently found themselves at cross-purposes.

He interested himself in sports as a boy because his brothers were outstanding, and suffered successive embarrassments. While Bill, Jr., could run the hundred-yard dash in ten seconds flat, and Tony could sink unsinkable baskets, Howard displayed no such muscular coordination. He was, to use his own word, lousy. His inferiority complex in sports led him to pound the tennis courts to exhaustion, and to team up to win the city doubles championship for a number of years hand running. It gave him profound satisfaction.

Pug shared with Tony's wife Margo the title of the family's practical joker. Subtleties were not for him. On one occasion he carefully planted the names of Piper and two other firms, Beech and Cessna, in a speech before a group of engineers.

"So tonight," he said, "we have with us the sons of Piper and the sons of Cessna. We also have the sons of Beeches." It brought down the house.

All three boys shared their father's abstemiousness.

"They don't smoke," he said proudly, "and if any of them take a drink, I don't know about it."

The Perfect Bankrupt

A SEQUENCE OF EVENTS HAD BEGUN
nine years before W. T. Piper's factory in Bradford, Pennsylvania,
went up in smoke and flame. It hinged on a man named Taylor.
C. Gilbert Taylor was of slight build, gifted in things mechanical,
and given to cantankerous outbursts. He was intense, brooding, and
humorless. Though he had never gone beyond high school, he had
a quick, native understanding of aerodynamics. He had to be in
complete charge of any project he undertook, making all the decisions,
no matter how minor, or he was unhappy. He walked with a pronounced limp from a polio affliction as a child. He was a nonsmoker,
a nondrinker, and a sparse eater. Because the first two initials of his
name converted readily into an aeronautical contraction meaning
center of gravity, he was known simply as "C. G." He was fascinated
by airplane design and was a competent designer. In the year 1926
he had fashioned a two-passenger airplane with side-by-side seating
called the Chummy. Its projected retail price was $4,000. That was
a lot of money for the times. In the eastern seaboard hinterlands ham
was twenty-eight cents a pound, potatoes twenty-three cents a peck,
and cigarettes $1.10 a carton. Taylor could see nothing wrong with
the price that he proposed putting on his airplane. A man who
in 1931 was to become his partner in a manufacturing enterprise,
W. T. Piper, could. It was the first of many disagreements between
them.

At the moment W. T. Piper's business of drilling for and selling
crude oil in Bradford was becoming progressively less profitable. A
half century before, Bradford had been known as the oil capital of
the world. In August 1881 the surrounding fields had produced an
all-time high of seventy-five thousand barrels a day. Now they were
playing out. Bradford was looking around for industry to supplement
its economy.

Taylor, in Rochester, New York, was looking around too. He
wanted someone to pony up some money for a Taylor Brothers Aircraft Corporation factory to produce the Chummy. He retained the
"Brothers" in the company name even though his brother-partner had

THE CHUMMY
The pilot departed the last one by parachute.

been killed shortly before in the crash of one of their airplanes. A year before the yet-to-become-famous Zippo founded its cigarette lighter factory in Bradford, the community's good citizens invited C. G. to locate in their midst. Their support was fifty thousand dollars in stock purchases, which built a modest sheet iron factory at the Harri Emery Airport, a field at the edge of town with a short cinder runway.

It was at this point that W. T. Piper was pushed backward into airplane manufacture. He and his partner in oil, Ralph Lloyd, had offices on the same floor of a building housing yet another oil man, Clayton Dorn. Dorn dropped by the Lloyd-Piper offices in W. T. Piper's absence one sunny afternoon with an announcement.

"We're bringing an aircraft company to town," said he. "I've bought some stock, and I think you and Bill ought to buy some."

"How much?"

Dorn figured on a pad. "With your gross, I'd say about four hundred dollars apiece."

When W. T. Piper got back to his office Lloyd broke the news. "You're in the airplane business."

"Hmm," said W. T. Piper. He knew oil. He knew nothing about airplanes. The previous year he had had his first and only flight. The man who ran the airport had stopped him on Main Street one day and invited him aloft in an open cockpit Travel Air.

"Know how fast we're going?" the pilot yelled above the roar of the engine as they swept over town. "Ninety miles an hour!"

W. T. Piper was not impressed. The contraption was noisy, the wind seared his face, and there were more comfortable ways to travel. It didn't look very safe, either.

Simple logic proved the case against commercial aviation: flying was dangerous; only daredevils essayed the dangerous; ergo, anyone who flew was a daredevil. Practically all flying in the 1920s was done in open cockpit airplanes, many of them Curtiss JN–4 ("Jenny") trainer relics of the world war, propelled by Curtiss OX–5 ninety-horsepower engines. The "flying circus" was a fixture at county fairs. Because the biggest hazard in flying was starving to death, there were pilots who resorted to flying contraband booze from Canada and contraband Chinese from Mexico.

As for the airlines—if indeed there were operations meriting the designation—most of them were fighting off pressures to make them carry passengers. Their reasons for being were contracts for carrying the mail. The Post Office Department subsidy became rather lavish when some of the operators discovered that bricks and telephone books could be used to pad out the poundage of lean mail sacks. They became robber baron counterparts, junior grade, of the thieves who built the nation's railroads.

And as for so-called private flying, an esoteric pursuit, the roster of the Long Island Aviation Country Club was a reprint of a portion of society's Blue Book. The *Aircraft Year Book,* which totted up aviation's achievements for the Aeronautical Chamber of Commerce, contained this entry for 1928: "Thousands of persons learned that they might own a machine and fly it at relatively the same expense as that involved in operating a good motor car. Lightplanes could be purchased for the price of a good car." How good? Of the typical airplanes for sale, a Ryan Brougham with a Wright Whirlwind engine retailed for $9,700. The going price of a Cadillac was $2,685, FOB Detroit.

"Hmm," said W. T. Piper.

He had five children: besides the three boys and Mary, he had a daughter Elizabeth. The eldest was about to enter college. This was no time to invest money frivolously. But the promise had been made and for the present he would go along.

His knowledge of private flying was limited to an abstruse recognition that overnight a flight by a man named Lindbergh from New York to Paris had evoked a national, if nonparticipating, passion for aviation—anything, everything that had wings—that bordered on hysteria. Stock in the Seaboard Air Line, which was a railroad, skyrocketed on the exchange. Flying schools mushroomed.

Here, now, was the "Air Age." Everyone in this dizzy era of Calvin Coolidge–Herbert Hoover prosperity would sprout his own wings.

Hardly before he could recover from the shock of becoming a stockholder in Taylor Brothers, W. T. Piper was pushed again. His commanding officer in the Spanish-American War had been a Lt. Col. Andrew D. Burns, at this time president of the Bradford Chamber of

Commerce. One touch of military service had rendered Burns a soldier to the marrow.

"Captain," said Burns to Mr. Piper in deference to his rank in the world war, "you're a stockholder in the Taylor company." Mr. Piper had an uneasy feeling that something was coming. "The welfare of the stockholders is my responsibility. I want you on the board of directors."

One of the products of the air age boom was a nationwide contest for a "safe" flying machine. It was staged in 1929, the year of Black Thursday in the stock market, by Harry F. Guggenheim, wartime flier son of a banker-philanthropist, Daniel Guggenheim. Prizes came to $150,000. C. G. Taylor decided that winning the competition was exactly the prescription to put his aircraft factory in Bradford on a sound footing.

The Chummy, a monoplane, looked somewhat like Lindbergh's Spirit of St. Louis, but then most small monoplanes of the period looked like the Spirit of St. Louis. A pilot flew the machine to Mitchel Field on Long Island, site of the Guggenheim trials.

W. T. Piper was dragooned into driving a secondhand Buick, his current mount, to Mitchel Field with Taylor beside him to oversee the performance of the Chummy.

Taylor and W. T. Piper were not long in getting the word.

"That thing," remarked a contest official, "hasn't got a prayer to qualify. Why don't you get it the hell out of here?"

The Chummy was not alone in being unloved, like a bastard child, except by its owners. Of the other entries, five withdrew and six failed to qualify. On January 1, 1930, the Daniel Gugghenheim Fund for the Promotion of Aeronautics announced that the winner was a machine named the Tanager, entered by the Curtiss Aeroplane and Motor Corporation. It was safe enough; it qualified on all counts; but it was a production engineer's nightmare. For this larceny, Curtiss collected first prize money of $100,000.

"What will it cost to build an airplane like that?" asked W. T. Piper. "How are they going to sell it?"

He was prophetic. It cost too much and they *couldn't* sell it. The Tanager never saw a production line.

Whether recognition in the contest would have preserved the Chummy as a viable piece of merchandise became at this point an academic question. The stock market had crashed. For the year 1931 the *Aircraft Year Book* listed forty-four aircraft companies in being. By 1934 two dozen of them had failed and most of those remaining were dormant.

By early 1930 the money that had come from the sale of stock in Taylor Brothers Aircraft was gone. On top of that, C. G. was into the Bradford National Bank for $15,000 in loans.

"See if you can salvage any of the money Taylor owes the bank," Burns told W. T. Piper.

Enter now an entrepreneur named Gordon Moore Curtis, Amherst educated, with considerable talents for imaginative thinking in making money. A few weeks before, in Dayton, Ohio, he had contrived a meeting of representatives of nine aircraft manufacturers. Taylor Brothers Aircraft was not among them. Curtis had an idea. He would form a company to finance the sale of airplanes at the consumer level. He would buy the manufacturers' "paper" at discount and take time payments from aircraft purchasers, thus boosting sales and making himself a bundle. Before the manufacturers' representatives walked from the Dayton hotel room where he presented his plan, he had signatures on nine articles of agreement with his Aviation Funding Corporation. These included one committing the Aeronautical Corporation of America—named by men who patently had dreams of glory—to the Curtis venture. The Aeronautical Corporation, little more than a backyard fabricator in Cincinnati, made a flying machine with the acronym, "Aeronca." The company was owned by the wealthy Taft family, and a member immediately concerned was Robert who, as "Mr. Republican," twenty-two years later failed of his party's nomination to the White House.

Robert Taft repudiated the agreement signed by his representative in Dayton. In a meeting with Curtis he simply reached across the table, seized the document, and shredded it.

"How much have you got invested in this company?" asked Curtis.

"Three-quarters of a million," replied Taft, "and we've got hundreds of thousands of dollars lying around that are not working. Why should we peddle our paper to someone else?"

"Mr. Taft," remarked Curtis, controlling his temper, "the day will come when you will have to sell out for $100,000."

Curtis began cultivating W. T. Piper. He would see that the Tafts paid for the cavalier treatment accorded him.

"Maybe you ought to dump the Chummy," Curtis said over lunch a few days after the Cincinnati incident. "What you need is an airplane like the Aeronca, only better."

Mr. Piper was already arriving at that conclusion. On a trip to Cleveland he and Taylor had seen the Aeronca, known irreverently as the Bathtub. The best that could be said for the machine as a mechanical device was that it *would* become airborne on its miniscule, two-cylinder engine, and it *was* small and it *was* simple. Beyond all else, it was inexpensive.

The sixth and last Chummy was built and finally sold on August 13, 1930. It was short lived. A delivery pilot, Tom Smith, flying it

Aeronca Aircraft Corporation

AERONCA BATHTUB
It didn't look like an airplane.

to a purchaser, bailed out with a parachute in West Virginia. Smith never bothered to report back to Bradford.

W. T. Piper's authority was growing. He had begun dipping into his oil profits to keep the company afloat.

"Taylor," he said to the president of Taylor Brothers Aircraft, "we've got to design something cheap." He delivered an identical report to the board of directors.

"Moreover," he remarked, "we're not going to aim at the private owner. If anyone wants a plane, he can have it, but we're going to sell to the man who gives flying lessons."

He had been nosing around. The cost of instruction in the rudiments of flying was astronomical—up to thirty dollars an hour in the big, clumsy airplanes that were in use by merchants known as "fixed-base operators." For want of students, they were going broke. If the hourly rate could be halved, it would attract more students. More students would induce the operators to buy more airplanes.

Mr. Piper had a parting shot: "Our airplane has to be easy to fly."

Taylor went back to his drawing board.

On the subject of lightplane manufacture in Bradford, W. T. Piper remarked to Gordon Curtis, "You know, I think this thing has possibilities. I've told Lloyd that if the company goes under the hammer, not to be surprised if I buy it."

THE GLIDER
You didn't get into it, you just put it on.

It was now mid-1930. W. T. Piper had become, by virtue of his investment, the company treasurer. He decided to file a voluntary bankruptcy petition. Considering its liabilities, Taylor Aircraft was broke. The referee in the bankruptcy proceeding was an old school-mate. They met on the street.

"You're a wonder," remarked the referee, "the most perfect bankrupt I've met in all my twenty years of experience. You've got more liabilities and fewer assets than anyone I've ever heard of."

When the assets were put up for sale, W. T. Piper offered $761. It was the only bid. Taylor Brothers Aircraft Corporation was re-organized as the Taylor Aircraft Company. Mr. Piper gave C. G. a half interest in the business, such as it was, and the presidency. He himself retained the key to the till.

It was uphill going. A flivver airplane? A personage no less then Henry Ford the elder, wizard of the River Rouge, had tried his hand at a tiny, cheap airplane. Ford had a highly competent pilot, Harry Brooks, in charge of the project. Brooks' credentials were so good that Lindbergh had entrusted his own mother to his care on a long flight to Mexico. Then on the evening of February 25, 1928, in good flying weather, Brooks and Ford's flivver with the curlicued Ford script painted on its flanks plunged into the ocean off Melbourne, Florida, never to be seen again. A disenchanted Mr. Ford promptly wrote off small airplanes in the consumer field as a bad idea.

Few firms besides the Aeronautical Corporation were exhibiting temerity enough to build small planes. Money was scarce, the light-plane as a piece of transportation was faulty, and engines quit. Yet C. G. Taylor and W. T. Piper proposed to launch light airplane man-ufacture.

"The fact was," Mr. Piper said in later years, "we didn't know what the hell we were getting into."

Taylor designed a glider, a test bed for a wing and control surfaces.

"You didn't get into it," said Tony Piper, "you just sort of put it on."

Taylor blueprinted an airplane with an engine. On his sixteenth birthday on August 13, Tony Piper was accorded the honor of sitting in the cockpit of what, with some charity, might be called the wood mockup of the corporation's first small powered flying machine. Taylor, Mr. Piper, and a handful of workmen walked around the mockup, looking. The thing had been built up of orange crates with a wood framework hammered together to the size of a cabin. The seat layout was tandem, the cockpit open. No one laughed—fortune or failure could hang on this contraption. One month after Tony performed his modeling chore, the Taylor lightplane was ready to fly. It had been a community effort, and everyone had pitched in. Even Alice Roberts, the strikingly pretty blonde who later became the bride of Rensselaer C. Havens, a test pilot, had done her bit by sewing fabric on the wings.

The airplane flew. That is, it got off the ground. How much flying it actually did was subject to compassionate interpretation. On its nose was a two-cyclinder, twenty-horsepower engine known as the Brownbach Tiger Kitten. The Bradford airport was fourteen hundred feet above sea level, the air correspondingly less dense, and the runway was seventeen hundred feet long, less than a third of a mile. Test Pilot George Kirkendall was about to run out of airport on his first flight by the time he achieved an altitude of five feet. With the trees getting closer at the end of the strip, he chopped the throttle and settled in.

THE FIRST PIPER POWERED AIRPLANE
"Cub" became a generic name for lightplanes.

"How is it?" asked Taylor in his unsmiling way.

"Fine, handles fine."

"Needs a bigger engine," said W. T. Piper.

At that moment Gilbert Hadrel, the company accountant, gave the airplane the name that in the coming years became generic for lightplanes. "The engine's the Tiger Kitten," he said. "Why not call the plane the Cub?" Cub it was.

C. G. and Mr. Piper had one thing going for them: their flivver airplane was simple, far simpler than an automobile. Workers on a Cub production line needed few acquired skills. That kept down fabricating costs. The factory needed little precision tooling. That kept down the capital investment.

A cursory glance would have equated the Cub's construction with that of airplanes of a decade before, wired together to keep the component parts flying in formation. It was nothing of the kind. Besides its sturdy steel framework, it had tubular struts, not flexible cables like the Aeronca, to supplement the anchorages of the wings to the fuselage. Wing spars were made of Oregon spruce. To absorb landing impacts, rubber "shock cord" served as springs. It was cheap but it worked.

For the neophytes to be introduced to flying by the fixed-base operators, Mr. Piper wanted a wing that would not sass back as it was maneuvered. Taylor chose the USA (for U.S. Army) 35-B, used in many other airplanes because it was stable at low speeds. Even if a student blundered into a spin, granted enough altitude, all he had to do was close the throttle, take his feet off the rudder pedals, and put his hands in his lap. The Cub, picking up speed as it spiraled down, "flew out."

Cockpit instruments were war surplus and minimal: one for oil temperature, one for oil pressure, a tachometer, and a Mickey Mouse altimeter. The airplane had no compass, no airspeed indicator. The fuel gauge was a wire with a cork on the nether end that thrust up out of the tank.

The Cub certainly needed more power. Taylor tried a French-made Salmson radial producing forty-five horsepower. The Cub soared but the engine cost too much. Besides, it ran backward— counter-clockwise as one sat in the cockpit—and it was built to metric measurements. In February 1931 Continental Motors, essentially an automobile engine maker, came up with a solution. Its A–40, four-cylinder engine of an advertised forty horsepower (on a dynamometer it actually produced thirty-seven) was imperfect, but it could be used to get the Cub licensed and into production. The Continental design in the succeeding years became classic in lightplanes. Like the Aeronca engine, it was "flat"—the cylinders lay horizontally, two on each side of the crankshaft. They were finned, like those of all lightplane engines, for heat dissipation to the air instead of through a heavy radiator. A flat engine enjoyed a plus: it afforded good visibility from the cockpit.

Four months after the installation of the Continental engine, the first production Cub, called the E–2, was ready for government inspection. "E–2" meant nothing; Taylor used it as a model number. It had a top speed, according to the sales literature that presently began pouring out of a lean-to office at the Bradford airport, of eighty-three miles an hour—that is, with its tiny, 115-cubic-inch engine beating its heart out. This was taking liberties with the facts; the top speed was closer to seventy-five, and the cruising speed at 2,550 revolutions per minute was no more than sixty-five. Fuel consumption was three gallons an hour. At the then current prices for automobile-grade gasoline, on which the Continental thrived, that meant a cost of a third of a cent a mile. The Cub toted two persons of 170 pounds each and nine gallons of gasoline. It had no provision for luggage, but it wasn't designed to go anywhere anyway. It was an airport puddle jumper. At a gross weight of 925 pounds, it took off in still air in three hundred feet, providing it was not a hot day, and it landed at thirty-five miles an hour. The price, flyaway factory, was $1,325, a far cry from the thousands of dollars asked for the bigger, heavier, more powerful, faster aircraft of the day. The Cub, in short, was exactly what W. T. Piper had ordered.

On June 15, 1931, the E–2 was licensed for manufacture by the United States Government's Department of Commerce. Where angels had feared to tread, Taylor and Piper rushed in. Whether they were fools was left to history to decide.

If the Piper family's fortunes were to be tied up with aviation, its members had best find out what it was all about. Under Bud Havens' tutelage, Mr. Piper, now fifty years old, and Tony began learning to fly. Tony first soloed three weeks after his seventeenth birthday in the first production Cub. Up from Pittsburgh presently came an official to put him through the required tests—takeoffs, landings, spin recovery, and a long series of questions on the regulations.

"A glider and a free balloon," Tony recited dutifully on the written test, "have the right-of-way over a powered aircraft."

"Now you've got a licensed pilot in the family," Havens announced to W. T. Piper on October 8. Tony had less than fifteen hours' solo time.

William, Sr., was more leisurely in acquiring his license. Between trying to keep the company afloat and run his oil business, he had limited time to devote to flying lessons.

By year's end practically everyone on the production line and in

1936
A bargain basement airplane was bound to sell.

the office of the Taylor Aircraft Company was taking flying lessons. It was a fringe benefit decreed by Mr. Piper over the grumblings of his partner.

"It's the least we can do," he explained. "We're only paying the production people twenty cents an hour for a nine-and-a-half-hour day and a five-and-a-half-day week, and sometimes they don't get that."

The charge for employes' flying lessons was one dollar an hour. It would be a disservice to Mr. Piper's native intelligence to say that he was without guile; it was a big thing to learn to fly at that price.

It was all too true that employes sometimes did not get paid. The Bradford railway express office kept the company inventory. Engines arrived from Continental on sight drafts. To get them out of hock while a customer awaited delivery of an airplane, Mr. Piper exhibited a savoir faire that put him in the acting class of the Barrymores and the Drews. Casually he accepted a check in payment for the airplane. At that point the tempo changed. He rushed to the bank for the money. At the express office, he paid for the engine, tied it to the front bumper of his secondhand car and hied himself back to the airport. The conspiratorial company staff, diverting the customer who had brought such largess to the coffers with such innocent ploys as another cup of coffee, awaited word that the engine had been mounted on the purchased Cub and test flown—once around the field. Then, with ceremony, the purchaser was presented with his aircraft.

To keep apace of his expenses Mr. Piper floated loans at banks, using a forthcoming production of oil on his leases as collateral. He and Taylor *were* selling airplanes. By year's end they had built and disposed of twenty-two.

"Everyone who was still flying," said W. T. Piper in later years, "was starved into using Cubs."

But profits were small. He clung to his credo: keep the price down. The dealers were allowed a 20 percent margin on the retail price. When the cost of production was subtracted from the wholesale price, there was precious little left to put in the company safe.

"We'll make it up," said Mr. Piper, "when we get the volume."

The factory was getting a constant feedback from dealers and owners on engine troubles. Crankshafts broke. Continental designed its products to meet the strains imposed by torque (rotational energy) in automobiles. Their little eggbeater engines being shipped to Bradford had one thrust bearing and that at the rear. Mounted on the noses of airplanes, the engines were subjected to the pull of propellers intent on making pretzels of the crankshafts. The Bradford factory had to replace crankshafts in the field. It was one circumstance that helped keep Taylor Aircraft in poverty.

The engine had other ills.

"When we flew as much as twenty miles," remembered Tony Piper, "most of the time we had a forced landing."

The Continental blew head gaskets with unnerving regularity. Magnetos gave up. Then there was the lubricating problem. Continental was not responsible for that. William, Jr., a senior at Harvard in the autumn of 1933, wanted to take a Cub to college. It would provide him cheap transportation between Bradford and Cambridge, and over the scalloped terrain of the eastern seaboard—provided the engine didn't quit—it would be quicker than a car or train.

"And safer," put in Mr. Piper. He believed it.

Beyond that, the Cub could be rented for instruction weekdays to a distributor, E. W. Wiggins, at Norwood, Massachusetts, just outside Boston. Mr. Piper was passing up no chance to turn a dollar.

On September 19 the two Williams, father and son, took off to fly up together. Lock Haven on the West Branch of the Susquehanna River was the first stop; Bloomsburg the second. Few airports of the period stocked lightplane crankcase lubricants. Big aircraft piston engines demanded a heavy, fifty-weight oil. The Continental could stomach no more than a thirty-weight. At Bloomsburg a mechanic poured fifty-weight oil into the Cub on its way to college. The Pipers took off again, Mr. Piper at the controls. At Shenandoah, in Pennsylvania's anthracite mining region, the Cub began getting the croup. The heavy oil was overheating the engine. William, Jr., recognized the symptoms.

"Well, Dad," he remarked calmly as the engine lost revolutions, "I guess I'll fly a little while now."

Mr. Piper relinquished the controls. The only landing site within gliding distance was a flat-topped mountain of slag. William, Jr., circled and stalled in. There wasn't a scratch on the airplane as he rolled to a stop. It was an hour before the Continental's temperature returned to normal. William, Jr., attempted a solo takeoff from the slag heap. A crowd had gathered. It pressed forward. The pilot swerved, piling up the airplane. Father and son abandoned it. When they returned days later to trailer the carcass back to Bradford for rebuilding, souvenir hunters had cannibalized it. It was more than a year before another Cub actually got to college.

Resistance to accepting the Cub and the Aeronca as genuine airplanes, not toys, came from a logical quarter. The "big airplane boys," as William, Jr., characterized them, tried to laugh the tiny aircraft out of business. Their scorn was real. To have any layman with a modicum of talent and application learn in a few hours to get an airplane off the ground and back again intact eroded the image of the Greek god that professional and sportsmen pilots so assiduously cultivated.

The lightplane people were not disturbed. They knew their market. In Bradford the sales literature was written for the garage mechanic and the grocery store clerk. For example:

"Flying, a sport for kings and millionaires, can be yours now with a Taylor Cub."

On safety, "What goes up must come down, but if the rules of good flying are observed, the 'Cub' will come down both SLOWLY AND SAFELY."

Hen Houses Always Face South

LATE IN THE FALL OF 1932 A MAN NAMED Walter Corey Jamouneau wrote the Taylor Aircraft Corporation from his home in Irvington, New Jersey. The surname implied a paternal ancestry that was as French as Bordeaux truffles.

"I am an aeronautical engineering graduate of Rutgers," he said, "and would like to talk with you about employment."

The "aeronautical engineering graduate" part of it was stretching a point. He had taken courses in airplane structures and aerodynamics; only three colleges in the country offered degrees in aeronautical engineering, and Rutgers was not one of them. But Jamouneau was a precocious young man of 19, and he was getting so restive under depression-enforced idleness that he was ready to work for anything. Inquiries to a number of other companies had brought no response. He was not hurting for money; his family was in comfortable circumstances. He had no illusions about making a fortune in airplane manufacture; flying intrigued him, and he had obtained a license.

C. G. Taylor replied, "Why don't you come to Bradford and we'll talk over the possibilities."

Jamouneau, a tall man with patrician features, conferred with Taylor and W. T. Piper in Bradford in December. He sensed a friction between the partners in the business and cautiously tried to steer a course between them. Mr. Piper did the talking.

"What do you think can be done to improve lightplane sales?" he asked, probing for a clue to Jamouneau's personality.

In the course of his job hunting Jamouneau had visited two manufacturers of rotary wing Autogyros in the Philadelphia area. Wallace Kellett and Harold F. Pitcairn, the proprietors of those establishments, had impressed him. He saw virtues in aircraft that could land on postage stamp fields. "If you made aircraft with folding rotors so they would fit in a garage," he told his interrogators in Bradford, "you might have considerable sales to private owners."

Mr. Piper spoke up. "We are not interested in selling to private owners, and we are not interested in rotary wing aircraft."

29

"How about something bigger than what you're building?" offered Jamouneau.

"No," said Mr. Piper, "the plane's big enough. If we stay out of Stinson's and Waco's business, they'll stay out of ours." Stinson and Waco were trying to survive in a shrinking market on four-place airplanes.

"Well," concluded Jamouneau, searching for a way to get off stage gracefully, "money is no object with me."

If the interview had not been disastrous, it certainly had seemed unprofitable. Little did Jamouneau know how much of a clout his last remark had fetched to Messrs. Piper and Taylor. As fast as the oil business made money for Mr. Piper, the airplane business was blotting it up.

"Come to work," Taylor wrote him less than two weeks later, "on the terms you specified."

Walter Jamouneau, in January 1933, went to work for the Taylor Aircraft Corporation at just what he had implied—no salary. The only man in the plant with a college degree that did, indeed, connote a knowledge of airplanes, he was glad to get the job. He was an odd fixture in the rough-and-ready Taylor Aircraft establishment. Proust and Thoreau were no strangers to him. He thought frankly that the airplanes being manufactured in Bradford were setting back the cause of flying for a decade. But at last he had a job. He was articulate and an eloquent phrase-maker.

Four months after Jamouneau joined up, Mr. Piper with unconscious humor told him, "I'm afraid we'll have to terminate this arrangement for the time being."

"I think," recalled Jamouneau later, "that he was getting embarrassed about not paying me."

A week later he was recalled.

"Do you want to go on the road selling?" asked the company treasurer.

Jamouneau was wary of asking for a salary. "Yes," he said.

He got one—fifteen dollars a week. But he had a fringe benefit—twenty-five dollars a week for expenses. He was also supplied with an airplane.

To Bradford in 1932 the sale of aircraft had brought a gross average income of $1,908 a month. Skidding sales in 1933 reduced this to $1,484. W. T. Piper, with two kids in college and an albatross in flying machine manufacture around his neck, continued to plod to the banks for short-term loans.

"Why," asked Harvey Haggerty, president of the Bradford National Bank, "don't you give up that damned thing at the airport and devote yourself to the oil business?"

Mr. Piper had begun to wonder why himself.

Periodically he loaded a couple of knocked-down Cubs on a trailer and hauled them behind his current secondhand car to Seattle, which from Bradford was practically all the way across the continent. To save freight charges, he loaded the trailer with spruce lumber for spars and drove all the way home. On the go from morning to night, he and Havens combed the countryside by automobile for business. William, Sr., a health food enthusiast, was big on bananas at the moment. As he cruised along behind the wheel, always straight down the center of the road, giving way only when he met an oncoming car, he would pull a couple of bananas from a jacket pocket.

"Lunch," he would tell Havens, dividing the spoils.

Dinner was better. Each had a banana *and* an orange.

When they were lucky enough to locate a prospect, Havens would return with a Cub for a demonstration. His performance was salesmanship in itself. He was an expert pilot. If a sale was consummated, the buyer had a choice.

"The price," said William, Sr., "is $1,325. Now of course if you want to become the Cub dealer in this area, we'll give you 20 percent off. In that event, you'll need another airplane at the same discount."

He prized Bud Havens. Fine airplane pilots came high even with the country economically prostrate. In the month of May Mr. Piper told Havens that in appreciation for his work, he was giving him a ten-dollar-a-week raise. In place of the thirty dollars a week that he had *not* been getting, he was *now* not getting forty dollars a week. It lifted his spirits.

Mr. Piper kept at everybody to give the Cub exposure. He could sniff a weekend air show a hundred miles away. "Go over there," he would order Havens, "and demonstrate the airplane." Havens went. He stunted. "Help develop airports," ordered the boss. "Airplanes are no good without places for takeoffs and landings."

The factory sales literature began acquiring proselyting rhetoric. "This is an airplane," it boasted in an obvious slap at the Aeronca with its wire-braced wings, "that looks like an airplane."

The Cub may have looked it, but its power problems continued endemic. Tony Piper once had to land on the Air Corps' Wright Field, Dayton, verboten to civilian aircraft without prior notice of arrival, when suddenly he was bereft of power.

At his wits' end to find an engine to replace the sickly Continental A–40, Taylor tried a three-cylinder Szekley radial of thirty horsepower. Designed by Otto Szekley, a Holland, Michigan, engineer, it had every known mechanical defect that could be built into a reciprocating, internal combustion engine plus some that were truly exotic.

The crisis had its effects on the fortunes of Walter Jamouneau, out in the boondocks trying to sell Cubs. For all his eloquence, magnificent salary, and expense account, he would not have been eating regularly had it not been for personal funds. Jamouneau's sales prospects burned his gas on demonstration rides and walked away without so much as a thank you. The public was not buying airplanes.

In the late summer of 1934 Jamouneau was recalled to Bradford.

"Continental's not going to make engines for us any more," Taylor greeted him. "We'll have to manufacture our own."

The Detroit company was balking not only because of Taylor's constant remonstrances on crankshaft failures, but also because the lightplane business was too tiny to bother with. With his uncanny gift in mechanics, Taylor designed and built a four-cylinder, air-cooled engine. Like the Continental, it had ailments. Like the Continental, it broke crankshafts. Only a change of heart at Continental kept Taylor from perfecting his power plant, and perfect it he would have. Continental offered to find the cause of its failures. It did. The addition of a thrust bearing at the front end obviated crankshaft breakage and no doubt contributed substantially to the proliferation of lightplane sales in the years preceding World War II. Continental did more. It added a second magneto and a second spark plug to each cylinder for fail-safe operation. Gaskets held. Taylor Aircraft was in business again—all that it needed was customers.

"Want to take a ride?" Mr. Piper asked an old friend at the Bradford airport on a hot July 4 in the midst of the engine crisis.

He had won his pilot's license and was getting to be a pretty good flier—nothing fancy, mind you, but competent. He was acquiring the bits and pieces of know-how that separated the good pilot from the dub. He could read clouds, and he knew when to land in advance of a storm. He could navigate by highway map, and if perchance he got lost he knew that a railroad track usually was the shortest distance to a town with an airport. He knew that in the Midwest the section lines, always defined by a road, ran north and south and east and west; this helped in keeping on course in a crosswind. In the absence of a compass, with an overcast hiding the sun, he knew how to check his directions: farmers always built their hen houses facing south for protection from the weather. He felt safe in one of his airplanes for, as he put it, "Anyone who hurts himself in one of these things ought to have his head examined."

He would never be an expert pilot, but he was accomplished enough to fly unaccompanied the length and breadth of the country, spreading the gospel of the lightplane. Like many a nonprofessional flier, he piloted by the seat of his pants. In later years, when the Cub's instrument panel became sophisticated enough to boast a turn-and-bank indicator with a little black ball nestled in a curved trough to proclaim a perfect or faulty bank, he seldom bothered to check anything except his altimeter, compass, fuel gauge, and the weather. He was satisfied if the black ball stayed in the cockpit.

On this July day Mr. Piper and his first passenger since he had been certificated climbed aboard a Cub. It was the passenger's first flight. Pilot Piper called out, "Switch on." Someone pulled the prop through, the engine caught, and he taxied to the downwind lip of the cinder runway. He ran up his engine and tested his magneto, taking care to keep his rpm well below one thousand, for the airplane had no brakes.

"All set?" he asked his friend.

"All set."

W. T. Piper opened the throttle and, holding rudder against the propeller torque, he took off. Once the airplane was airborne, no one on the flight line or at the hangar gave it a second thought. Twenty minutes elapsed and the two men had not returned. At thirty minutes the men on the flight line began watching. Forty-five minutes after their departure, Mr. Piper and his passenger were glimpsed walking toward the hangar from the far end of the runway, dragging the machine on its wheels. One wing was in tatters. In they trudged and sat down to rest from their exertions.

"Wonderful day," observed Mr. Piper.

"A little warm, though," said his companion, "walking in the sun."

"Thanks for coming along."

"Thanks for the ride."

"What in hell happened?" exploded a pilot who had witnessed the charade.

"Oh," replied Mr. Piper in the indulgent tone of an elder to a child, "I couldn't gain any altitude and we wound up in the creek."

Help on propagandizing the lightplane began coming from an unexpected quarter. Intercollegiate air meets had been held, incredibly enough, as early as 1911 at Harvard. Never very lusty, this type of flying had been resumed after the war, and to strengthen it, Grover Loening, a pioneer in the design and manufacture of aircraft, had established an intercollegiate flying trophy. It was lodged with the National Aeronautic Association in Washington, D.C. For more than three years the depression wiped out college flying. Then in 1934 students at Amherst, Purdue, the University of Minnesota, and a dozen other institutions began campaigning for a resumption of the meets. Undergraduates—among them Thomas Watson, Jr., who was attending Brown University in Providence, Rhode Island, and in later years was president and then board chairman of International Business Machines—participated in events that were staged like a track meet. They competed in "spot" (precision) landings, "bomb" dropping with paper bags of flour, balloon busting, and intercepting rolls of toilet paper tossed from the cockpit. The experts among them early learned that the quickest way to intercept a roll of toilet paper was to loop.

Then, as now, most college students were reduced to hot dogs and milk shakes by the time the old man's check arrived on the first of the month. To participate in the activities of the National Intercollegiate Flying Club required no great sum, one that could be amassed with three straight passes in the Saturday night crap game if side bets were placed judiciously. A used Cub fitted neatly into the corporate structure of a college flying club. One such machine, bought by the Amherst club, was the third Cub ever produced by the Taylor Aircraft Corporation, licensed NC 12610. It cost five hundred dollars. W. T. Piper, his antenna picking up the vibrations from the college campuses, began compounding the newspaper publicity issuing from the intercollegiate meets. He cultivated the clubs. He corresponded. He listened to complaints. He offered advice.

One of the most enthusiastic fliers at Amherst was a chunky student named William Dengler Strohmeier, the first president of the revived Intercollegiate Flying Club. "Our trouble with the Cub," he wrote Mr. Piper, "is that it's down for engine repairs more than it's up."

"We are making progress on the engine problem," replied Mr. Piper, "and we'll see to it that your Cub is up more than it's down."

W. T. Piper's dogged insistence that a bargain basement airplane was bound to sell began to pay off as the books were closed on the year 1934. Nothing really spectacular happened. Sales quadrupled, but that meant only seventy-one aircraft. It was not the volume that pleased the company treasurer; it was the evident upturn. The national economy had rounded the corner of the Great Depression. A little jingle money began appearing in the pockets of wage earners.

"Next year," said Mr. Piper, the perennial optimist, "we'll really sell airplanes."

No basic changes were being made in the design of the Cub, but small refinements were being added. Jamouneau engineered a winter enclosure for the open cockpit. Optional, its price was forty-five dollars. On the right side was a horizontally split window for getting in and out, a feature that remains to this day in the Super Cub, lineal descendant of the first E–2 in structure and looks. A cockpit heater was still a long way off.

Every so often in the relations between C. G. Taylor and W. T. Piper a storm warning flew from the company masthead. In one of C. G.'s increasingly frequent absences, experimental, bigger, lower-pressure tires were put on the Cub's landing gear.

"Who authorized that?" asked Taylor.

"I did," said the treasurer.

"What do you know about such things?" demanded Taylor.

Mr. Piper was not one to argue, but he was reaching the point of protest. "You're constantly criticizing," he told Taylor. "If you keep interfering with everyone else's work, we're not going to turn out airplanes and we're not going to make any money."

To Jamouneau he said, "When Taylor isn't around, you feel free to make any changes in the design of the E–2 that you think will make it more salable."

Not in the best of health to begin with, Taylor got acute appendicitis. In a months-long convalescence, C. G., ensconced in a house on the edge of the airport, sat at a window dourly watching the factory and the flight line.

Whether it was prescience, or hope, or plodding determination, or luck, or the policies of a politician in the White House dedicated to banishing fear from the human heart, or just the recovery potential of a national economy that had plumbed rock bottom and had nowhere to go but up, or everything in combination, Taylor Aircraft at the close of 1935 had begun putting black ink on the books. It was producing one Cub every working day. More important, the airplanes were selling, thanks in part to Gordon Curtis and his funding company.

William T. Piper, Sr., in 1935 supplied the ultimate proof of his optimism over the future of lightplane manufacture. After his long string of secondhand cars, he blew himself to his first brand new one, a Ford V–8. He paid cash.

Gordon Curtis hit it on the button on that day in 1930 when he remarked that the Taft family ultimately would have to sell the three-quarter-million-dollar Aeronautical Corporation of America for one hundred thousand dollars. In 1935 Walter J. Friedlander bought out the Tafts for that sum, exclusive of the building in Cincinnati where the Aeronca airplane had been fabricated. He turned the company over to his son Carl, and presently Carl established a manufactory upstate in Middletown.

Two Bills of Divorcement

WILLIAM D. STROHMEIER, LATELY OF
Amherst, was a lucky young man on an early summer day of 1936.
He had achieved the payroll of the Taylor Aircraft Corporation. He
had his own sales airplane, and on its side was emblazoned, "BILL
STROHMEIER, FACTORY REPRESENTATIVE." Most of his
classmates were still job hunting; there were precious few jobs to be
had. He had his own ideas about demonstrating the utility of lightplanes and the ease of flying them.

Buoyed by his good fortune, he cruised along in his airplane,
still fragrant with the nitrate dope that smelled like banana oil, used
to treat the wings and fuselage. It was noon. He was hungry. He
would put on a show. He would land alongside a highway and eat
at a hot dog stand. He picked a field, "dragged" it, throttled back to
look it over for impediments, wheeled around, and flared out. Too
late, he saw some telephone wires in his flight path.

"Mr. Weld," he telephoned the Taylor sales manager in Bradford, "I've had an accident."

"Are you hurt?"

"No."

"What parts do you need?"

"I spread the landing gear, is all."

Strohmeier had had only a portion of his baptism as a company
sales rep. Airplanes the factory could mend. Parting with money for
salesmen was something else again.

Weld and Mr. Piper had had their heads together on policy
matters, and the subject, bluntly, was parsimony. The fifteen-dollar-
a-week salary that Walter Jamouneau had been paid when he was
beating the bushes for customers would stand, but wouldn't it be a
dandy idea to keep the men on the road a mite hungry? An expense
account of twenty-five dollars a week was cut to fifteen. But ah,
there was a bonus! A salesman was given an extra dollar a night for
every different place he bedded down in the course of a week. That
kept him on the move. If he elected to spend two or three nights

RAY MILLAND AND CLAUDETTE COLBERT
The Cub was as much a product of publicity as of the assembly line.

in the same place, he lost his bonus. There was another emolument: if he sold a prospect his airplane on the spot, he collected an extra twenty-five dollars.

The expense allowance called for some inventiveness. A man spent an entire morning trying to cadge a ride to the airport to save a taxi fare. Sometimes taxi drivers could be suckered into a free trip in return for a flight once around the field. The rules were firm on the compasses that, by now, were being installed on the instrument panel. They cost the company three dollars. When a demonstration airplane was sold, the buyer had to pay an extra ten dollars for it. If a customer didn't want the compass, the salesman was to wait until the deal was concluded and then surreptitiously remove it. On a trip to Maine Strohmeier forgot.

"There's a new airplane for you on the flight line," Weld told him on his return to the factory. "Where's your compass?"

"I forgot to take it out."

Weld was sorrow incarnate. "Gee," he said, "that's too bad."

Strohmeier took off in his new airplane without a compass. He never forgot again.

It began to be said of the Cub that it was as much a product of publicity as of the production line. This was the indelible imprint of William, Sr. He was indefatigable, always on the go. If a man bought an airplane and agreed to be a duly annointed dealer for his area, the Taylor Aircraft treasurer managed to be on hand to officiate at the sacred rites. Any grass field that any wag decided to dedicate as an airport found him there to deliver a speech. He was the author of one publicity ploy that for a time revived the days of barnstorming. He organized teams of three pilots, three Cubs, and a trailer. The trailer was a perambulating parts depot and bedroom. The teams toured small towns where airplane hops were a novelty. Rides were a dollar on a production line basis.

The professional stunt pilot and a sophisticated version of the postwar flying circus became Piper allies in exhibiting the Cub—a natural showpiece. Pilots trusted it. The National Air Races at Cleveland were becoming an institution. They ran for ten days, drawing enormous crowds that waited with nervous, hopeful expectancy for an accident. Now and then they got a gory reward in the crash of a racer that had too much power on the nose and too little judgment in the cockpit. The fast airplanes were built with so little wingspan that they earned the name of "prostitutes"—they had no visible means of support.

But it was the aerobatic exhibitions that drew the cheers of the spectators. Here the Cub was in its glory.

Two of the most nerveless stunt fliers in the business were Beverly (Bevo) Howard of Charleston, South Carolina, and Mike C. Murphy of Findlay, Ohio. They were personality contrasts. Howard looked like an ascetic. Murphy was robust and ebullient. But put them at the controls of an airplane, and their behavior was that of identical twins. Howard was the first man in the world to perform an outside loop in a lightplane—instead of putting his cockpit in the inside of the maneuver, he pushed forward on the control stick to ride the outside. His mount was a Cub.

Mike Murphy, too, was a precision pilot, but his specialty was stunts. One of his choice acts was landing upside down in an airplane with wheels on both top and bottom. At the All-American Air Maneuvers in Miami, a counterpart of the Cleveland show, he proposed flying a Cub off the top of a speeding car.

"Let me borrow your airplane," he said to the ubiquitous Bill Strohmeier.

Strohmeier swallowed hard. Ted Weld was arriving. If Murphy cracked up, Strohmeier and Taylor Aircraft would part company.

"Okay," he said finally, with grave misgivings.

He could have saved his adrenalin. Murphy had been practicing in Findlay and had the act down pat. He winged off the top of the car without incident.

Landau-Meister

LANDING ATOP A SPEEDING CAR
Stunt pilots helped publicize the Cub.

"Gee," breathed Weld, to Strohmeier, "how did you arrange that?"

The following year, at Cleveland, Murphy topped his own performance. He *landed* a Cub on the top of a speeding car.

Danny Fowlie flew a Cub in air shows in Canada, Cuba, and the United States. At rest his airplane bore lettering that was upside down—because he flew that way, clipping a ribbon stretched between two poles. Like Murphy, he took off from a speeding car. In the days before drunken flying, like drunken driving, drew public censure, Dick Grenier flew a Cub in a simulated alcoholic haze.

Alfred B. Bennett, a Cub distributor, stunted too, but only to display the business value and inherent safety of small airplanes. Daily he commuted off his home lawn, only 450 feet long and surrounded by high trees, to an airport a few miles away, by tethering his airplane to a sturdy pole and flying around it until he had enough speed to cut loose. He repeated his performance at the air shows. Annoyed by the pontificating of the armchair experts on the dangers of landing with a flat tire, he deflated one and took off and landed. Then he removed the tire altogether, and then the entire wheel. He suffered not even so much as a damaged spindle.

In 1936 Taylor Aircraft sold 515 airplanes, and the gross infusion of money into what had been an ailing business came to a half-million dollars. The net wasn't much. The treasurer's scalpel was cutting close to the bone.

Lightplane fabrication had begun to coax investment money out of hiding. To Aeronca and Taylor were added names like Luscombe, Porterfield, and Rearwin. There was another: Cessna. The Cessna Aircraft Company as yet was not in the lightplane business, as the term then was interpreted in Bradford. It was producing a somewhat heavier airplane of outstanding performance, the Airmaster.

Dwane Leon Wallace, a man with Lincolnesque facial features who stood six feet, two and a half, took over the company from his founding uncle, Clyde V. Cessna, in 1936, and thereupon with verve, nerve, work, and guile, piloted it ultimately into the blue chip list of five hundred leading U.S. corporations as listed by *Fortune* magazine. A graduate aeronautical engineer, he kept his company afloat by winning airplane contests wherever the opportunity offered and courting publicity even when it didn't. He turned the corner on profits at the start of World War II when, in New York, he approached a British purchasing commission for a contract to produce twin-engine trainers for the Royal Canadian Air Force. The commission was interested in Wallace's ability to produce, and in something more.

"We would like to know your financial condition," it said.

Wallace telephoned his office in Wichita for a statement. The bank reported a cash balance of less than five dollars. Wallace made another call, to the bank. In an hour he had a credit line of a half-million dollars. That did it. He returned home with a contract for 180 airplanes.

"Boss," said Gordon Curtis to W. T. Piper early in 1936, "I think we need some help."

He was becoming a familiar fixture in the office. Mr. Piper had come to trust his judgment.

"The business," said Curtis, "is growing so fast that you aren't going to be able to finance the expansion you need out of your own pocket."

"What'll it take?"

"At this point, about $100,000."

"That was a figure I'd begun thinking would do it," said Mr. Piper. "But you're not going to get an investor in this thing, making light airplanes."

Curtis had connections. He was on a first-name basis with James Paul Warburg, president of the Bank of Manhattan Company, who dallied with other trinkets like a majority interest in Kuhn, Loeb &

Company, investment banking house, and the chairmanship of the board of the Southern Pacific Railroad. Curtis and Warburg had become friends in the Navy Flying Corps during the war. Back in New York, Curtis telephoned Warburg at his 40 Wall Street office.

"How'd you like to get into the aviation business?" he asked. He explained the dilemma of Taylor Aircraft.

"I'll take half the company," said Warburg, "for $100,000." That was only pocket money to the banker.

For the present, Curtis put the offer on ice.

In the autumn of 1935 C. G. Taylor commissioned Walter Jamouneau to do a little touching-up on the Cub for more sales appeal. Jamouneau's authority was severely limited. He was to keep his hands off the airplane's basic configuration.

With some irritation at this point, Jamouneau, taking William, Sr., at his word that he could make any changes he saw fit, proceeded to alter the plan form of the wing and tail surfaces. Taylor had designed everything at right angles. Wingtips were square. The horizontal and vertical stabilizers were square. The rudder was square. Jamouneau rounded off these members. He disturbed nothing aerodynamically.

By now Taylor was not speaking to his treasurer. He insisted on communicating only by note. His indirection extended to everyone in the company. Their natural response was to go to Mr. Piper with their problems. Taylor let it be known that he felt the treasurer was deliberately proselyting the loyalty of the personnel to him, the president of the company. A forthright man, Mr. Piper had difficulty understanding what was transpiring.

On the day that the first of the production Cubs with the rounded-off corners was wheeled from the assembly line for a test flight, Taylor, recuperating from his illness, was sitting in his window, watching. The altered appearance smote his eye. He reached for a telephone and called Jamouneau.

"Nobody told you to do that!" he stormed.

At that moment Gordon Curtis was talking with Mr. Piper in the tarpaper clad office that had been glued to the side of the factory. Jamouneau strode in.

"I'm fired," he announced. "Taylor just fired the entire engineering staff." That took no heroic effort; the staff consisted of three men.

"Take it easy," counseled Mr. Piper. "You've done a great job. There are adjustments to be made here."

"I knew right then," Curtis said later, "that the boss had decided Taylor had to go."

The denouement was anticlimactic. "You can buy me out or

I'll buy you out," said William, Sr., when at last he managed a confrontation. He had to escape a partnership that was in the advanced stages of decay.

Taylor went searching for money. He found none. William, Sr., had none either, but he had credit.

"I'll pay you a salary of $250 a month for three years," he offered Taylor, "and keep up the payments on any life insurance policies you hold."

Taylor accepted and moved out, but not without a parting, dark prophecy. "This company," he said, "will never survive."

If Taylor proved right, only W. T. Piper would be responsible. He was now president, treasurer, and chairman of the board.

"He was a fine airplane designer," he said of Taylor in later years. "Give him that. He just had a hard time getting along with people."

As the door closed on C. G.'s coattails, Mr. Piper asked Jamouneau, "Do you want to be chief engineer?"

"Yes." Jamouneau was twenty-four years old.

The new chief engineer enjoyed a bonus. The reconfigured Cub was given the designation J–2. The "J" was for Jamouneau.

The year 1937 held promise of being a good one for Taylor Aircraft. Orders were necessitating two shifts of workmen. The second shift went off at midnight. The production schedule was eighteen airplanes a week. W. T. Piper and his eldest son, now secretary and assistant treasurer, figured that income would put the company well over the hump by December 31. The plant was a messy hodgepodge. The original building, of sheet iron, measuring 80 by 120 feet, had suffered ramshackle additions from time to time as production demanded more space. One of these was the paint shop, filled with drums of highly flammable nitrate dope. Bradford's fire protection system was nowhere near adequate at the airport; the plant had no sprinkler system, and this, coupled with the presence of flammable materials, rendered the premiums on fire insurance staggering. William, Sr., couldn't afford them. A recent addition to the factory, costing $10,000, was the only portion covered. A building and loan association, which had done the financing, had insisted on that.

At 10:30 P.M. on March 16, a cold, blustery, snowy night, two men in the dope and finishing department were holing through an airplane firewall with an electric drill. Warren Finch, a deaf mute who had been Taylor Aircraft's first production line employe and was now department foreman, saw a spark spin off the drill and land in some dope-soaked debris on the floor. The stuff flamed. Finch jogged off after a fire extinguisher. By the time he got back the fire plainly was out of hand. All too well aware of the flammable nitrates in the paint shop, he and the other workmen made for an exit.

The *Bradford Era* ran this story in part on March 17:

> The plant of the Taylor Aircraft Company was almost destroyed in less than two hours last night by mad, billowing flames that swept through the frame and metal sections of the factory with almost unbelievable speed. . . .
>
> Firemen, called just before 10:45 P.M., were confronted with flames shooting high above the roofs of the place upon their arrival. It appeared for some time that the metal building, the main sector of the plant, could be saved, but a strong and shifty wind aided the fire.
>
> Flames shot at least 50 feet in the air as one explosion followed another to various parts of the plant, which spread over considerable ground adjacent to Harri Emery Airport in West Branch. Employes said the blasts were from five-gallon cans of "dope," liquid celluloid paint used to treat the fuselages in the finishing processes.
>
> About 20 employes, working on a night shift when the fire started, wheeled 15 planes, most of them almost completed, onto the snow-covered landing field.
>
> Nobody was badly hurt. John Putzman of Wellsville, a riveter in the plant, received burns on the left hand, singed hair and scorched face. . . .
>
> W. T. Piper, principal in the company, is in Los Angeles, Calif., attending the Pacific Aircraft Show. He was notified of the fire early today by T. V. Weld. . . .
>
> Wooden spars, lacquer thinners and gasoline added to the holocaust.

Bill, Jr., was in Bradford the night of the fire.

"Some fire!" remarked a neighbor the next morning.

"What fire?" He had slept through it.

Jamouneau had been in Ottawa seeking a certificate of airworthiness for the Cub for manufacture in Canada.

Tony Piper was on one of those peregrinating sales trips with three airplanes and a trailer in the Waycross-Jesup area of southeastern Georgia. Pug Piper was in college. Bill Strohmeier was in Key West. He didn't see a newspaper account of the fire and didn't telephone the factory until he reached Miami on the 20th. Weld was too busy to talk to him. He got Weld's wife.

"The factory burned down," said she, "three nights ago, and you haven't got a job." It was Strohmeier's birthday.

In Los Angeles, in the early morning hours of the 17th, Saint Patrick's Day, W. T. Piper went out under the darkling sky looking for Gordon Curtis. Weary of the boisterous merrymaking of friends in the aviation business, Curtis had gone to bed at his hotel. At 1 A.M. someone knocked on his door. He didn't answer. The knocking persisted. With some annoyance, he opened the door a crack.

"I've got some bad news," said Mr. Piper. "I'll need some of the financing we were talking about."

"Boss," said Curtis when the president of Taylor Aircraft had described the extent of the loss, "you're going to need more than $100,000. I'd say a quarter of a million."

They talked until 3 A.M. Taylor Aircraft would "go public." Curtis would browse around. In the morning he telephoned George M. Brashears, a Los Angeles investment banker who originally financed the Lockheed Aircraft Corporation. The Warburg offer was still on tap, but Curtis wanted to stake out some other sources of money. Nothing was as hard to sell in a public offering in New York as a fraction of a million dollars. A million came far more easily.

"Sure," said Brashears.

Curtis hung up the telephone. Instantly it rang.

"This is Franklin Field," said the caller. Field was a partner in J. E. Swan & Company, a New York brokerage house. "If there's going to be some financing, we want in on it."

Curtis telephoned Mr. Piper, packing to leave for home.

"We're all set," he said, "whenever you're ready."

There was hand-wringing in Bradford. Weld's customary aplomb was shattered. New-fallen snow blanketed the black ruins of the factory. Acrid odors lingered in the air. Jamouneau, Weld, and Hanford Eckman, a monosyllabic Swede who was in charge of experimental construction, directed employes to begin digging through the rubble. Of raw materials there were scarcely any left. An entire railroad car of dope and another of aluminum had been consumed. But some jigs and fixtures, lathes, and milling machines could still be used when they were cleaned up. Weld set up an office in the airport administration building. He had good reason to worry—the factory was on the threshold of the summer selling season; already it had seventy-five unfilled orders on hand.

"There's got to be an empty building somewhere in town," said Jamouneau, "that we can use."

He and Eckman searched. They turned up an iron foundry that had been abandoned for years. Into it they moved the salvaged tools. Patterns for parts had been destroyed, but these could be duplicated if unassembled parts could be found. A notice to employes was posted: "If you have any parts at home, please bring them in. No questions will be asked." Out of employees' basements and attics and trunks of automobiles came wing ribs, landing gear legs, and engine mounts. Draftsmen in the engineering department copied a set of Cub drawings, borrowed from the U.S. Department of Commerce where they were on file. As components began to trickle from the foundry, an assembly line was set up in a hangar at the airport. Weld and Jamouneau contacted suppliers by telephone.

"We aren't honoring sight drafts," the suppliers were told.

Not one refused to extend credit.

Distributors and dealers began descending on Bradford to snatch up flying machines to fill customers' orders. One, Jake Miller of Lock Haven, Pennsylvania, was in the south central part of the state on a selling trip when the fire occurred. Incredibly, he had not heard of it when, more than a day later, Weld collared him by telephone in the hamlet of Gallitzin, west of Altoona, as he was in the act of selling a Cub to a man who ran a garage. With orders for seven airplanes in his pocket, Miller raced to Bradford. He managed to talk the factory out of two.

The employes had no guarantee that they would get paid. None raised the question. To a man, they went to work. It took W. T. Piper four and a half days of hard driving to get back to Bradford, and by the time he rolled into Main Street some order had begun to emerge from the company's shambles. Rubbing his chin appraisingly at a council of war in the temporary office at the airport, he announced that everything was going to be all right.

"We're going to get refinanced," he said.

He would keep the Curtis offer in Los Angeles on tap. An idea had begun taking shape in the back of his head.

One week after the fire, the first Cub built from scratch was assembled and flown. Now that the crisis had been surmounted, he sat down to take stock of his immediate plight, the makeshift production facilities. Either the factory must be rebuilt soon, or he must find another one in being. Even before the fire, orders for airplanes were taxing the production line. Now he faced up to another consideration: Bradford and Taylor Aircraft had not been completely comfortable with each other since the company had moved in nine years before.

"I get the feeling," William, Jr., had said to his father on one occasion, "that the town regards us as more of a nuisance than an asset."

There was reason. The factory's wage scales were low. Bradford essentially was still an oil town, and the men who worked at enticing crude from the earth—drillers, pumpers, riggers—were well paid. Taylor Aircraft did not generate much spendable income for the town's merchants. Oil field workers made no secret of their conviction that the factory tended to demean wage levels. Moreover, attempts by organizers to interest Taylor Aircraft workers in a union evoked a tight-lipped response from that archconservative, W. T. Piper.

At this moment an unforeseen high card was dealt the management. Within twenty-four hours after the fire, telegraphed offers began arriving to move the factory bag and baggage to Oklahoma, California, Illinois, Texas, Indiana. At first there were a couple of dozen. In two weeks this became a hundred, and in a month a couple of hundred. Cities were looking for new industries and payrolls. The inducements were seductive: manufacturing facilities, bank credits, tax incentives.

As a token of the state of the U.S. economy almost eight years after the stock market crash that initiated the Great Depression, all these communities were angling for a manufactory that had an annual payroll of only a bit more than $100,000. But these were "real dollars" in the lingo of the economists—the FOB Dearborn, Michigan, price of a Ford V–8 four-door sedan was $670.50.

With almost indecent haste, the *Lock Haven Express,* downstate, on March 19 ran a page one story that smelled more like an editorial than news and in disarming simplicity was a model of proselyting technique:

> Lock Haven is inviting the Taylor Aircraft Company to locate in this city, taking over the property formerly occupied by the Susquehanna Silk Mills. . . .
> Theodore Weld, president [*sic*] of the company, is now considering plans for either rebuilding at Bradford or accepting one of the many offers to locate in another city.

"I've been downtown talking," said Mr. Piper to his eldest son, "and nobody seems interested in putting up any money to get us started again. I've been thinking."

"So have I," said William, Jr. "Let's move."

W. T. Piper the elder had been mulling the idea over ever since he got back from Los Angeles.

JAKE MILLER
"Everyone remembers Paul Revere, but nobody remembers the name of his horse."

William, Sr., and Ted Weld began safaris to cities of likely prospect. Each time they returned to Bradford it was evident that the head of the company had not found what he was looking for. To abide by his thesis of underselling the market, he could not, he stated, move to a place where he would have to compete for a labor force accustomed to wages paid by steel mills or automobile factories.

On an early Spring day in 1937 William, Sr., met his match in a man of sheer energy and persuasiveness. His name was Jake Miller. He had a goal. His patient persistence could have worn down the pyramids. He talked William, Sr.'s language. He was small town. He knew flying. He knew selling.

Jacob Willard Miller had been born in Lock Haven, and there he had lived all his life. He was still shy of thirty, slender, black haired, and given to weighing his words. He got his introduction to airplanes while still in high school when a flying circus roared into town. To the worry of his mother, he had been diving off the fretwork-railed Jay Street bridge that spanned the West Branch of the Susquehanna River. It was a long drop. On this day he was swimming with friends around a pier.

"Hey, kid!" a man yelled to him from the bridge. "Let's see you dive from up here."

"No."

"I've seen you do it."

"I hurt my back doing it a couple of days ago."

Just then one of the flying circus biplanes cruised by overhead. Young Jake eyed it.

"I'll buy you an airplane ride if you'll dive off the bridge," said the man.

Suddenly Jake's back didn't hurt any more. Clutching the five dollars that he collected for his feat, he ran the mile and a half to the airfield. A long line of customers were waiting for rides. He was not going to get aboard before darkness closed down operations. As Jake watched, one of the circus airplanes turned turtle on landing, skidding to a stop in a billow of dust. The line of people melted away. Jake clambered into the cockpit of a second airplane, a wartime Jenny with an OX–5 engine.

From that moment on, Jake Miller was lost to anything but flying. He lusted for wings. He took lessons during his college career—majoring, of course, in aeronautical engineering.

By 1937 Jake Miller was a competent pilot and a partner with William and John Widmann, whose family owned a chain of drug stores, in Bald Eagle Airways, a rather grandiose name for a shoestring operation. For five years Bald Eagle had been a Taylor Cub distributor, and Miller ranged central Pennsylvania to separate prospective airplane purchasers from their money. It was Miller who climbed into W. T. Piper's secondhand car one day at Lock Haven to find the floor awash with peanut shells.

He had been a beneficiary of the Taylor Aircraft treasurer's philosophy on lightplanes. Prior to the appearance of the Cub, he had had to charge twenty-five dollars an hour for student instruction in big, lumbering, expensive biplanes. Cubs cut that to ten dollars. A lot more people could afford that. In a modest way Bald Eagle Airways was prospering. Of the five airplanes it owned, three had been made in Bradford.

No sooner had Jake Miller talked the Bradford factory out of two of its sketchy supply of new airplanes than he marched into the precincts of the Lock Haven Chamber of Commerce and seized the attention of Edward Heffner, its chairman.

"There's the silk mill," he said. "It's just the thing."

"They were burned out in Bradford," said Heffner. "They'll need financing."

"They can get it. We can help." Miller had his teeth in something, and he would not let go. "Come on, let's talk to them."

The silk mill had gone bankrupt five years before. It was huge. It was empty. It abutted the airport. Expensive looms, bolted to the floor, were rusting away.

"You can knock a hole in the west wall to bring in the raw materials," argued Miller to the Pipers and Ted Weld, "and knock one in the east wall to wheel out your finished airplanes."

"We could never use that much room," said Mr. Piper, "never."
"But you can get the mill for a song."
"How much?"
"We'll find out."

In Lock Haven, Miller pushed the newspaper campaign. Rebecca Gross, a reporter for the *Express,* became an ally. In a page one statement, Frank O'Reilly, publisher of the newspaper, opened the city gates to the aircraft manufacturer in Bradford:

> Lock Haven rightly feels that it has much to offer in its negotiations with the Taylor Aircraft Company on the company's taking over the plant of the Susquehanna Silk Mill to replace the Bradford factory. . . .
>
> We have a population inspired by high ideals of Americanism. . . .

In truth, Mr. Piper had made up his mind. He was just toying with his options. Besides, the cardinal rule of good salesmanship was to let the opposite party generate the anxiety. The price, whatever it was at the moment, might come down.

On a bright day in May Ted Weld and Gordon Curtis made a reconnaissance of the Lock Haven property. They were under meticulous orders from the boss. A full-dress meeting of chamber of commerce officials was held around a table in the office of Calvin R. Armstrong, president of the Lock Haven Trust Company and the town's most prestigious banker. Armstrong presided. Weld and Curtis proceeded to pin down the price for the silk mill.

Mr. Piper had had an appraisal made of it by an industrial engineering firm.

"Of course," said the firm's report, "the downstairs will give you all the room you will need for years." The fifty thousand square feet downstairs was eightfold what Taylor Aircraft had had in Bradford.

The negotiations in Armstrong's office appeared to be a bit complex. His bank had been involved in the silk mill. New York's National City Bank had an interest in the proceedings as a creditor. Brown, Crosby & Company of New York were realtors for the failed mill.

"A lot of people have to be satisfied," said Armstrong. Weld and Curtis sat poker faced. "The price will be $130,000." He added hastily, "But $30,000 can be handled in notes."

Unknown to Curtis and Weld, a representative of the realty firm, which had reached a conclusion with the National City Bank, was listening in on the conversation through an open telephone line.

Armstrong excused himself and picked up the telephone. "Yes,"

THE SILK MILL
One way to make $35,000 was to keep your mouth shut.

he said, "yes." He returned to the table. "The price," he amended, looking slightly crestfallen, "is $95,000. That includes ten company houses on the property and sixteen acres of land."

"One way to make $35,000," commented Curtis to Weld on their way back to Bradford, "is to keep your mouth shut."

"Good heaven!" exclaimed William, Sr., when the two had reported. "When will we ever use the second floor of that silk mill?"

Within two months of initial occupancy, the airplane company's engineering department had purloined part of it.

Of Bankers, Brokers, Barristers, and Hanky Panky

AT THE INTERSECTION OF EAST WATER and Jay streets in Lock Haven hard by the bridge from which Jake Miller won his first airplane ride stands a block of granite:

> *Erected July 29, 1899*
> *By the Hugh White Chapter*
> *Of the Daughters of the*
> *American Revolution*
> *Of Lock Haven, Pa.*
> *Located in the Stockade of*
> *Fort Reed*
> *Built in 1775 for Defence* [sic]
> *Against the Indians*

This was the community that in mid-1937 was about to take to its bosom a manufacturing firm that would make "Lock Haven, U.S.A." known throughout the world of air transport.

A tarnished jewel of the Alleghenies, the town had been, in its 160 years, the site of the westernmost of a string of military bastions against marauding red men, the subject of real estate investments by a queen of Spain who was jittery over the permanency of her crown, a roistering lumber and sawmill port on the West Branch of the Susquehanna River, and during the Prohibition Era, the locale of some of the noblest houses of assignation between New York and Pittsburgh. In the 1920s it supplied a good part of the northeastern seaboard with as fine a cask of bootleg whisky, trucked openly down its Main Street, as was obtainable from rum runners lying warily offshore in the Atlantic. One of Lock Haven's legendary boasts was that it was largely responsible for the nomination in 1924 of John W. Davis as a compromise Democratic candidate for the presidency on the 103rd ballot of the national convention in New York. Lock Haven's output of alcoholic spirits, distilled in a lovely valley across a mountain ridge to the southeast by a man known even to the local parsons as Prince Farrington, did much to prolong the wrangle between William Gibbs McAdoo and Alfred E. Smith. The delegates were under no compulsion to adjourn for a drink. At least three of the "prince's" bootleggers were, two and three decades later, respectable Lock Haven businessmen in good standing at the chamber of commerce.

The venality of Lock Haven's own politicians was no more, no less, than that of any other semirural, lightly industrialized town. Their peccadillos now and then provided juicy gossip after hours in the city room of the daily press.

Brought to justice on a charge of having pushed a customer to his death down a flight of stairs, the blonde, buxom inmate of one of the brothels was asked by the prosecutor, "Now, how far would you say it is from the door of your bedroom to the head of the stairs?"

"Why, Homer," exclaimed the innocent, if soiled, lass, "you ought to know!"

Biggest of the establishments for the purchase of transient love was Nell Bowes' house on Brown Street in the south of town. Nell was a rather stunning woman, her 140 pounds appropriately distributed, and her taste in fillies was exquisite. Her competition included two ladies known as Big Anne and The Mink who, it was said, grew so popular that they incorporated themselves. The end of Prohibition was the end of all this hanky panky in Lock Haven, and of course there hasn't been a single prostitute in the town since.

Planted between the West Branch and Bald Eagle Creek and walled by "brooding, misty mountains" in the words of author Isabel Winner Miller, Lock Haven had been known as Old Town in pre-Revolutionary days. Old Town and the upper reaches of the West Branch knew violence. With a talent for intrigue during the Revolution, the British played footsie with the Indians and established a going price of ten dollars for every Colonial white scalp delivered, whether of man, woman, or child. In 1778 Indians, Tories, and British soldiers slaughtered hundreds of settlers in upstate Pennsylvania. At Fort Reed, Old Town, the inhabitants were warned, and the annals tell of the Great Runaway down the river in flat boats, batteaux, canoes, rafts, and even pig troughs. It was five years before they returned.

As early as 1830 Old Town was a lumbering center. The industry reached its pinnacle in the 1880s. The wealth that was timber created lumber barons who in the mid-nineteenth century built mansions in the communities of the West Branch. Some of them in Lock Haven still stand today.

A twelve-hundred-mile state network of canals described by Rebecca Gross, the tart-tongued newspaperman's newspaperwoman, as "a magnificent pipe dream inspired by New York State's Erie Canal," reached Lock Haven in 1834. They endured for fifty-five years, and in their heyday were highways for boats and barges that carried passengers, mail, express, farm products, lumber, and coal. They gave Lock Haven, established by a businessman-adventurer, Jeremiah Church, its name. On the Susquehanna the town was called the "head of navigation." It had canal locks, and it was a haven for lumbermen of the working echelon who crawled ashore to sleep off the effects of potions purveyed by boats that plied the West Branch with bottled goods. Periodic floods, the ravishing of the forests, and the construction of a railroad to Lock Haven ultimately did in the West Branch canals. Today a canal segment still serves a purpose as a sedimentation pool for a paper mill.

A respectable hostelry, the four-story Fallon Hotel opened in 1855. It was named for the Fallon brothers, John and Christopher, agents in the United States of America for Her Majesty, Queen Maria Christina of Spain. Maria must have been loaded. She invested five million dollars in this country, including a substantial sum in the Fallon. The highest mountain in Clinton County was named for her consort, the Duke of Riansares. So, later, was the barroom in the Fallon.

A silk manufactory, one in a chain known as the Susquehanna Silk Mills, had come to Lock Haven seventeen years before Taylor Aircraft's arrival. By June 1932 the depression had caught up with the Susquehanna Silk Mills. Operations in Lock Haven closed down. It was a sick town. A devastating flood in 1936, the worst since the year 1889 (a product of the lumbering period that had denuded the mountainsides), had left it prostrate.

A community of ten thousand souls, Lock Haven was 120 miles by road and 80 by air south by east of Bradford. Bellefonte, in the mountainous "Hell Stretch" for pilots flying the mails in open cockpit biplanes during the decade of the 1920s, was less than 25 air miles to the southwest. Compared with Bradford's valley, Lock Haven's was broad. This raised fewer problems for aircraft operation. Lock Haven was a thousand feet lower in altitude, with a corollary improvement in winter weather, and yet it too was heir to some of the "lake effect" storms. In minutes, snow showers sweeping across the spires of the hills could blot out the sun. But there were added compensations. To a man contemplating the manufacture of aircraft, the sinuous West Branch could be an asset in testing floats, and both the New York Central and Pennsylvania railroads provided freight service.

There were other entries on the right side of the ledger. Prices

GORDON CURTIS
A presidential aspirant tore
up his contract.

were much lower than those in Bradford. A small house rented for twenty dollars a month. In Bradford that was the cost of a single room. Lock Haven stores advertised men's suits for twelve-fifty and steak for eighteen cents a pound.

In 1937 Lock Haven needed industry. The flood of the year before had created some jobs of reconstruction, but that wasn't enough. The town needed W. T. Piper's aircraft factory so badly that it paved the single, 2,800-foot airport runway. The aircraft factory needed Lock Haven's abandoned silk mill.

William Thomas Piper had come into a bonanza. He kept saying he was going to find a tenant for the upper floor of the silk mill, but he never got around to it. The mill at 820 East Bald Eagle Street abutting the airport had been built to stand. Constructed of steel, brick, and reinforced concrete, it had a total floor area equal to that of two football fields. The mill had been built late in 1919 and early 1920 at a cost, including a sewer system and the company houses, of $831,000. It had a sprinkler system for fire, fed by a fifty-thousand-gallon water tank. On the property was a Pennsylvania Railroad siding. The price of $96,146.61, including accrued taxes, was a shade more than eleven cents on the dollar of original investment.

Taylor Aircraft moved. By June 15 the hegira was well under way. Salvageable tools and jigs rolled south on trucks along with aluminum sheeting and steel tubing. Employes moved, too—some two hundred of them.

An audit was taken. The company's physical assets and materials inventory would bulk big in the public financing that Mr. Piper and Gordon Curtis had discussed. An inventory was in progress at the time that the company's goods were in transit from Bradford.

Meantime, the silk mill had to be paid for. W. T. Piper was about as broke as he ever had been since he went into the oil business more than thirty years before. The fire had wiped him out. By now he had sunk $150,000 of his own money into Taylor Aircraft. What with the intricacies of floating a stock issue under the rules of the new Securities and Exchange Act—designed to forestall any more debacles in Wall Street—funds from public financing were some months away. Gordon Curtis, the financial marriage broker, knew what to do. He called his friend Joe Swan, the stockbroker, in New York. Franklin Field of Swan and Company had been breathing down Curtis' neck for a piece of the Taylor Aircraft financing ever since he made the telephone call to Los Angeles on Saint Patrick's Day. Joe Swan himself was no less anxious than Field.

In the end the company had less than $5,000 in cash, notes to banks and creditors of $100,000, and net working capital of $2,000. Its president was wagering everything that at last it was on the high road.

As a manufacturing enterprise, Taylor Aircraft had been unique from the start, and it remained in character. To the employes it brought down from the Bradford area it began adding others from the local labor force. They were not the prototype of the industrial production line laborer. For the most part they were young, with an average age of twenty-three, caught up in the romance of fabricating flying machines. Their wage rate for welding, stamping and riveting wing ribs, and sewing and doping fabric was considerably

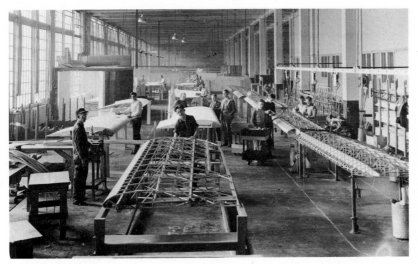

MAKING WINGS
It was the day of soft-skinned airplanes.

FINAL ASSEMBLY
Henry Ford had nothing on W. T. Piper.

less than that at the local paper mill, but then the paper mill didn't let a person skip off the job at will to take flying lessons for a dollar an hour, subject only to making up the time later. Within a year one of every ninety residents of Lock Haven was a pilot. The employe flying program embodied a substantial fringe benefit for the company, and while W. T. Piper was never so gauche as to voice the thought, he was well aware of one reason that his youngsters did no shoddy work. If they skimped it was their necks.

In the company's growing years the informality of the production line encompassed other phases of the business. Someone was always off in a corner inventing something. Hanford Eckman, a gruff Swede who had assumed the responsibility for production on the departure of C. G. Taylor, was a genius with metals.

"All Swedes," generalized Tony Piper, "are natural tinsmiths."

It was Eckman who, with the merest smattering of aerodynamics, designed the first side-by-side seater in the fall of 1937. Known as the J–4, or the Coupe, the airplane went counter to Mr. Piper's philosophy. It implied private ownership, and that was exactly what he had argued against from the beginning. His airplanes were for instruction.

"Raise the roof," he commanded as he sat in the wooden mock-up. "More headroom. If we're going to do this, let's have some comfort."

The sales staff grew planlessly, by accretion. Jake Miller, who had played a starring role in inducing the company to move, somehow never returned to the management of Bald Eagle Airways and his Cub distributorship after the arrival of the trucks from Bradford.

"Why don't you look around the east coast," Ted Weld suggested, "and see about setting up some more distributors?"

Perhaps as a reward for his labors with the chamber of commerce the previous March, he was paid ten dollars over the going rate for salesmen—twenty-five dollars a week, plus the customary twenty-five for expenses. Like Strohmeier, he always bummed rides to and from the airport.

"At that money," he recalled in later years, "I had to."

Taylor Aircraft was on the doorstep of two major events in its short history. It was growing up. In the wake of C. G. Taylor's departure, and the acquisition of a respectable manufacturing facility, it needed a new identity. And it needed money. That would come from its first venture into public financing.

William, Jr., three years out of Harvard, had become his father's right arm in company management. Two years of selling in the western states had given him a good grounding in merchandising. He knew the elements of production, having taken over the supervision of the plant in Bradford when the Piper-Taylor partnership was dissolved. He was no dilettante. He could spray paint with the best of the hourly paid employes.

By November 1937 William Thomas Piper, Sr., of Knapp Creek faced up to the first brush in his life with those strange denizens of the big cities, the bloodless financiers. First would come a new name for the company. The Pipers, senior and junior, Joe Swan, Curtis, and Weld sat down in the president's office in Lock Haven which served also as the board room to dream up a good handle.

"I see no reason," said Swan, "why you should go on giving free advertising to C. G. Taylor." Taylor, by now, had established a new and competitive company first in Butler, Pennsylvania, and then in Alliance, Ohio.

"I've been thinking," said William, Sr., "about one of those contractions—like Aeronca for the Aeronautical Corporation."

"It doesn't mean anything," interposed Bill, Jr.

"We ought to tie the company into a personality," put in Weld.

"Like Piper," said Curtis.

So it would be the Piper Aircraft Corporation. It was so chartered under the laws of Pennsylvania. A board of directors was elected: the Pipers senior and junior, Weld, Gordon Curtis, Douglas Parmentier of the Swan organization, and Joe Swan.

Drawing up a launching plan for public financing was something else again. Under the rules of the Securities and Exchange Commission, public offerings had to be based on an audit that was no more than three months old. An audit by Lybrand, Ross Brothers and Montgomery, nationally known, had been made in June. A new one was ordered. This one was conducted by the same firm but by a different man over a period of six weeks.

"Get a good attorney," Mr. Piper's old friend Harvey Haggerty of the Bradford National Bank had told him, "or those New York bankers will steal your eyeteeth."

The anatomy of a $250,000 stock issue proved to be an affidavit to the admonition. On the day that the details finally were hammered out, Curtis got the Pipers into a private huddle. "Two things," he said. "This is only the beginning, and the brokers are our markets for the future. So we take care of them. The second is the distribution of stock."

William, Sr., nodded. "I've been thinking that we ought to avoid a concentration that might threaten the management of the company."

"Right. Let's arrange for 250,000 shares of common at a dollar par, 21,500 shares of convertible preferred at 2½ to 1, no par, with a cumulative sixty-cent annual dividend, and 100,000 warrants at fifty cents to buy the common. The boss will get 80,000 common and 57,000 of the warrants."

It sounded simple. But nobody was paying any heed to the two audits.

Everybody concerned was jittery over the SEC regulations. There was enough legal talent on the payroll at the moment to start a legislature.

The man who had made the second audit telephoned Curtis from Lock Haven at this point and asked him to come over to look at the result. He confided that he had sent a copy to Joe Swan. Curtis, arriving by overnight train, glanced over the auditor's findings and sucked in his breath.

"Now, what?" asked Bill, Jr., who was getting a surfeit of the goings-on among the alleged experts.

"It's the registration," said Curtis, lying in his teeth. "I'll be in touch."

He hurried back to New York and called Swan.

"The whole deal's off," announced Swan almost before Curtis could say hello. "That company can't conceivably make any money."

"Joe," said Curtis, "you sit still."

"I'm about to call Piper."

"If you do, I'm going to come down there personally and commit mayhem on you."

Racing from his office at 270 Madison Avenue, he caught the subway to Swan's office at 20 Broad Street in lower Manhattan. "I want a closed room and the two audits," he said on arrival.

Subject to headaches, he began taking aspirin. He studied the two audits. At length he had an answer. The second audit was correct. Somehow a mistake had been made in taking the first audit. It showed a substantial profit despite the devastating fire and the cost of moving from Bradford to Lock Haven, as compared with a very small profit for the four months that the company operated in the new plant. The plunging profit curve would make it difficult to market the stock, but even more important, the discrepancies in the audits might make it hard to obtain an approved prospectus from the SEC.

"Gordon," said Swan as Curtis emerged from several hours of study, "you've got to make Lybrand admit in writing that their first audit was wrong. They ought to pay the $7,500 it cost too."

"No," said Curtis. "Our problem now is to decide what changes can be made in the prospectus to make it acceptable to the SEC."

To the Pipers he said, "Swan wants Lybrand, a respectable, nationally known company, to cut their own throats. I've decided that both audits have got to appear in the prospectus, with an explanation of the discrepancies."

"I won't be a party to damning Lybrand," said William, Sr.

Curtis composed a footnote to the prospectus. The lawyers were satisfied. Lybrand was satisfied. The company was satisfied. Best of all, the SEC was satisfied.

On Thursday, March 3, 1938, the newly minted Piper Aircraft Corporation at long last made its first public offering of common and preferred stock, plus subscription warrants. While brokers were still studying the issue on Tuesday, March 8, "They all," in the words of Gordon Curtis, "left town for ten days." Richard Whitney and Company, headed by a man who five times had been president of the New York Stock Exchange, was suspended for insolvency. The charge was appropriating customers' securities. Whitney subsequently was convicted and sentenced to prison.

When the brokers decided it was safe to look their customers in the eye again, the Piper stock was sold.

The cost of the operation had been astronomical—$38,000 for a mere quarter million dollars of capital. A few months later the company floated another issue for three-quarters of a million at a cost of a mere $1,200.

"I guess," remarked Mr. Piper ruefully to his eldest son, "that's what Haggerty meant about those New York fellows."

While Piper Aircraft was refinancing in the presence of a market for airplanes that was experiencing a slow but steady growth (Piper's sales alone in 1938 were 701 aircraft, forty-one *times* the number sold only five years before), competitive enterprises began angling for a piece of the action. The magazine *Aero Digest* for March 1939 listed seventy-three aircraft manufacturers, fourteen in Piper's weight and price brackets. Fourteen was stretching the truth. The bulk of them were in the fringe category, fashioning flying machines with one eye peeled for any well-heeled stranger to the business who could be gulled into investment. Beech Aircraft in Wichita, founded by Walter H. Beech, made superlatively good airplanes, but its prices were manyfold those of the Cub class. Dwane Wallace of Cessna was yet to get into the lightplane business. Only the Porterfield, manufactured in Kansas City, C. G.'s Taylorcraft, and Carl Friedlander's Aeronca represented any kind of challenge, and that as yet was minimal. Porterfield's production was too sparse to merit mention. The Cub completely dominated its market.

The only person in lightplane manufacture whose imagination and sales sense matched that of William, Sr., was Friedlander. A big, handsome, outgoing man and avid horseman, he promptly junked the Aeronca wire-braced Bathtub when his father bought out the Tafts and, casting a speculative eye at the strut-stabilized Taylor design, brought out a similar model, the "K," subsequently renamed the Champion. He also produced a low-wing, two-seater with a cruising speed of 108 miles an hour and a high-wing, side-by-side Chief. Like the Cub, the Friedlander airplanes were stable. They played no tricks. Aeronca abandoned manufacture of its flat, two-cylinder engine, installed the forty-horsepower Continental and, later, a Lycoming of similar design. This made the "K" model at $1,290 competitive with the Cub in performance and price.

Friendlander's only problem was the same one that plagued the rest of Piper's competition: limited production.

"Let's see what we can do to improve the product," William, Sr., kept saying to Jamouneau.

Under no circumstances would he make any basic alterations in his tandem trainer. It was his bread and butter. But he could and did refine it. In automobile manufacture this was known as face-lifting.

Late in 1937 the J–2 metamorphosed into the J–3. William, Sr., named it the Cub Sport, which sounded festive, which was exactly what he intended. The J–2 had hard seats on a plywood frame. The J–3 substituted a chair-type front seat and a bench-type in the rear, both upholstered. The panel was improved. It now contained as standard equipment, in addition to an altimeter and gauges to

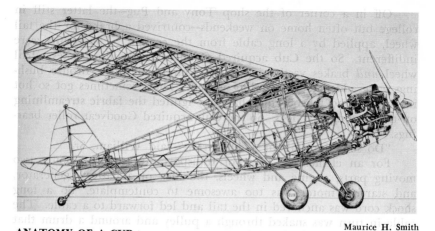

ANATOMY OF A CUB   Maurice H. Smith
It had only two moving parts.

show engine revolutions and oil temperature and pressure, a compass
and an airspeed indicator. The instruments didn't cost the factory
much. A tachometer, essentially an automobile speedometer with a
different face, came at five dollars wholesale, the compass at eleven
dollars, and the airspeed indicator at twenty. But to a youngster
aglow with the pride of a first solo, the panel was a case of jewels.
Hand and foot controls were prettied up. Control cables were buried
under the floor. Jamouneau's winter enclosure, the upper part of the
split window on the starboard side, became standard. An aluminum
sleeve around the exhaust pipe collected warm air for the cabin and
carburetor. (The Volkswagen car after World War II adopted the
same thing to heat its passenger compartment.) The J–3 was given a
balanced rudder and a modified fin.

Some other changes were being forced by Friedlander. The
"K" boasted both brakes and a tail wheel. In the private, proud,
esoteric world of the airplane pilot, these were accoutrements equat-
ing with a "Hollywood muffler" on a car. It was downright mortify-
ing to a Cub pilot, with only a tail skid and no brakes, to taxi down
the flight line weaving to and fro to see past the engine by application of rudder and throttle. His reflexes had to be especially nimble
in maneuvering downwind. If he blasted the prop with his elevators
depressed, he could be up on his nose, hanging by his seat belt in a
twinkling, and if a spanking breeze caught his vertical stabilizer, he
could groundloop. So the Cub acquired a tail wheel. Now, without
the restraint of a tail skid, a man could be thrown into a panic if
he headed for the hangar at too fast a clip. His only recourse was to
jump out, grab a strut, and yell for help.

"Do something about a brake," Mr. Piper said to Tony.

Off in a corner of the shop Tony and Pug—the latter still in college but often home on weekends—contrived a brake for the tail wheel, applied by a long cable from the cockpit. The results were indifferent. So the Cub acquired Goodrich hydraulic brakes. Tail wheel *and* brakes vastly simplified ground handling. Bronze bushings were added to the landing wheels. These sometimes got so hot in landing and takeoff runs that they ignited the fabric streamlining on the landing gear legs. So the Cub acquired Goodyear roller bearings.

"Do something about a self-starter," said William, Sr.

For an elementary piece of transportation that had only two moving parts, engine and wheels, the idea of a battery, generator, and starting motor was too awesome to contemplate. So a long shock cord was anchored in the tail and led forward to a cable. The cable in turn was snaked through a pulley and around a drum that could be engaged by hand lever to a starter dog on the engine. A pilot cranked the shock cord taut and released it. Sometimes the engine started. It was simpler to pull the prop through by hand.

"If the thing hadn't been so underengineered," mused Jake Miller later, "it might have been around longer."

The Piper training plane up to now had been painted a solid blue, or green, or red. The J–3 for the first time standardized on yellow because it was the most readily visible color in a sky where the rule was, "See and be seen."

Engines had been vastly improved in the short space of two years, and now there were three suppliers, not one. To Continental Motors were added Franklin, a former car manufacturer, in Syracuse, New York, and Lycoming, at Williamsport, later a division of the AVCO Manufacturing Corporation. All the engines were flat fours, all essentially of the same design. Horsepowers ran from forty to fifty and were expandable. Of the three, the Lycoming held the most promise; it was this same Lycoming engine, stepped up in power, that in 1940 carried aloft the world's first successful helicopter designed by Igor Sikorsky.

There was a fourth brand of engine, the three-cylinder Lenape radial. While it was a livelier piece of machinery than the flat fours, it had vibrations that were harrowing. Piper never mounted more than a baker's dozen Lenapes on the noses of Cubs.

The new families of engines emancipated the light airplane. A ceiling of 10,000 feet was commonplace, and a cruising speed of eighty to eighty-five miles an hour easily obtainable if protuberances on the airframe were cleaned up. Some training school proprietors shook their heads disapprovingly—with a mammoth fifty horsepower, a student got aloft too fast to learn how to hold his airplane straight and true against torque and a quartering wind.

J–3 MODEL
Mr. Piper named it the Cub Sport, which sounded festive.

The wood spars that carried the air loads, made of Oregon spruce because of its resilience and high ratio of strength to weight, had become an annoyance. The wood itself was becoming scarce—World War I had made big inroads on the available stands—and lumbering companies were loath to harvest trees to meet the small demand from aircraft manufacturers. Government inspectors, allowing a minimum amount of grain to the inch, too frequently were forcing the factory to junk a substantial portion of a carload. This was costly.

William, Sr., conducting a visitor through the plant, would point to the floor under a planing machine and remark, "There's the most expensive pile of shavings in the world."

Wing ribs had been fabricated of aluminum alloy since the first E–2 model. Now, working with the Aluminum Company of America, Piper began switching to metal spars. They were quite a sales feature. Unchanged in the J–3 was its essential simplicity. Unchanged too was the total lack of insulation against the clatter of the engine. Noise was the hallmark of the Cub.

To speed production, the factory developed a "ferris wheel" holding twelve wings and six fuselages. As it rotated, workmen sprayed dope on the fabric. By the time one cycle was complete the skin was ready for the second coat. An overhead monorail conveyor system was installed, complete with switches, crossovers, and sidings, to connect all departments of manufacture. Henry Ford had nothing on W. T. Piper.

The Piper policy of keeping the salesmen hungry had deleterious effects on the competition. While it sold airplanes, it left the individual drummer with the approximate moral compunctions of an Indian bent on horse-stealing.

The technique of picking the other man's pocket for a sale was demonstrated one day by Strohmeier in Cocoa Beach, Florida. Strohmeier had a hot prospect, but the man was enamored of Friedlander's refurbished and elegant Aeronca, then still powered by a two-cylinder engine. Strohmeier theatrically invited his prospect to watch him wire off one cylinder of the four-cylinder Cub. He screwed out one spark plug, wrapped it in paper, and wound it with a rubber band so it wouldn't short out.

"Now," said Strohmeier, "watch."

He chocked the wheels, cracked the throttle, and pulled the prop through. Climbing in, he took off, circled the field, and landed. It was no sweat—he still had three-quarters of his power.

"When the Aeronca man comes by again," said Strohmeier, "ask him to disconnect one of *his* spark plugs and see what happens." He got the order.

Piper Aircraft's banditry on the sales echelon went hand in glove with its imaginative press-agentry. Early in the spring of 1938 the factory asked one of its test pilots, Kenneth T. Kress, if he would be interested in celebrating the anniversary of the inauguration of air-mail service by the U.S. Army in 1918. Just how the Cub would fit into the ceremonies of this auspicious occasion went unexplained.

"Celebrating like how?" asked Kress.

"Like flying a round trip between Newark and Miami," he was told. Then there was an afterthought, like the thump of a man dropping the other shoe on the floor above: "Nonstop." It was only something more than eleven hundred miles each way.

Kress was a careful, cautious pilot. He planned a fueling pickup at Raleigh, North Carolina, and at Jacksonville, Florida, both coming and going. The J–3 to be used, with registration 20280, was equipped with a fifteen-gallon belly tank and a wobble pump to transfer the fuel to the main tank. Kress had a radio receiver but no transmitter. Eastern Air Lines would provide weather forecasts. Glen Englert, Kress' assistant in factory test work, would be copilot.

Bill Mann, a confederate, would drive the gasoline-laden truck at Raleigh, and Romer Wyant, a Lenape engine representative, the one at Jacksonville.

Kress and Englert took off from Newark early in the morning of May 18. The weather went sour. Winds were contrary to the forecasts. Yet they made Raleigh, and Mann, tied to a rear fender of a Chevrolet pickup, tied ropes to gas cans as Kress and his companion made passes over the airport and lifted them up. It was a bit touch-and-go because the Chevy was slow to accelerate, and the heavily laden Cub had a stall speed somewhat above the normal thirty-eight miles an hour. At Jacksonville things went better. Wyant used a Ford pickup; it was faster.

Now the Piper celebrants of the airmail anniversary began encountering other problems. The hour was late, ceilings were low, winds buffeted them, and the "night effect" on the low-frequency radio range navigation signals left Kress with doubts about their accuracy. He spent several hours southbound before giving it up as a bad job, and returned to Jacksonville to orbit. At daylight he flew low over the downtown hotel where he knew Wyant was staying, trying futilely to tumble him out of bed. By luck, the airways weather bureau man at the airport had watched the refueling procedure the evening before. Racing the Ford pickup along the runway, he gave the Cub another prodigious swallow of gasoline.

Kress had not planned to refuel at Miami because the gravel runway at the 36th Street Airport (now Miami International) was short. The Lenape engine people, worried over the winds and weather, had had the foresight to fly a man to Miami and arrange for fuel. He transferred fifteen gallons from a Ford roadster.

Northbound, Kress topped off his main and belly tanks at Jacksonville and then, worried over the persistent low ceilings, proceeded to store extra five-gallon cans behind the rear seat to orbit the area again. He had not installed a static line on his altimeter, and it lagged by about twenty feet. During one pass he went through a treetop and broke loose the right wheel pant fitting. That was only a minor fret. He snatched up a new battery for radio reception while he was about it, refueled at daybreak, made his rendezvous with Mann at Raleigh, and a few minutes after 8 P.M. on May 20 greased his Cub onto the runway at Newark.

Kress and Englert had flown 2,390 miles nonstop, not counting the orbits at Jacksonville, behind an engine that shook out their eyeteeth. Aloft for sixty-three hours and fifty-four minutes, they were bone tired.

"Good show," pronounced the Piper press department.

It made all the newspapers.

Piper people took all such promotion exercises in stride. There were others.

Item: Briefly, in 1939 W. T. Piper, Sr., reduced the price of his lowest-cost Cub, with a forty-horsepower engine, to $995 FAF. This was considerably more than the $700 that Eugene Vidal, the director of the then Federal Bureau of Air Commerce and father of the latter-day author and playwright, Gore Vidal, had been plugging for two years, but it was still a good sales ploy. A world's fair was opening on New York's Flushing Meadows. Piper Aircraft suggested that a Cub be put on a pedestal in front of the fair's aviation exhibit. The fair management agreed, provided, however, that it would bear no price tag. The Piper press agents were delighted to discover that the aircraft registration number 995 was available. When the Cub was unveiled in its pristine glory, someone, somehow, had put a dollar sign in front of the registration on the tail.

Item: On the west coast a team of three men, Tom Smith, Harley Long, and Clyde Schlieper, with on-the-fly refuelings, kept a Cub, the "Little Bear," aloft for 218 hours, 23 minutes, for a new world's lightplane endurance record.

Item: At Miami's air show in 1939, out of 625 airplanes of every description that participated in a fly-down from all parts of the United States, 261 were Cubs. Scribes dubbed the affair the "Cub Convoy."

Item: Piper collected newspaper and magazine clippings by the bale when it announced eight hours of free dual instruction with the purchase of a plane.

Item: Forty-eight Cubs, one for every state in the Union and each toting a toothsome girl in the rear seat, were flown to LaGuardia

Airport, New York, for the benefit of the Royal Canadian Air Force Benevolent Fund. The news media tripped over each other's feet to cover the event.

Item: Frank Hawks, one of the most famous fliers of his day, was making news with a superfast monoplane, a Texaco Oil sign emblazoned on its sides, called "Time Flies." Presently the great aviator was supplementing his speed runs with flights in a plane named "Time Flits." It was a Cub.

Item: Piper "Taxicubs" appeared. It was a publicity gag.

Item: Millions of book matches were handed out by cigarette merchants, each carrying a message from Piper Aircraft—send in ten cents and receive a Cub pin for your lapel. The promotion was self-liquidating. The matches cost two cents and the pin even less.

Item: Any bonafide aviation writer in the United States could get free instruction and solo time at Lock Haven. Dozens did. His readiest qualification was membership in the Aviation Writers Association (later the Aviation/Space Writers Association). Every time that one such journalist showed up, bright-eyed and bushy-tailed, the publicity was in the bag.

Item: A cigarette-manufacturing company purveying a brand called Wings bought one Cub a week (at cost) equipped with a Continental engine (at cost) to be given away on a radio program called "Wings of Destiny." A smartly uniformed pilot, Arthur Segar Pierce, delivered each airplane personally to successful contestants. Scheduled for a run of six months, the stunt got so popular that it lasted a year and a half.

Item: By June 1940 the sheer flamboyance of the Piper sales operation had so impressed the magazine *Fortune* of the Henry Luce publishing empire—selling for a dollar a copy, it was a bible to the American business community—that it ran a seven-page article on the man who, at the moment, was making more airplanes "than any other manufacturer in the world." *Fortune* customarily leavened its praise for man or enterprise with a certain biliousness to bolster its equity in dispassionate reporting. Not this time. The magazine was all kudos. It surprised no one in Lock Haven that its headline, "COUNT THE CUBS," just happened to be a new slogan coined by William, Sr.

The corporation could have had even more publicity. Fliers, some of national renown, regularly descended on Lock Haven to ask the loan of aircraft on the plausible argument that they could give the product exposure in the public prints. A few were accommodated, but Jake Miller lowered the boom on most of them.

"Everyone remembers Paul Revere," said he, "but nobody remembers the name of his horse."

Piper had, indeed, become the world's biggest manufacturer of aircraft. The previous year it had turned out 1,806 and production was still rising. By Pearl Harbor a third of all civil airplanes registered in the United States and 60 percent of all lightplanes would be Pipers. In an obvious effort to improve social status, factory deliveries were going by rail instead of car trailer.

Business was so good that William, Sr., for a time toyed with the idea of selling his airplanes at cost and, like a famous razor manufacturer who made his money on blades alone, confine his profit-taking to accessories. Inevitably his domination of the market subjected him to pressures. Gordon Curtis hatched an explosive plan. He would form a General Motors of lightplane manufacture with Piper as his centerpiece. It would be a cartel, plain and simple, but would escape the charge of monopoly by the presence of other, if small, companies in the field. Piper would consolidate with Taylorcraft and Aeronca. The details on control could be worked out later; obviously Piper would have the major voice.

"No," William, Sr., told Curtis. "I've got enough of a headache right here in Lock Haven. Why should I take on two more?"

Pilots by the Peck

IF PIPER AIRCRAFT WAS PROSPERING, William T. Piper was the first to admit that luck and circumstance had something to do with it.

Adolf Hitler and his toady, Benito Mussolini, were redrawing the map of Europe under a threat of war spearheaded by bombing raids that could kill millions. It was the year of Munich and the dismemberment of Czechoslovakia. Spain, in the grip of civil war, was being used as a laboratory by the German Luftwaffe. Under the guise of running commercial airlines, Berlin was funneling millions of dollars into Latin America to woo its peoples and threaten the U.S. defensive flank and the Panama Canal. Japanese armies were advancing in China.

In Germany 65,000 men between the ages of eighteen and thirty-five were being trained as pilots and airplane mechanics in defiance of the Treaty of Versailles. Three times that number were taking glider training. In Italy the government sponsored an aeronautical society with 120,000 members and paid flying schools $210 for every man who won a pilot's license. The personnel of Japan's army and navy air forces was growing. On the eve of Pearl Harbor it would number, with reserves, 51,500. In Russia 600,000 youths were reported studying aeronautics. In France 153 civilian training centers were schooling 20,000 men between seventeen and twenty-one, and they had an option of taking advanced training in the air force. England had dawdled, but in 1938 the government established a civil air guard to flight-train men and women between eighteen and fifty.

The United States had no formalized aeronautical education programs. Its certificated civilian pilots, including those on airlines, numbered 23,236. Most of them knew only the rudiments of taking off and landing. The air arms of the U.S. military establishment were in a sorry state, victims of years of short rationing.

On Tuesday, December 27, 1938, President Roosevelt told a press conference that a plan was under way for the federal Civil Aeronautics

Authority (CAA) to train 20,000 private pilots a year in the nation's colleges and universities. He proposed to give it a tryout with 330 . students in twelve schools during the opening semester of 1939, financed by $100,000 from the National Youth Administration. If that proved successful, the training program would be expanded. The objectives, he said, were twofold: to stimulate private flying and contribute thereby to the growth of civil aviation, and to create a reserve of qualified pilots on which the armed forces might draw. Colleges could charge up to $40 for such curricular extras as "laboratory fees" and insurance. The CAA would pay the college $20 and the participating flying school from $270 to $290 for each student who qualified.

In a nation divided between interventionists and America Firsters, the Civilian Pilot Training program (CPT), as the project became known, was a political porcupine. Would Congress fund it? A politically sensitive president had sounded out the Army Air Corps and the Navy Bureau of Aeronautics. Louis Johnson, assistant secretary of war and later the first secretary of defense, was enthusiastic. So was Charles Edison, assistant secretary of the navy. All this was duly publicized in the press. The Gallup poll reported an overwhelming public support.

There was haggling. The whole thing bore the odor of yet another Roosevelt alphabetical boondoggle. One college president thought the selection of college men for the training unnecessary because, as he put it in a curious, backhanded slap at airmen, "the successful pilots of the country today are, in general, I believe, not college men."

The Civilian Pilot Training program had its defenders. The president of the University of Alabama said: "To those who will work in aeronautical construction, design, or transportation, or use flying in business or profession, this training should be of great value." Dr. Edward C. Elliott, Purdue's president, stated, "The flight training program . . . affords an unusual opportunity for engineers and scientific institutions . . . to round out our aeronautical training and experience of students in preparing them for more competent service in the development of an industry of critical value in time of peace as well as in time of emergency."

On January 12, 1939, when the rhetorical winds had blown themselves out, the president dispatched a pointed message to Congress asking for $10 million a year to give primary training to twenty thousand citizens.

The ante shortly was raised from twenty to ninety-five thousand over a five-year period.

Congress voted the money, if only half in the beginning, what the president asked. Politically attuned, the nation's First Lady took a flight in a Cub, adequately photographed.

ELEANOR ROOSEVELT
She was a politically attuned First Lady.

The Civilian Pilot Training program, like most imaginative concepts, could only have originated with one man. He was Robert Henry Hinckley from Ogden, Utah, the son of Mormon pioneers and himself a fixed-base operator. He had been in charge of building airports in seven western states for the Works Progress Administration, a product of the Great Depression, when Harry Hopkins was its director. Brought to Washington as Hopkins moved into the White House as assistant to the president, Hinckley had access to the presidential ear. He was a man of considerable presence, a natural administrator, and a quick student of the national capital's political infighting. He had watched the growth of military-oriented air training abroad with increasing worry. He was smart enough to know that any parallel program in the United States would have to be sugar coated with a primary emphasis on civil flying if it was not to experience a backlash of opposition in Congress and in the public mind. He knew that the military services' capacity for turning out pilots was something less than a thousand a year. It was Hinckley who, almost single-handedly, bulled CPT through the White House and by adroit architecture made it palatable to senator, representative, and the electorate at a time when Roosevelt was just scraping by the threat of a halt in the recovery from the depression. The economy had had a scare in 1938.

Hinckley was appointed chairman of the CAA on April 12, 1939, and automatically became administrator of the CPT.

Thus was launched the most ambitious air training program in the nation's history. The CPT primary instruction was in lightplanes exclusively, and those by the thousands. Three of each four airplanes used were Cubs. The program was thoughtfully detailed. Instruction was divided between textbooks and the cockpit. Four women's colleges were accepted in the program, and women students were admitted in other colleges at the rate of one to every ten men. In a noncollege adjunct, women competed with men in entrance examinations. Nine Negro colleges were in CPT. Latin American students were invited to train at U.S. expense.

In 1939 only 130 out of 28,000 high schools were teaching aviation in any form. By January 1942, Hinckley had helped institute preflight aviation instruction in more than 14,000 parochial, public, and private high schools with an enrollment of 250,000.

The CPT turned out to be a stunning success. In its first year it qualified 313 private pilots. A dozen students dropped out. One was killed. In its second year CPT graduated 10,000. By January 1, 1941, CAA listed 63,113 pilots qualified to fly. The program advanced ambitious graduates to secondary training in bigger airplanes—Beechcrafts, Stinsons, Cessnas, and Wacos—and to commercial-rated pilot training.

The CPT's safety record was phenomenal. Students in the 1939–40 expanded program flew 96,009,000 miles. Thirty-one died in accidents, an average of 3,096,797 miles per fatality. In 1941 the fatality rate dropped to one for each 7,620,000 miles, the best figure that private flying had ever posted.

Among those who won their private pilots' licenses in CPT was John H. Glenn, Jr., the first U.S. astronaut to orbit the earth. He trained in a sixty-five-horsepower Taylorcraft in New Philadelphia, Ohio. Other men whose names became page one news in the Second World War were graduates of Hinckley's CPT, among them Joe Foss, Kenneth D. Bailey, Ralph Cheli, and James E. Swett, all Medal of Honor winners. Still another CPT graduate, Richard I. Bong, from Poplar, Wisconsin, won the Distinguished Flying Cross, the Distinguished Service Cross, a Silver Star, and the Air Medal with fourteen Oak Leaf Clusters. Nineteen of the seventy-nine airmen who slashed at Tokyo on April 18, 1942, were CPT products.

By the time the Civilian Pilot Training program was announced, Piper Aircraft—now beyond the clutches of wall-to-wall poverty—had begun to experiment with variations in products. A split-level research assumed two directions. One was the design of aircraft of nontrainer utility, the other, exercises in sheer demoniac futility.

W. T. Piper was by no means abandoning his conviction that the lightplane was essentially a trainer. His devotion to the Cub Sport attested to that. But he was willing to concede that low-production airplanes of other configurations could be added to his output for additional profit. Hanford Eckman had come up with the J-4, the Coupe. So be it. If the company was going to produce the machine, the president would go all out to make it attractive. It offended him to see potential customers walk around a showroom doing nothing more than kick the tires.

A stylist, Harry Pack, was imported from Detroit to put sequins on the Coupe. Shades of the auto industry! The airplane had a hand-rubbed finish, a 105-pound-capacity luggage compartment, a fabric-lined cabin, a floor mat, a landing gear sprung with springs, not rubber bands, and an instrument panel to render a newly licensed pilot, parchment clutched in hand, delirious. Mr. Piper ordered that at a flyaway price of $1,995, a purchaser must have no extras to buy save a radio receiver. The advertised cruising speed in still air on a fifty-horsepower engine was ninety miles an hour. That was stretching it. Properly trimmed, a Coupe could knock off only eighty-five, but no owner would ever own up to it. Proud pilots were notorious liars.

To the Coupe was added the Cruiser. This was more to Mr. Piper's liking. Designed for the fixed-base operator, it had a pilot's seat up front and a bench-type seat for two behind, and was promoted for low-cost, profitable charter work despite skimpy hip and leg room. With seventy-five horsepower, it could do a commendable job on cross-country if the headwinds were not formidable.

As an affidavit to his business sense, 1,254 Cruisers were sold in the two years prior to Pearl Harbor. What shook him up was the sale of 1,224 Coupes in the same period. He began to ponder the advisability of establishing a full line of aircraft.

The nuttier parts of the experimentation at Lock Haven derived less from any far-out ideas dreamed up by the resident engineers than from inventors who saw all that money flowing into the Piper coffers. A brilliant inspiration could put them on the gravy train too. Ray Applegate was one such character. A World War I navy flying boat pilot, he believed devoutly in amphibians. They could fly off both land and water and therefore had a limitless number of airports. To Lock Haven he brought an amphibian of a design that

APPLEGATE AMPHIBIAN
The propeller was put on backward.

Hans Groenhoff

he had contributed to. It had a strut-braced high wing topped by an engine and pusher propeller. The wheels for land operation were racheted up and down manually by chain and sprocket. Piper Aircraft agreed to play guinea pig for the Applegate amphibian on the broad bosom of the West Branch.

"Might as well see if it's worth anything," said Mr. Piper.

He should have been forewarned when Applegate arrived with his prize not by air but in a truck. Piper put its own wings on the contraption and replaced Applegate's Essex automobile engine with an air-cooled Franklin. For one test flight Applegate succeeded in attaching the prop on its flange backward. The airplane didn't fly very well that day. Even when everything was properly installed, the amphibian made a lot of noise but didn't go anywhere.

"The drag," recalled Jamouneau, "was spectacular."

Then there was the Rose Slotted Wing. Harrison R. Tucker was the protege of a New York financier, William K. Rose, scion of a Cleveland sewing machine family. Rose himself was a man of considerable capriciousness. He kept an accumulation of years of the *New York Times* stacked on the floor of his home. He had convinced Tucker that a way could be found to give an airplane wing more lift. Tucker designed tremendous flaps for the trailing edge. To those he added slotted ailerons and a slat on the leading edge to prolong the flow of laminar air over the top of the wing and reduce stall speed. Piper Aircraft gave Tucker a spot in the cut-and-try department to prove out his theories. He put his wing on a Coupe.

The Coupe did, indeed, get airborne, but it staggered in flight like a man emerging from a gin mill.

"What do you think?" Tucker asked Jamouneau.

"I think, Mr. Tucker," replied Jamouneau, "that you're on a path strewn with primroses."

A man came by one day with another wonderful idea. He had devised rubber floats—a natural. An airplane owner with two thousand dollars invested in aluminum floats was always straining his eyes at takeoff and landing for fear a piece of jetsam would poke a hole in them. Approaching a dock, especially in a wind, he jockeyed his throttle nervously to prevent collision. Now, a pneumatic rubber float was resilient, it could take all kinds of abuse. Piper put the floats on a J–3. They worked fine. It took a little longer to get them on the step, but they were everything that the inventor said they were. The only trouble was that when a pilot got up a few thousand feet, the reduced ambient air pressure caused them to blow up like balloons. The increase in drag was immeasurable.

The gimmick inventors left a few gray hairs among the test pilots, including Pug Piper. Pug, now out of college and wholly immersed in aircraft design, was running evaluation tests on anything new introduced by competitive manufacturers as a matter of comparison shopping. At the moment it was retractable landing gears. Piper had no plans for putting retractables on a production airplane, but the day might come. Pug flew the powered gear on a four-place, low-wing Bellanca, and found it good. Then a pilot dropped by with a Culver Cadet, designed by one Al Mooney. This sleek airplane got 120 miles an hour out of a mere sixty-five horsepower. It was tiny. One man and a briefcase could barely crowd into the cockpit. The Cadet too had retractable gear, but with two differences: it was manually operated, and it had a trick arrangement to prevent

ROSE SLOTTED WING
On a path strewn with primroses.

ON FLOATS
At altitude pneumatic shoes became balloons.

a pilot's throttling back for a landing if he had forgotten to lower his
gear. A sequencing procedure had to be followed. Nobody told
young Piper that the Rube Goldberg device worked in reverse, too.
Trying it out, he closed the throttle and dropped the gear while flying
at low altitude. It was dandy. Then, deciding on another test, he
raised the gear while the throttle was closed. He tried to open the
throttle. It was no dice. He pushed harder. It wouldn't budge.
When he smacked the throttle a third time he bent the rod on the
linkage. Without power, he had run out of time. He managed to
put his mount down in a hayfield without a scratch. The Mooney
retractable landing gear was one that Piper Aircraft never adopted.

In a growing affluence, W. T. Piper remained a cautious man
with a personal or corporate buck. Regularly he hopscotched over
the landscape in one of his tiny airplanes to visit distributors and
dealers, and returning, would announce with a straight face, "You'll
never believe it, but I've been all the way to Boston and back for
only ten dollars, and how come the company salesmen are always
running up such big expense accounts?" No wonder. On his trips
the distributors and dealers picked up his tabs. They fed him, paid

his hotel bills, and supplied his gasoline, and they presented the bills to the first luckless salesman from the home office in Lock Haven who happened by. Mr. Piper knew that.

He believed devoutly in a man's earning his keep. If his income from the corporation provided only porridge three times a day, it was a splendid thing for morale—it kept his ambition aflame to better himself during the learning process. And employes should start at the bottom and work up. One such recipient of the Piper philosophy was Michael J. Strok, a Cornell graduate. Strok wrote William, Sr., that he would like to get into aviation. "Son," wrote Mr. Piper, "come see me."

"The pay," announced William, Sr., at the interview, "will be $13.75 a week. That's while you're apprenticing. As a matter of fact, I may have some plans for you. You'll get more. And"—the clincher—"you'll be around airplanes."

Strok went to work as a mechanic's helper on the night shift in the repair department. Had it not been that he got flight instruction for pennies, he never would have stayed on. For weeks Strok traded off eating for the opportunity to fly. In 1939, a year later, he was raised to twenty dollars a week and, suffused with the wonder of it all, got married. William, Sr., was as good as his word. Strok advanced through the ranks and was assistant purchasing agent at a comfortable salary by the time he went off to war. He had glimpses of the president of the company that were afforded few of those on the payroll outside the immediate Piper family. William, Sr., wearing a suit that always looked as though it had been freshly slept in, would drop by the Strok apartment of an evening to talk. He would just stay a minute. The minute stretched until bedtime. Pulling the stub of a pencil from a vest pocket, he sketched and dallied with figures on any subject that came to mind. Gradually from bits and pieces of conversation the Stroks began to realize the reason for the visits. It was implicit only in his behavior. Marie Piper, the quiet, self-effacing homemaker to whom he had been married almost three decades, the mother of his five children, had died just before Christmas in 1937 after a short illness. He didn't know what to do with himself.

The Piper Aircraft Corporation's annual report issued September 30, 1940, showed sales of $3,230,086.50 and net profit after taxes and depreciation of $157,823.46.

"This profit," the president advised his stockholders, "plus the money received from the sale of common stock is being put back into the company."

Preferred dividends of $12,419.10 had been paid during the year on 19,564 shares outstanding. Additional working capital of $241,-740 had been obtained through a public offering of 41,290 shares of common the previous February. It was snapped up the day it was announced. Total company assets were $1,192,751.77 and total liabilities, less contingencies, $444,209.29.

Besides the Pipers, senior and junior, and Ted Weld, the board members were Franklin Field, John E. P. Morgan, J. E. Swan, and Gordon Curtis.

The entire report was covered in eleven pocket-size pages measuring 5½ by 8½ inches, unembellished except for a couple of airplane pictures.

"We hold too many talk-talk meetings around here," Mr. Piper was beginning to say. "Let's get out and do some selling."

War Breeds Grasshoppers

AT DAYBREAK ON SEPTEMBER 1, 1939, Hitler's armies poured across the Polish frontier to launch World War II. Fighter airplanes and bombers, spreading destruction and terror, apprised Europe, America, and Asia that a new, strategic dimension had been added to man's gift for annihilating his own kind. To the U.S. military, the defeat of Poland in one week was a profound shock.

On February 18, 1941, W. T. Piper, Sr., wrote the Honorable Henry L. Stimson, secretary of war:

> The Piper Aircraft Corporation, representing 50% of the Light Aircraft Production in the United States, is anxious to know what it can do to further aid in the defense of this country. Although I cannot speak for the rest of the industry, I am sure that their desire and willingness to help is no less than ours. . . .
>
> On a separate sheet attached hereto are a number of suggestions for semi-military and non-military cooperation. . . .
>
> John E. P. Morgan, who presents this letter, is a director of our company and has my authority to discuss this matter with whomever you designate.

William, Sr., William, Jr., and Morgan had spent a lot of time phrasing the proposal. Notwithstanding the fact that President Roosevelt had begun galvanizing the nation the previous May against the chance of being drawn into the war in Europe, the possibility of using lightplanes as military instruments had received no official encouragement whatever. The jungles of Washington politics were impenetrable to the layman, and it was Morgan's commission to do a selling job at the War Department, on Washington's Constitution Avenue. William, Sr., suggested that lightplanes on the semimilitary side could (1) control troop movements, (2) evacuate wounded, (3)

79

carry messages, (4) ferry personnel, (5) scout, (6) patrol, (7) drop bombs or torpedoes, and (8) be used for blind flying training. He appended a list of nonmilitary uses.

On March 24 Robert A. Lovett, special assistant to the secretary of war for air (and later secretary of defense), a man of delectable political acumen, replied that he liked the nonmilitary suggestions, "but neither personnel nor funds are at present available within the War Department." As for the semimilitary, items (1) to (4) "would appear to have elements of real interest to ground forces, whereas items (3), (4), and (8) would particularly concern the air forces."

Much that bore on the proposed use of lightplanes in war had happened in the seventeen and a half months between the invasion of Poland and the dispatch of the Piper letter to Stimson.

In July 1940, 1st Lt. James M. Watson III asked Piper Aircraft if it could send some airplanes to Fort Beauregard, Louisiana, for army maneuvers in August. Tom Case of the Piper staff flew a Coupe to the camp on August 12 and demonstrated that it could land on and take off from a dirt road.

Henry S. Wann, Piper district sales manager for the far western states, was doing some missionary work on his own. He telephoned Fort Lewis, Washington, to make a pitch on lightplanes and got a lieutenant colonel named D. D. Eisenhower. Yup, said Eisenhower, he was aware of the lightplane's uses.

Brig. Gen. Adna R. Chaffee called Lock Haven on February 9, 1941, to ask if a Cub could be flown to Fort Knox, Kentucky, the Armor School, to direct armored columns and adjust tank fire. Case flew a J–3 in the following day and conducted tests through February 15.

All this was informal. Nobody in uniform had any authority to use, much less buy, an airplane for the ground forces. Assistant Secretary Lovett made the situation clear between the lines of his March 24 letter: Anything that had wings was the province of the U.S. Air Corps. For years the Air Corps had been bucking for a separate service, coequal with the army and the navy. As the German panzer columns spearheaded by Stuka dive bombers knifed through Belgium in May 1940, the shock of the Polish campaign was compounded in political and military Washington. The Air Corps (to become the U.S. Army Air Forces a month later) was feeling its oats.

Notwithstanding the fact that U.S. aircraft factories had produced only 568 military aircraft in 1939, on May 16, 1940, Roosevelt told Congress: "I should like to see this nation geared up to the ability to turn out at least 50,000 planes a year . . . I believe this nation should plan at this time a program that will provide us with 50,000 military and naval planes."

United States production of all types of aircraft currently was about 12,000 units a year. Of 6,500 military aircraft owned by the U.S. Army and Navy, only a third were combat-ready.

It was in this climate that John Edward Parsons Morgan assumed the job of extracting an admission from Constitution Avenue that puddle-jumper aircraft had a role to play, should war come. He didn't know a spinner from a tail cone, but like Gordon Curtis he got around. He was blessed with a lot of bounce. He had been voted onto the Piper board at the request of Jim Warburg, the banker and his friend and mentor, and had been a vice president of Warburg's Bank of the Manhattan Company. As a token of his imaginative thinking, Morgan had founded the National Ski Patrol to rescue skiers in distress. This became the basis for U.S. ski troop training in World War II. As assistant to the chairman of the Union Pacific, he built the country's first ski lift at Sun Valley, Idaho, a resort in which both Warburg and Averell Harriman, the man who would become governor of New York and diplomat with and without portfolio to four presidents, were financially interested.

Morgan's qualifications in 1941 for merchandising lightplanes in the national capital included the persuasiveness of a confidence man and friendships in the vast shoal of prominent civilians being drafted by Roosevelt to help run a government swollen by the rearmament effort. Among those he could call by their first names was Robert Lovett, who had been a private commercial banker and a partner in Brown Brothers, Harriman & Company. The two had been friends since their college days when Lovett was at Yale. Lovett had a sympathetic ear. A former U.S. Naval Reserve pilot—his wings bore the number 66—he had taken some lessons in lightplanes at the Hempstead Aero Club on Long Island to renew his hand just before heeding Roosevelt's call to Washington. Lovett, of all people, was aware of the simmering feud between the Air Corps and the ground forces. Was a lightplane a method of transport or an operational aircraft? Was it an airplane or a "vehicle"? The army was entitled to vehicles. But if lightplanes were airplanes, they belonged on the Air Corps' pad.

"Obviously," Robert Lovett commented in later years, "they were both. And awfully easy to fly."

Immediately following Roosevelt's fifty-thousand-airplane message, all airplane manufacturers large and small had been summoned to Washington to get production rolling. William, Sr., attended for Piper Aircraft. A panel of army and navy brass, and Henry Morganthau, secretary of the treasury, representing the president, sat at a table in the front of the room.

"General," asked Ed Porterfield, a lightplane manufacturer, addressing one of the beribboned panel members, "will there be any place in the program for light airplanes?"

"No," said the general, "at least not in the army or Air Corps. They're impractical for military use."

"How about the navy?"

"I'm afraid not," replied a navy captain.

"It seems to me," said William, Sr., getting to his feet, "that the lightplane hasn't been given a chance to show what it can do. Now that we're here," he waved to his cohorts in the small plane business, "we'd like to explain our side of the picture to somebody, some sergeant or corporal, maybe."

The ensuing laughter was largely mirthless. It was no sale.

With Morgan's arrival in Washington in the late winter of 1940–41, there began one of the most adroit, unremitting public- and government-relations campaigns in the history of the American business community. By common consent Morgan was named lobbyist-in-residence not only for Piper but for Aeronca and Taylorcraft as well.

"What we've got to do is demonstrate our aircraft," he told his clients.

Cynics could have charged him with concocting a scheme to extract money from the federal treasury for a handful of industrialists. That much was true. The rest of the story was too corny to be credible. The lightplane makers actually were convinced that their minuscule machines, with a top speed of less than one hundred miles an hour, could help defend the United States.

"We only have to paint the Cub olive drab," said William, Jr., in the course of a family council with Morgan and Curtis, "to produce a military airplane. It can go into active combat."

The price tag could do part of the convincing. A couple of Air Corps observation-type airplanes currently on test at Wright Field, the engineering and evaluation center, cost $25,000 each. Even if the U.S. Army asked for modifications in the Aeronca, Cub, and Taylorcraft, the three little planes would cost a tenth of that per copy.

In June, Morgan got a break. The Second Army was about to embark on maneuvers at Camp Forrest, Tennessee, and the Air Corps was asked to supply some observation aircraft. It had none to spare. Assistant Secretary Lovett wrote Morgan suggesting the use of lightplanes. At their own expense Piper supplied eight airplanes, Taylorcraft and Aeronca, two each. All were fitted with two-way RCA radios for communication. All had sixty-five-horsepower Continental engines.

The experiment at Camp Forrest was hardly an unqualified success. Someone had failed to pass along the word. The army was puzzled by the presence of civilian pilots flying outsize kites. The utility of the things was too simple for the military mind to grasp. Lightplanes were not in the table of organization and, ipso facto, did not exist. Their pilots were given few orders. They slept under the wings of their planes. They scrounged their food. Some messenger, reconnaissance, and spotter flights did get flown. In the fourth and last week of the maneuvers the umpires discovered that they could find out what was going on only if they covered the terrain from the backseat of the civilian planes. That helped.

Okay, the puddle jumpers would try again, still at their own expense. This time it was the Third Army maneuvers at Fort Bliss, near El Paso, for two weeks dating from the middle of July. Two more Cubs were added to the liaison fleet. West Texas blistered under a copper sun. The orders cut for the signature of Maj. Gen. Henry H. Arnold, chief of the Air Corps, specified that the lightplanes were to report to Biggs Field, Laredo, for assignment to the 1st Cavalry under command of Maj. Gen. Innis P. Swift. The pilots would be billeted by the air forces and eat in the officers' mess. But Arnold's orders meant nothing to the post commanding officer, a national guardsman called up to active duty. What were civilians doing on his post?

"I know nothing about you," he snapped, "or why you're here."

The lightplane pilots, hot, tired, dirty, and nettled—Strohmeier and Tony Piper among them—flew to the Laredo civil airport and checked into a downtown hotel. For two days Ted Weld and John Morgan, who had come down to oversee the operation, argued with the Biggs commandant.

"What do you have to have," demanded Morgan, "a verbal command from a big shot?"

"Yes, if you dot the 'o'."

In desperation Morgan telephoned Lovett in Washington.

"Be in the commanding officer's office at 10 A.M. tomorrow," said Lovett.

Morgan and Weld were there when the telephone rang.

"Yes, sir," responded the C.O. "Yes, sir! Yes, SIR!"

Whereupon the lightplane contingent moved onto Biggs Field and into the officers' mess.

The Texas maneuvers proved to be the payoff. In the biggest desert operations ever undertaken by the U.S. Army, in temperatures ranging up to 115 degrees, the little airplanes bounced in and out on blistering runways hastily scraped by army engineers on dry lake beds, on the slopes of hills, and through cactus with spikes that left festering sores if a man brushed against them. The lightplanes not only were durable, they were easily repaired as well. In

STROHMEIER AND GRASSHOPPER INSIGNIA
"What's a Grasshopper?" asked General Swift's aide.

one instance three of them were ordered to land on an unprepared field. The first two pilots stubbed their toes on landing and spread their gears. The third got down without damage. He radioed the base for repair parts. In one hour and twenty minutes both the damaged airplanes were flying again. The air force fly boys crash-landed their big Consolidated-Vultee O (for Observation)–Ones so consistently that orders were finally issued that no military aircraft was to use a newly prepared field until the lightplanes had been in and out of it for forty-eight hours. Any damaged air force observation plane had to be trucked to a main base for repair.

General Swift was impressed by the ease with which the small planes carried out their courier duties. At his headquarters fifty miles north of El Paso he growled about the delay in getting radio messages through.

"Send a Grasshopper down to Biggs Field," he told an aide.

"What's a Grasshopper?" asked the aide.

"They'll know when you tell them."

The name stuck. Within a month Grasshopper lapel pins had been struck and distributed.

As for the Grasshopper sent to Biggs Field, its pilot arrived thirty minutes ahead of the radio message announcing its dispatch.

John Morgan's propaganda campaign had all the subtlety of a

bank holdup. "Give the officers a ride," he kept saying to the light-plane pilots, "especially the generals." By the time the Third Army had been trucked to Fort Beauregard, Louisiana, for August maneuvers, Morgan could count on the fingers of one hand the top brass he had not had aloft in a Grasshopper.

Participating in the August Third Army exercise in Louisiana was a colonel who was himself a lightplane pilot.

"Watch him," said an aide to assembled newsmen over the evening's Scotch and sodas, "he's going places."

On a given day the colonel was assigned Strohmeier as a pilot to go aloft and check the worth of the camouflage used by the troops for their equipment. The colonel had won a private flying license in the Philippines in 1936 but hadn't flown much since. Strohmeier was nobody's fool. He was there to sell Cubs.

"You fly it," he said to the colonel as they climbed into the airplane.

The colonel was a good pilot. After a time he feather-landed on a road to gas up from a truck convoy, and returning to a firing range that was being used as a landing field, squared away for his approach. The field was narrow, though its length of eight hundred feet offered plenty of room for the Cub to get down. The problem was that the strip was surrounded by trees, and a brisk crosswind was blowing. The colonel put the plane down with the aplomb of a seasoned fly boy.

"That was a good job, Colonel Eisenhower," said Strohmeier.

It was the same Dwight David Eisenhower that Henry Wann had talked with on the telephone the previous year at Fort Lewis, Washington. On the friendliest of terms with the Grasshopper squadron, each evening in the oppressive August heat the colonel borrowed an airplane to go aloft and cool off.

But this was not resulting in any contracts for aircraft, and Morgan began getting testy feedbacks from the home offices of Aeronca, Piper, and Taylorcraft. A giant war game for the Second and Third armies was being planned for the month of September at Camp Polk, Louisiana.

On August 23 Lovett wrote Morgan at Camp Polk, "It may interest you to know that we (have been) notified that the Third Army would like to have the planes that have been on maneuvers. We suggested that they rent them. . . ."

While the air force would have to approve any outright purchase of aircraft, *renting* them was something else again.

Eisenhower, chief of staff to Lt. Gen. Walter Krueger, Third Army commander, called Morgan into conference.

"You're not getting paid," said Eisenhower.

"No."

"Would you like to?"

"We'd be delighted."

"Get me a figure."

William T. Piper, Sr., had arrived at Lake Charles, Louisiana, to watch what everyone assumed would be the last chukker of the Grasshopper squadron vs. the U.S. Army Air Forces.

"We're going to get some money," Morgan told William, Sr.

"If we *don't* get it, said William, Sr., "let's not get hasty and pull out our planes. The army needs the planes more than we need the money."

Morgan reported back to Eisenhower.

"Okay," said Eisenhower, "but nobody in the army has ever rented an airplane. You'll have to find out how to go about it. Try the quartermaster in Lake Charles first." Eisenhower knew the niceties of chain of command. He handed Morgan what he called a "maneuver order" for $24,000.

Morgan telephoned John J. McCloy (later U.S. high commissioner to Germany and president of the World Bank), Lovett's opposite number in the ground army, and Lovett. At 3 P.M. of the day following his interview with Eisenhower he was ushered into the presence of the quartermaster general himself, Maj. Gen. Edmund Bristol Gregory. Morgan told his story and showed Gregory the maneuver order.

"Draw up a contract," said Gregory. "Make it short and simple."

Morgan was no lawyer, but his banking experience helped. The quartermaster general signed the contract. So did Morgan—with no legal authority whatever from Aeronca, Piper, and Taylorcraft. The U.S. Army was now fighting a mock war with hirelings, Hessians all. Not a word of the Morgan contract was ever questioned. The army paid the succeeding bills promptly as they were presented.

The role of the lightplane pilots in the war games did not end in September. They flew, often twelve to fourteen hours a day, with the First Army on through October and November in the Carolinas. The story was the same wherever they performed: the Grasshoppers were indispensable.

"Do you mind putting that in writing?" Morgan told the soldiery when he was offered verbal testimonials.

No less than General Krueger himself had beseeched a lightplane pilot for help on a hot day when a column of armor had entangled itself in a pretzel-shaped traffic jam.

"I've got to clean up that mess," he told the lightplane pilot who was the namesake of his father, Gordon Curtis.

"Get a megaphone," said young Curtis. They shoehorned into

a Grasshopper. The general was a big man. It is doubtful that Lt. Gen. Walter Krueger, former chief of the Tank Corps, American Expeditionary Forces in 1918, former executive officer of the War Plans Division of the General Staff, former commander of the Eighth Army Corps, and now commanding general of the Third Army, ever before had been given the order now barked by a Grasshopper pilot. "Suck in your gut," said Gordon Curtis, Jr.

With Krueger bellowing orders from an altitude of two hundred feet, the armored column got straightened out in scarcely more than twenty minutes.

Morgan missed no tricks. He organized a congressional flying club. Representative (later Senator) Jennings Randolph of West Virginia was the first president. Morgan arranged for Jack McCloy to take flying lessons. Morgan's secretary, Jean Ross Howard, herself a pilot and an inventive propagandist, organized a Fuddy-Duddy Flying Club. Piper supplied it with an airplane. Miss Howard, always with a pocket of Grasshopper pins to distribute, cajoled scores of newly minted light and bird colonels into taking lessons.

Morgan cultivated the generals, among them Devers of the Tank Corps, Hodges of the infantry, and Huebner, chief of the training branch of Operations and Training. His campaign was paying off in kudos. It remained to be seen whether the lightplane, despite the opposition of the U.S. Air Forces, would become a viable piece of military equipment.

As the weary Grasshopper pilots returned home, an order was transmitted through the air forces for Grasshoppers—a mere eight airplanes each from Aeronca, Piper, and Taylorcraft. Morgan and the officers of the three lightplane companies held a council of war. Morgan trudged back to Constitution Avenue.

"On our echelon," McCloy told him, "we can't recommend the procurement of planes unless the ground forces demand them and give them a priority." Lovett echoed him.

On the eve of Pearl Harbor two dozen companies were manufacturing light aircraft. In volume, only three continued to count—Piper, Aeronca, and Taylorcraft. Piper continued to dominate the field. In three years the company had built and sold 8,020 aircraft of the 17,727 in the "private" category that had been manufactured by the industry. These included a generous sprinkling of planes that were far too big and powerful to be classed as lightplanes. Even so, Piper had 45 percent of the total market. In 1941 alone, Piper turned out 3,197 airplanes. Taylorcraft and Aeronca, expanding production, produced 1,000 and 999 aircraft respectively.

The company had been forced into an expansion of its physical plant. A huge new warehouse was in being. In all, the facilities measured 204,000 square feet, more than twice what they were when it moved to Lock Haven. A manufactory was operating in Canada. The Piper payroll numbered almost two thousand persons.

On June 14, 1941, Walter Davenport, an internationally known scribe for *Collier's,* published an article titled, "Impregnable Pearl Harbor."

The Wild Fliers

THE U.S. MILITARY ESTABLISHMENT in mid-December 1941 was a clutch of paradoxes. Its increments were an air force engaged in a pushing-and-hauling contest with its parent army in the sublime belief that bombing with conventional explosives was the be-all and end-all of warfare (though England had survived the Luftwaffe); ground forces that were still equipped with horse cavalry, moved from site to site by trailer (though the German armies that had overrun most of Europe and were deep into the U.S.S.R. were spearheaded by motorized armor); and a navy that insisted its battleships were the backbone of its fire power (even after the holocaust of Pearl Harbor and the swift destruction on December 10 by Japanese aircraft of two British battle cruisers, the Prince of Wales and the Repulse, off the coast of Malaysia).

These arthritic postures were overdue for change.

In 1940 Maj. Gen. Robert M. Danford, chief of Field Artillery, witnessed a demonstration of the use of lightplanes as spotters at England's Royal Artillery School in Larkhill. Thereupon he applied for permission to undertake field tests of the system. The authority given him to stage (in the gobbledegook of the military) "organic air observation for field artillery" was implemented late. It was not until December 22, 1941, fifteen days after Pearl Harbor, that Col. R. W. Beasley, in Danford's name, wrote the Civil Aeronautics Authority confirming a telephone conversation. "It is understood," he said, "that the CAA will arrange for . . . the training of Field Artillery pilot-mechanics at Fort Sill, Oklahoma, during January and February, 1942."

The plan contemplated the employment of six flight instructors "to be experienced pilots and instructors in flying of the barnstorming type[!]; at least two men to be pilots who had taken part in this year's maneuvers." Tony Piper, W. T.'s son with the analytical approach and a wholesome irreverence for authority, was one of the two veterans of the maneuvers chosen for Fort Sill. The other was

89

Henry Wann. The program was strictly experimental. It had air-craft. The U.S. Air Forces offloaded to it the two dozen Grasshop-pers, dubbed O–59's, that had been purchased reluctantly at the end of the maneuvers in November. Away they went to Fort Sill.

Training started on January 13 under the direction of Brig. Gen. George R. Allin, commandant of the Field Artillery Training School. The first class consisted of a group of field artillery officers and enlisted men, 90 percent of whom were graduates of CAA pilot training or of the War Training Service (WTS) that followed it. General Allin, only nominally in control of the program, sprouted some gray hairs when he found out what was going on.

Lt. Col. Wallace W. Ford, himself a lightplane pilot, was in im-mediate charge of the training. A deliberate Jeckyll-and-Hyde per-sonality, Ford was the soul of friendliness after hours. During the day he had an epic command of abusive language. It got results. His deputy was Gordon Wolf, a reserve major and an attorney for Aeronca. A flight curriculum was set up by Lt.–later Maj. Gen.– Robert R. Williams, assisted by, among others, Tony Piper and Henry Wann, both still in mufti. Richard Alley directed short field precision and low acrobatic flight instruction. Maintenance instruc-tion was given by Stanley J. Stelle. Both were loaned by the CAA. Piper contributed the services of a mechanic to do the greasy-finger airframe work for Stelle, and Continental Engines another one for engine maintenance.

The instruction began innocently enough. Students were en-couraged to smarten up their air work. They did chandelles, lazy eights, dead-stick 720-degree landings, and coordinating exercises. Then all hell began breaking loose.

"Turn short!" ordered the instructors. "Get that wing down 90 degrees! You've got a fighter after you! You've got to turn inside of him! Put the stick in your gut, chop the throttle, spin! It's the only way to save yourself!"

Grasshopper pilots would have to land anywhere and every-where if ever they saw combat. Satellite fields were carved out of the surrounding hills. They were primitive. Trainees practiced tak-ing off over barriers. They landed over obstacles like bamboo poles, side-slipping to within a foot of the ground.

"You knocked off a pole!" an instructor would bark. "Hit the top of a tree like that in combat and you'll be dead!"

All this was only lesson one. The purpose of the training was to turn out pilots for elevated observation posts. They would be the eyes of the artillery. The guns below opened up with live ammuni-tion. The Grasshoppers got so good that they were on target in four rounds. The gunnery officers weren't happy even with that. So the Grasshoppers were sent out in advance of the guns, over "no man's land." The added visibility cut the rounds for on-target to three—one over, one short, wham!

"But if we fly out front," objected a trainee, "we'll draw enemy ground fire."

"Yup," agreed his commanding officer cheerfully.

Instructors, the key to the operation, were hard to come by, and here the Civilian Pilot Training program (CPT) and WTS were the final justification of Robert Hinckley's faith. Nine out of ten were drawn from civilian ranks.

Ultimately lightplane training got under way at eighteen fields in eleven states.

War Training Service collected other credits. A cross-country course turned out airline copilots. Concurrently, the CAA was training navy combat pilots and pilots for the ferry command. WTS instituted classes in meteorology to fill vacant forecasting slots in the armed services and the U.S. Weather Bureau.

The accident rate at Fort Sill, for all the wild, evasive flying that was taught, was low. The first man killed in the program, Lt. R. P. Stallings II, spun in in a Taylorcraft. The instructors learned early that the L-2, as the airplane was known, was not suitable for short fields and was touchy when speed was reduced to just above the stall point. With any abuse of the controls, it whipped off into a spin with little warning. Presently Taylorcrafts were phased out of the program. The Aeronca fared little better. While used for elevated OP training, it was dropped from combat liaison plane manufacture in order to standardize on parts shipped overseas. Only the Piper L-4 remained until later in the war the Stinson L-5, a heavier machine with three times the horsepower, began to supplement it.

Civilian-owned Cubs were organized into a U.S. Army Air Forces auxiliary, the Civil Air Patrol (CAP), enrolling in work suggested by William T. Piper, Sr. Before the navy took over the job in August 1943, twenty-one CAP bases were in operation on the Atlantic and Gulf coasts from the Canadian border to Tampico, Mexico. The puddle jumpers had flown 24 million miles on 86,685 missions.

While the eccentric syllabus at Fort Sill was scaring the pants off trainees and old-line artillery officers alike, John Morgan was drumming his fingers on his desk in the national capital. Adopting the idiocies of the historical, ecclesiastical debate over how many angels could stand on the point of a needle, the Establishment on Constitution Avenue had decided that lightplanes were, indeed, airplanes and not "vehicles" and therefore the niceties of military protocol demanded the signature of the air forces' Wright Field on any contract for the delivery of the things to the ground forces. The Establishment had an ace up its sleeve—a complete divorce between air forces aviation and organic army aviation.

On January 16 Morgan heard from Lovett. "I believe," wrote the assistant secretary of war for air, "the bottleneck is about to be broken." On February 10 he got the word. Wright Field at last had signed an order for 1,500 Grasshoppers. That was far below the number Morgan and the ground forces had been talking about for months, precisely 4,629, of which ground units other than the artillery would get 1,879.

As the first summer of the war neared, one more step to the deployment of the lightplane to combat was vital.

That was taken on June 6, 1942. The words "Piper Cub" were engraved on the birth certificate of ground forces aviation. Addressed to Lt. Gen. Lesley James McNair, it read in part:

> MEMORANDUM FOR THE COMMANDING GENERAL ARMY GROUND FORCES:
> Subject: Organic Air Observation for Field Artillery.
> Your recommendation that organic air observation units be included in Field Artillery organizations is approved. . . .
> Liaison airplanes will be authorized for Field Artillery units at the rate of 2 per light and medium Artillery Battalion, 2 per Division Artillery Headquarters and Headquarters Battery or Field Artillery Brigade Headquarters and Headquarters Battery.
> Personnel will be authorized at the rate of 1 pilot and $\frac{1}{2}$ airplane mechanic for each liaison plane authorized. . . .
> The Commanding General, Army Air Forces, will be responsible for the procurement and issue of airplanes, spare parts, repair materials, and the necessary auxiliary flying equipment required by this program. The airplanes will be commercial low performance aircraft of the "Piper Cub" type . . .
> By order of the Secretary of War:
> I. H. EDWARDS,
> Brigadier General,
> Assistant Chief of Staff

McNair was authorized to organize at Fort Sill or other stations he selected a course of instruction for pilots, mechanics, and observers. That relieved the CAA of a job already begun.

A copy of the order went to General Arnold.

In August 1945 the War Department gave lightplanes to the cavalry, engineers, infantry, and armored and tank destroyer divisions as a direct outgrowth of the creation of artillery aviation three years earlier.

In the national spasm of sudden war, only hours after the Japanese initiated hostilities, factory wheels at Lock Haven, Alliance, and Middletown, Ohio, and everywhere else that civilian-type, non-transport planes were being fabricated were stilled. Four hundred Cubs with a wholesale value of close to $400,000 squatted immobile, wingtip-to-wingtip, on the perimeter of the Lock Haven airport. Washington froze any movement of them on security grounds. After a lapse of weeks Piper Aircraft began facing up to a problem, a growing money crunch. It didn't owe a great deal—$150,000—but a New York bank, the chief creditor, began getting difficult. Nothing was resolved at a meeting in the financial district. The bank wanted its money, and now. Mr. Piper pushed back his chair, crammed his battered hat on his head, and made for the door.

"Where to?" he was asked.

"We're not getting anywhere here," he said.

"We'll send a man to Lock Haven," said a bank official, relenting.

Official U.S. Marine Corps photograph

HOSPITAL CUBS WERE TRANSPORTED BY AIR
In the Pacific the first airstrips were for lightplanes.

Dolan, he said his name was on arrival. Thomas James Dolan was a tall, brusque Irishman in the auditing business with a Toledo firm, Wideman, Madden and Company. For two days the man Dolan walked through the plant and went over the books.

"I want to telephone the bank," he announced finally.

"Alone?" asked William, Jr.

"No, you fellows sit right where you are." He was put through. "Hello, Rock," he said to someone in New York. "Listen, these people are in good shape. If anything, I'd advance them some more money. They need it right now more than you do. Okay, very good, thanks." He hung up. To the assembled Piper officials he said, "That was Rock Kent, a vice president. Everything's okay."

Privately, over dinner with his family, William, Sr., said, "If that guy can tell the bankers where to head in, we ought to hire him." Forthwith, Tom Dolan was hired.

The money situation turned out to be self-solving. The navy bought the bulk of the Cubs on the field, and the air forces the rest, for primary training.

As the company settled into the grind of turning out warplanes, it chafed at the restraints put on its production.

"We were never turned loose," Bill, Jr., said in later years. "We could have done a lot more."

At no time during the war was more than a fifth of Piper's capacity channeled into aircraft manufacture. Now and then an order for a few hundred L–4's, with wood spars to save aluminum for air forces planes, came through. The company funneled its resources to the output of aircraft other than combat Cubs. It made a hundred

AMBULANCE CUB
Official U.S. Navy photograph
They raised the turtle deck and put a stretcher behind the front seat.

MILITARY GLIDER
The factory made "bedsprings" too.

ambulance planes, the HE–1, a converted Cruiser, for the navy. Jamouneau's department simply raised the turtle deck and put a stretcher behind the front seat. Much later Piper produced an army version, the L–14, that carried four persons and could be used as an ambulance.

For a time Piper produced canopies for Stearman and Fairchild trainers. It made gliders. As early as the spring of 1941 the air corps began to experiment with gliders and graduated 150 pilots in its first program. It was high time. Hitler had 200,000 glider pilots when he launched the attack on Poland. Glider-borne troops helped reduce the Maginot Line.

As a first training step in what proved to be a mammoth program with a concomitant in glider construction by other elements of the U.S. aviation industry, Piper suggested that trainees simply go aloft in the lightplanes and cut their ignition. The factory supplemented that with genuine gliders without engines. Six thousand glider pilots were trained in lightplanes at Lamesa, Texas; Wickenburg, Arizona; Stuttgart, Arkansas; Twenty-nine Palms, California; and Mobile, Alabama.

Piper thought it had something valuable for additional weapon manufacture when it undertook development of a pilotless glider-bomb dubbed the GLOMB—two tons of TNT with wings. A fighter pilot flying the thing by remote control would direct it at Japanese warships.

The electronics experts had a continuing field day with the weapon. The component parts they devised—more than four hundred in the end—kept the thing in a state of incompletion. Piper worked on it nonetheless until a year before the war's end. The factory produced a handful. They never saw combat. Some with modifications had an inglorious death when they were guided through a mushroom-shaped cloud to get radioactivity readings in the postwar test at Bikini Atoll.

The biggest wartime product by far at the Piper factory was bedsprings. At least that was what they were called. If a man wanted to invite questions on security, he mentioned radar. Piper turned out thousands of them in the course of the war.

Things were not all that mundane in lightplanes on the home front. Col. John C. L. Adams of the infantry saw to that. Adams was coltish. He was the kind of man who would try to fill an inside straight. He had a genius for staging stunts that backfired. A devout believer in Grasshoppers, he talked the C.O. at Fort Belvoir into letting them try to lay a smoke screen. A squadron of lightplanes swooped in low over the parade ground, depositing a barrier of chemical smoke between a grandstand and the opposite border of the field. When the smoke cleared, the humorless brass in the grandstand were looking down the muzzles of a line of machine guns. Adams wanted realism. At that moment confederates touched off an explosion behind one of the post's buildings. A couple of days later the paint on some of the post's automobiles began blistering, and officers' uniforms unaccountably began developing holes. Only then did Adams realize that the smoke he had generated contained a caustic. The C.O.'s staff hinted darkly of a court martial. That didn't deter Adams. He purloined a bazooka from army stores to mount on an L-4. He got as far as the door before they caught him. He ran a demonstration on lightplanes for Wild Bill Donovan's Office of Strategic Services.

Then there was that thing that happened at Congressional Airport, a small field northwest of Washington, and that was the end of Adams' exploits. He induced a group of officers to be targets for a lightplane "bombing" run. The group included quite a sprinkling of men with stars on their shoulders. Worse, they had as guests some officers from the British army.

"Lightplanes can drop hand grenades or even bombs," argued Adams as the arrangements progressed.

"But what will we use to bomb the brass?" asked Jake Miller.

"Flour."

The Cubs were jerry-rigged with bomb racks. Into them were loaded half-pound packets of flour in paper sacks.

It had begun to rain. The officers stood their ground. The attack was launched. It was from low level as befitted warplanes of a Grasshopper fleet. The pilots' aim was unerring. Out tumbled the flour. Smack on the officers' uniforms burst the bags. Any school child could have told the pilots that flour plus water equals paste.

Adams was no dunce. Practically all his preachments on the use of lightplanes, including indeed mounting bazookas on them, were realized in the next two years.

The factory at 820 East Bald Eagle Street in Lock Haven began to show war's erosion of personnel. Tony Piper was committed for the war's duration at Fort Sill. By now he was a captain and a flight commander with a half-dozen instructors in his detail. He got through one combat-pilot class and part of a second before he was put to training flight instructors. The school put forty to fifty men in the combat-pilot classes, and Tony was still around when it graduated class number ninety. Tom Case, the Piper pilot who with Stroh-meier had flown in the 1941 maneuvers, went into naval aviation. Strohmeier became a primary training instructor at Bevo Howard's Hawthorne Aviation School at Orangeburg, South Carolina. Mike Strok in the factory's purchasing department went through the school at Fort Sill, won a gold bar for his shoulders, and fretting that the war would be over before he could get into it, arrived at Casablanca in January 1943 as assistant air officer with the 5th Armored Artillery Group.

Howard (Pug) Piper, the son carrying on the enduring love affair with airplanes, went through navy flight school at Pensacola, Florida, and was assigned to operations at the Quonset Point, Rhode Island, Naval Air Station. He got just what he wanted—at the moment. He flew everything with wings that the navy had—fighters, dive bombers, torpedo bombers, patrol bombers, and transports such as the twin-engine Douglas, Lockheed Lodestars, and Neptunes, Beeches, and Grumman amphibians. Presently he realized that he was stuck state-side with a war on. His repeated requests for sea duty brought no response until after V-E Day. Then he got his orders. He was on his way to the Western Pacific when the war ended.

But Bill, Jr., was the genuinely unhappy member of the clan. He wanted combat. On a trip to Washington with his father he visited the naval recruiting center.

"Forget it," said the officer on duty, who had been a friend in prep school. "You don't want to get into this rat race."

Bill, Jr., wrote Pug about it. "I'm going to enlist," he said.

"You stay where you are," Pug shot back. "You can do more in Lock Haven than you can in uniform. Someone's got to help mind the store. You're it."

It was a hell of a way to participate in a war. Twenty-five years later he was still smarting over it.

The Most Lethal Warplane
in the World

THE PIPER CUB'S ENTRY INTO COMBAT
as an olive drab L–4 was hardly auspicious. A covey of three airplanes was loaded aboard the U.S. aircraft carrier Ranger to direct
artillery fire during the invasion of North Africa. This was a pincer
movement to catch Field Marshal Erwin Rommel's combined
German-Italian army, including the elite Afrika Korps, between
British General Bernard Montgomery's Eighth Army and Anglo-
American troops under General Eisenhower.

At 1:30 A.M. November 8, 1942, Eisenhower hit the beaches of
Morocco and Algeria. At daybreak on November 9 the lightplanes,
led by Capt. Ford E. Allcorn, rolled down the Ranger's flight deck.
The Ranger's skipper, launching the Grasshoppers sixty miles at sea,
refused to break radio silence to tell the Allied soldiery and, indeed,
the ships of the convoy, that the airplanes were on the way. He
had been under torpedo attack and was running at his full speed of
twenty-five knots. The Grasshoppers had to take off into a thirty-five–
knot headwind.

The news ashore was not good. Several of the Ranger's own
planes had been shot down by inexperienced American troops on the
beach.

Captain Allcorn in Cub No. 204 was followed by Lt. John R.
Shell and by Lt. William H. Butler with Capt. Brenton A. Devol,
Jr., riding as observer. The planes were airborne almost instantly.
They proceeded toward the beach in an echelon right formation at
two thousand feet. Their orders were to fly to Fedala where a racetrack would serve as a landing strip. Three miles from shore, for no
apparent reason, the formation switched to an echelon left. Within
seconds Allcorn saw a gun flash aboard the cruiser Brooklyn, standing inshore with the rest of an armada of two hundred ships. Almost
instantly a round exploded in the position where Shell had been
flying. The three planes dived for the surface.

As Allcorn headed toward shore, almost all the ships in the

convoy opened fire on the Cubs with twenty-millimeter guns, even though they had been painted with invasion markings. Allcorn skipped the waves and headed toward the beach. A hundred yards out he turned and paralleled the beach to reach Fedala. Allied shore installations fired at him most of the way. When he pulled up to head inland, units of the U.S. 2nd Armored Division riddled his airplane with machine gun fire. His windshield disintegrated. Portions of his cockpit were shot away. Then Vichy French opened up on him. He was hit in the right leg. His engine, hit also, burst into flames. He slipped his plane to the ground in a controlled crash, crawled from the cockpit, and dragged himself fifty feet. The Cub exploded.

Butler and Shell meanwhile decided to try to make an airport just north of Casablanca. That was a mistake. German planes had bombed and strafed the field a few minutes before, and nervous antiaircraft gunners let go at them. They managed to put down near a Vichy French fort, were captured, and briefly held prisoner.

Allcorn was found by friendly civilians and taken to an American first aid station. In a period of an hour he had achieved some dubious distinctions: He had been the first army aviator in combat, the first to fly a Cub from an aircraft carrier, the first army aviator to be wounded in combat, and the first to be shot down.

Years later a navy gunnery officer was asked why he had worked the Cubs over. "We looked through the silhouette charts," he explained, "and didn't see anything that resembled those planes. If you were at sea and saw a Cub putt-putting by, would you believe it?"

That was not the first humiliation visited on the newborn Army Aviation. Late the previous month the War Department had directed Fort Sill's Field Artillery School to send ten pilots and ten mechanics to the 13th Field Artillery Brigade in England. This was the first group that the school sent to tactical units. In England it was put into an infantry replacement battalion. Lt. Delbert L. Bristol, in charge of it, breathed fire. Before leaving Fort Sill, Bristol had been told by Col. Wallace Ford to contact Brig. Gen. A. M. Gruenther, chief of staff, Headquarters, II Corps, if anything went wrong. Bristol spoke his piece to Gruenther. Gruenther promptly had the group transferred to the 13th Field Artillery Brigade to become the flight instructor nucleus of the II Corps Air Observation Post School on a strip of grass along the edge of an olive grove at Sidi-bel-Abbes, Algeria. This was more like it. The group arrived by ship convoy late in November.

Attempting to thwart the mission of artillery aviation appeared to be standard operating procedure by some commanding officers at that point in the war. As late as mid-1944 some ground force officers, including artillerymen, militantly opposed the use of light-planes on the battlefield. The tiny planes embodied a new concept of command field performance, and it frightened many old time artillery officers. How could one little guy in one little airplane influence the course of an artillery battle? It boggled the military mind.

Few artillery commanders wanted to be bothered with the light-planes or their pilots. Faculty and students at Sidi-bel-Abbes lived in wooden crates that their airplanes had been shipped in. Frequently commanders failed to provide for feeding operational air section personnel, and on many a night an entire artillery unit would move, leaving its air section somewhere back in the desert.

Yet the Grasshopper pilots were irrepressible. In March 1943 at El Guetter, they uncovered a major thrust being launched by the German 10th Panzer Division. They called down a withering artillery barrage that helped stop the assault. Not content with belling the cat, they caged it. Two Grasshopper warriors calmly landed on a beach between Carthage and Bizerte and captured a half-dozen German soldiers.

As the Allies proceeded to protect their rear for the invasion of Sicily and Italy by sanitizing North Africa, it was the top-drawer field commanders who rescued the Grasshoppers from the military's bureaucratic odium. Their personal mobility was vastly increased by using lightplanes as airborne Jeeps. From aloft they could make quick, personal assessments of their tactical situations.

A hint of the utility of the lightplane for transportation and communication had been transmitted to the British as early as April 1940, when the Nazis seized all the chief Norwegian ports and began pouring in troops. King Haakon VII fled to the mountains in the north, and for weeks a lieutenant of the Norwegian Air Force used a Cub on skis to maintain liaison between the government in exile and loyal officials in Oslo—under the noses of the enemy.

In Africa, Lt. Gen. Mark W. Clark, who had been smuggled into Morocco by submarine to treat with the French before the invasion, used his Grasshoppers regularly as transportation while he was readying the U.S. Fifth Army for the assault on Italy. Once he had his pilot land alongside a field where some G.I.'s were playing baseball, Clark performed creditably at the first bag for a couple of innings. On another occasion he flew over his headquarters and bullhorned an order to have a car meet him at the airport. He got action. *Three* cars met his plane.

Clark himself related a classic story about himself and his Cub.

GENERAL MARK CLARK LANDING ON A NAPLES STREET
"Sir," said his pilot, "you have just witnessed a miracle."

He was taking off from Anzio during the fighting in the Anzio-Cassino sector. Maj. John T. Walker, his pilot, had put pontoons on the general's airplane. Since the Italian peninsula was surrounded by salt water, it let him get around more.

On this day the waves were high. Several soldiers pushed the Cub into waist-high water for takeoff. Walker bounced from wave to wave, trying to get airborne. The pontoons whammed on the crests. Major and general hit one wave with a crunch, but a moment later gained the air. A few minutes later Walker asked, "You see what happened?"

Clark looked over the side. Both pontoons had broken free and were hanging to the craft by a single wire.

"I see," said Clark.

"What," asked Walker, "do you want to do now, sir?"

"Hell, you're the pilot. Don't ask me."

"The only reason, sir," persisted Walker, "that I asked the question, sir, is that it is merely a matter of where the hell would you prefer to crash?"

"In that event, make it Sorrento, it's a pretty place." Sorrento,

L–4 OVER AN ARTILLERY BATTERY
If a passenger carried a revolver aboard, the fire power was doubled.

hard by the fabled Isle of Capri and a rest-and-recreation site for U.S. soldiers, was 100-odd miles away.

"Okay, it's Sorrento."

Walker put the Cub down in four feet of water, and they waded ashore. There wasn't enough left of the airplane to salvage.

Only once did General Clark have a close call despite his addiction to travel by putt-putt. On an observation trip in an L–5, the Stinson version of the unarmed liaison plane, Walker hooked the cable of a barrage balloon with a wing. The balloon had been run up as protection against a German air attack. The cable broke. Gasoline poured from a wing tank. Walker cut the ignition and made a dead stick landing. A bomb had been tethered to the balloon and rigged to slide down and explode if anything struck the cable. It didn't.

"Sir," announced Walker as they recovered their breath, "you have just witnessed a miracle."

General George S. Patton, Jr., the brilliant commander of the U.S. Third Army, survived dozens of lightplane flights on the battlefield—to be injured mortally in an automobile accident at war's end. General Eisenhower, who became theater commander after the invasion of Africa, regularly used Cubs for transportation, to the delight of a press that cabled the news home. So did Lt. Gen. Omar Bradley, later in immediate charge of the assault on Hitler's Fortress Europe under Eisenhower; General George C. Marshall, Army Chief of Staff; and on at least one occasion, Prime Minister Winston Churchill of England. King George himself flew on an inspection trip in an Auster, a British version of the Grasshopper. In Burma, Donovan of the OSS flew 150 miles inside the Japanese lines in a lightplane on an inspection trip.

The war correspondents discovered the Cub. In Italy, the Pacific theater, and later in Europe they rode in it to write of battle as it was seen from the air. Some even datelined their dispatches, "PIPER CUB BASE. . . ." Daniel De Luce of the Associated Press wrote in a dispatch datelined "FIFTH ARMY BEACHHEAD IN ITALY," "I looked from a winged armchair today at Rome, peacefully basking

GENERAL EISENHOWER AND HIS PILOT, T. J. WALKER
The brass used Cubs as airborne Jeeps.

RUNWAY ON AN INVASION BOAT
Landing ships became aircraft carriers.

on the seven ancient hills in the pale sunlight of a winter afternoon." Margaret Bourke-White, probably the war's most famous photographer, flew over the front lines in Italy with Mike Strok, by now the Fifth Army's air OP engineering officer, at the controls, to snap pictures for *Life* magazine.

Transporting the brass that ran the battlefield war, though vital, and the correspondents, was secondary to the principal function of the lightplane. On its scouting missions, it was the eyes of the artillery, even as General Danford (and W. T. Piper) had proposed.

Almost invariably the Grasshopper flew unarmed.

"The armament is so limited," reported Murlin Spencer of the Associated Press, describing a covey of lightplanes in the Southwest Pacific, "that when a passenger armed with a .45 caliber automatic climbs in, the plane's firepower is doubled."

Yet the Grasshopper proved to be the most lethal airplane for tactical land warfare flown by friend or foe in World War II. An air observation post had at its command the most formidable array of guns in the history of warfare. A single artillery battalion could deliver fifty tons of exposive steel an hour. One tiny L-plane could and did command the fire of several battalions on one target.

It was in the assault on Sicily and Italy—the "soft underbelly of the Axis," as Churchill described it—that the liaison planes won their spurs.

For the Sicilian operation, a flight deck seventy yards long and twelve feet wide was built on an LST (Landing Ship–Tank) under the supervision of Capt. B. A. Devol, Jr., one of the men who had taken off from the Ranger for the African invasion. The framework was timbers anchored to the deck by wires. The floor of the flight deck was steel matting. A slight rise in the runway began three-quarters of its length toward the bow. With ballast added to the ship's bow, a liaison pilot had a slight downgrade for takeoff for three-quarters of his run and a level deck for the rest of it. With a ship speed of ten knots into a ten-knot wind, the Grasshoppers were airborne in fifty yards. They flew out to sea several thousand yards, far enough to escape antiaircraft and small arms fire, and paralleled the beach. Lt. E. R. Smartt, the observer on a typical flight, reported the results:

Along the northern Sicilian shore an Allied 155-millimeter howitzer position was being shelled mercilessly by German artillery. In the rough terrain, positions to withdraw to were far to the rear. Forward ground observers could not spot the enemy. A message for help was sent several miles behind the Allied guns to a small landing strip being used by the Grasshoppers after their launch from the LST. Smartt and a pilot took off. They spotted the flashes of the German artillery.

"I made a quick estimation on my map," related Smartt, "coordinates 41.5–60.5. At that location I reported, 'Enemy battery, request battalion'. . . . The [Allied] cannoneers had scrambled out of their foxholes and loaded the pieces. 'Battery has fired.' I replied, 'Roger . . . four zero zero right, repeat range,' and on the next volley, 'one zero zero left, one zero zero short, fire for effect.' The guns gave me what I asked for. . . . The enemy did not fire from that position again."

Another kind of target in Sicily was the truck convoy and infantrymen. A Grasshopper nicknamed Fanny Rouge, puttering back and forth above its artillery battery, saw just such an inviting place for the lodgment of some shells. It radioed the range. The first burst was wide. "Five zero zero right, two zero zero over," advised Fanny Rouge. The second shell was closer. Again the artillery airplane radioed corrections. The third burst was on the nose. "Target, target," said Fanny Rouge. "Fire for effect, one round." "On the way," said the ground. "Mission accomplished," said Fanny Rouge.

In less than five minutes (reported *Time* magazine in its issue of September 16, 1943) Fanny Rouge had located and directed the destruction, with eleven shells, of a target that would have demanded a flight of medium bombers, plus more than an hour of communications, preparations, and operations.

The landings at Anzio for the assault on Italy proper spawned conditions that were tailor-made for the liaison aircraft. While the

Fifth Army was still fighting to get out of its beachhead, Capt. William H. McKay, of Arp, Texas, commander of a divisional Piper Cub section, discovered from his moving perch considerably more than he had been looking for.

"I nearly fell out of the plane," he related, "when I looked down. There were more than 2,000 (later confirmed at 2,400) Germans walking across a field toward our lines in parade formation. They had a lot of tanks with them."

Five thousand artillery rounds were fired into the area under McKay's direction. A captured German officer said later that casualties had been more than 50 percent. The enemy had been stunned by the ferocity of the barrage. Their orders had been to split the beachhead in two with a drive to the sea.

Cubs directed naval gunfire. More than 370 guns of all calibers were fired TOT (time on target) at one particular objective at Anzio, all aimed by one observer. This included naval gunfire from three cruisers, the USS Brooklyn, the HMS Dido, and the HMS Orion.

To this same bloody beachhead two Cubs flew fifty pints of whole blood to treat the wounded.

One German gun position had been not only dug in on the reverse face of a mountain but hidden in a tunnel as well. For firing, it was wheeled out on tracks. A Grasshopper pilot and his observer spotted it. They radioed. A gun from each of three U.S. battalions made a leisurely precision adjustment on the tunnel entrance. The Grasshopper flew off. The Germans waited half an hour, apparently concluded that it was safe to roll out their gun, and fired a round. Three shells fired simultaneously destroyed it.

When bad weather grounded the regular photoreconnaissance planes during the Volturno offensive in the drive on Rome, the entire Fifth Army, massed for battle, was immobilized for days. Unable to wait any longer, yet unwilling to advance without intelligence, General Lucian Truscott, who had taken over the Fifth Army as Clark took command of the 15th Army Group, sent up a Cub. The Grasshopper flew right up the Apennine River valley under the overcast, snapping pictures as it went, returned without a scratch, and the assault began.

In the first two days of attack on Monte Cassino, in which both the air forces and artillery units participated, the artillery delivered eleven thousand tons of ammunition on the target, the equivalent of 1,100 missions by four-engine bombers. One eight-inch gun delivered more firepower per hour than three bombers.

Allied ground forces bestowed affectionate names on the Grasshoppers: J. C. Penney Pursuits, Maytag Messerschmitts, Mail Order Monoplanes.

Mike Strok designed a parachute apparatus to supply troops marooned on a mountain near Venafro. The air forces contributed release devices originally manufactured for light fragmentary bombs. These were welded beneath the Cubs. Two cans tied together supplied water. C rations were 'chuted in fiber cases that had held 105-millimeter shells. The drops were made from a height of four hundred feet.

On June 3, 1944, in the march on Rome, a Cub piloted by Capt. John W. Oswalt, air officer of the 1st Armored Division, landed on a racetrack on the outskirts of the city to contact the lead Allied tanks and armored cars, and when the Germans had withdrawn and Jeeps cruised past Saint Peter's, Cubs flew overhead.

As Germany's Field Marshal Albert Kesselring retreated north to establish his Gothic Line, command became increasingly difficult. Truscott found it hard to get around by Jeep to visit his units in the mountains south of the Po Valley.

"Build me an airstrip near the CP (command post)," he told Capt. Jack Marinelli, Fifth Army air officer, "and the closer the better."

With a lightplane Truscott got the mobility he needed.

On October 28, 1944, a correspondent with the Fifth Army, Pat Frank, wrote of smashing the Gothic Line, then based on Futa Pass.

> Without the air OP's, such was the nature of the terrain, our artillery would have been blind. The Gothic Line was an unbroken barrier of mountains stretched across central Italy. The Huns held every inch of high ground. Everything we did they could see, even the Jeeps that moved miles from the front. . . . Behind this mountain barrier, on the reverse slopes, the German had his artillery. . . . He could drop shells on every crossroad at will. Except through air OP's we could never have located his batteries. Except for air OP's, victory, if it came at all, would have been enormously costly.

For the first time, in Sicily the liaison pilots began encountering attacks by enemy fighters. A German document that fell into the hands of U.S. Army Intelligence offered German pilots points toward the award of the Air Medal in these quotients: three for downing an escorted four-engine bomber, two for an escorted twin-engine bomber, one for a fighter, and two for a liaison plane. Ground troops who brought down a Cub were awarded fifteen days' leave. Numerous forays were made on the small planes by Messerschmitt 109's and Focke-Wulf 190's, often in groups of six. The Fort Sill training paid off. The artillery planes dived for the deck. Enemy pilots seldom could get them in their sights.

The first kill of an enemy fighter credited to a Cub—and there were others—was made by Capt. V. J. McGrath, a Royal Artillery officer flying for the Fifth Army. For several days McGrath had been chased home by the same Messerschmitt. He developed a distaste for the German pilot when, on one foray, his liaison airplane got ventilated by several machine gun slugs.

"I'm sick of this game," McGrath told his mechanic.

He devised a trap. On his next mission he flew in wide circles over the mountains. The German took the bait and dived out of the sun. The Grasshopper swept low and scuttled into a ravine. McGrath knew the ravine. He had flown it before. Tracers from the Messerschmitt were zinging by him as the German fired to establish range. McGrath turned a bend in the ravine. The German, intent on his prey, followed. McGrath banked vertically, reversed his field, and flew under the Messerschmitt. The ravine was a dead end. The German, unable to turn his fast fighter, splattered himself and his airplane on the face of a cliff.

That is not to say that the Grasshopper fleet suffered no casualties. The first pilot fatally wounded flew into a hail of enemy machine gun ground fire in the disaster at Kasserine Pass in Africa. He died in a prison camp. In Sicily, S. Sgt. James T. Smith, Jr., and his observer died when a Messerschmitt clipped off a wing.

Ernie Pyle, best-beloved of the war correspondents, writing from Italy, reported:

> The saddest story I've ever heard about a Cub happened here on the Fifth Army beachhead. A (friendly) "Long Tom"—or 155 rifle—was the unwitting villain in this case. This certain gun fired only one shell that entire day—but that one shell, with all the sky to travel in, made a direct hit on one of our Cubs in the air and blew it to smithereens.

For the entire first year of air OP, these men were the sum of those killed. It was a fair average, in relation to the number of missions flown, for the entire war.

Then there was the story of Captain Oswalt and his descent into a field of high explosives. Oswalt, subsequently chief of military requirements planning for the Bell Helicopter Company, Fort Worth,

had on this December 4, 1944, a before-daylight call from the headquarters of Combat Command A of the 1st Armored Division.

"Can you put up an air OP?" asked Maj. George B. Moore, a
friend. "We're getting severe shelling. It looks like a battery of
three German 150-millimeter guns."

"The weather's marginal."

"People are getting killed in CCA headquarters. Please send up
a plane even if it has to crash-land on some mountain pasture."

The division was in the North Apennines, just over Radacosa
Pass along Highway 65 north of Florence. It had moved through
Futa Pass in the early fall and now could look down on Bologna in
the Valley of the Po. Oswalt had a flight strip, a short, muddy section of pierced steel planking, in the Firenzuola Valley between the
two passes. Mountains shot up to 4,500 feet. A drizzle was falling
from a low overcast, and there was wind. But Radacosa Pass was
open.

"You could see out from under the overcast through the pass,"
Oswalt recounted, "almost as though the cloud layer over the valley
were a sliding lid on a cookie jar."

Under the circumstances, he elected to fly the mission himself
rather than assign it to a subordinate. He had three L-5's and six
L-4's in his detachment. If he had to crash-land, he wanted a plane
that would come in short. He chose his own Cub, "Sooper Snooper."

He took off, cleared the pass, located the enemy battery about a
quarter of the way between the U.S. forward positions and the auto-
strada to Bologna, and called down fire from the division artillery.
For good measure he brought in some heavier corps artillery on the
target. Some Thunderbolt fighters from Pisa swept over just then to
dive-bomb other targets. German 88-millimeter antiaircraft opened
up on the fighters, and Oswalt transferred fire to the AA guns to
suppress them.

By now, in the air for two hours and a quarter, he was getting
worried about fuel. He had been slow-flying while he adjusted fire
and figured that his normal two and a half to two and three-quarters
hours of gas probably was worth three hours and fifteen minutes.

To the fire direction center he reported, "I've got to leave station
and return."

"Will you stay for one last volley?" he was asked.

This was a TOT on the original target. It took additional minutes. Oswalt flew back toward Radacosa Pass. The cloud deck lowered.
In the venturi-like mouth of the pass, he fought a southeast wind.
This was no good. He was barely making headway. His options were
two: He could turn around and land in a mountain pasture within
friendly lines, or pull up through the cloud deck, chancing lighter
winds at a higher altitude, and let down on the far side of the pass

through three thousand feet of gray gauze. He chose the second alternative. His fuel was almost gone. Descending blind, he established a crab angle that would bring him out over his valley. What he didn't know was that a mountain to the east was blocking off some of the wind, so his crab was drifting him into it. Breaking out suddenly, he saw just below and ahead some pine trees, and then a line of six-by-six trucks on a muddy road. He pulled back on the stick and slapped the throttle open, but too late. His left wheel bounced off the top of a truck. The plane mushed nose-high into a muddy slope. Fifty feet to the left was a tent full of truck drivers getting ready to pull out. A half mile to the right was a huge fuel and oil cache. And he had landed squarely in the middle of an ammunition dump.

He radioed his coordinates to his fire direction center.

"That can't be right," he was advised. "We plot you on the side of a mountain."

That was exactly where he was. The Cub had a bashed-in left landing gear, a broken prop, and a wrecked oil radiator. It was flying again the next day. Oswalt's hurts were confined to a skinned nose and shins.

"Someone," he said, "had me by the hand."

The end of the war was not the end of John Oswalt's cockpit chores. When General Mark Clark was made senior commander of Allied occupation forces in Austria, Oswalt was his staff aviation officer and pilot. Some years later when Clark became commanding general of the Army Ground Forces at Fort Monroe, Virginia, Oswalt again was his pilot. In both cases the general's choice of a mount was a Cub.

Pilots became attached to their particular airplanes.

It was that way between Lt. Wilfred M. Boucher and his series of L-4 Sad Sacks. Boucher had three. The first, he had rolled into a ball in a forced landing during maneuvers with the 76th Division back home—his ground crew had failed to refuel him between two long missions. Sad Sack II took off from the runway of decked-over LST 906 on the morning of August 15, 1944, for reconnaissance in the invasion of southern France, described at the time as "the worst-kept secret of the war." Called Operation Anvil-Dragoon, it was designed to hold the German First and Nineteenth armies immobile and prevent their deployment against the Allies in Normandy. Lt. Gen. Alexander M. Patch's Seventh U.S. Army hit the beaches on this mid-August day southwest of Cannes. Boucher was a liaison pilot assigned to the 41st Field Artillery Battalion of the 3rd Division, one of three in the action that had been pulled out of combat after the Anzio breakout and the investment of Rome. But for the day he was on temporary duty with the VI Corps.

Boucher wasn't carrying his rabbit's foot. During his passes along the invasion beaches he flew into a barrage balloon cable that tore a foot off his right wing. He recovered from the resulting dive and since the Cub was ignoring the amputation, continued his mission. Then, after three hours and twenty minutes, his engine quit. Dirt in the gas or wobble pump lines from emergency cans could have caused it. Boucher flipped over in putting down in the Mediterranean a half mile off the beach at Saint Tropez. He got out. The plane, only lightly damaged, floated. Hours later a navy vessel eviscerated Sad Sack II in attempting to take it aboard.

Sad Sack III participated in a lightning thrust of twenty-four days up the Rhone Valley. It was during this sweep that, in the absence of ground transport for five days, Cubs performed resupply for some of the walking soldiery by dumping their loads on the fly at the top of a ski slide at Saint Etienne. The stuff skidded down to the waiting troops. It accelerated things—the planes didn't have to land.

On the evening of September 7 Sad Sack III was on the southern approaches to Besancon. The mission: to take Besancon and speed to the Belfort Gap to trap retreating German troops. Boucher's battalion air section was doing reconnaissance, calling down fire on targets of opportunity, and reregistering battalion howitzers on base points. Boucher set his alarm clock for 7 A.M. That was all that he remembered until he found himself standing in a courtyard in formation and asking the classic question, "What happened?"

An American lieutenant standing next to him muttered, "Shut up, we're being counted."

Another captured lieutenant from his outfit later filled him in. On the morning of September 8 he had flown forward to drop artillery fire on a convoy of German trucks pulling out of Besancon. Antiaircraft fire downed him. A head wound gave him a concussion. How Sad Sack III had brought him and Lt. Paul Alpert of Sedalia, Missouri, his observer, to earth alive, he did not know. Alpert hid out with French civilians until U.S. troops overran the area. Boucher spent the rest of the war in a prison camp.

In the Southwest Pacific, curiously enough, the ground army cottoned to the unarmed liaison airplane far more readily than in Europe. Still more curious, the U.S. Navy clasped the thing to its bosom. Perhaps its acceptance rate was affected by the fact that months elapsed between the time the Cub became operational in Sicily and Italy and its appearance as a weapon against the Japanese. In the interim there was a feedback on its usefulness. The navy's posture toward the Cub could have been conditioned by the traditional professionalism of that branch of the armed forces. The navy was the first to bestow the imprimatur of "Grasshopper" to its list of official aircraft. General Douglas MacArthur, once he had recognized air power as an indispensable adjunct to the walking soldiery, used the liaison airplane up to the hilt of its capabilities.

As MacArthur's slow return across the Southwest Pacific began to pick up momentum following the victory at Guadalcanal by the marines and army units, lightplanes began participating in liaison and spotter work. They were the first U.S. airplanes to use the Salamaua airstrip in New Guinea in September 1943. "We have landed Piper Cubs there," the briefing officer told surprised war correspondents to signalize the fall of that port on the world's second largest island.

A patrol, pushing into the dank jungle, was ambushed by Japanese. Outnumbered, it reported by radio, "We are holding on." Food and ammunition were running short. A Cub was dispatched to drop supplies until a relief party could fight its way through.

A Cub piloted by Capt. Sydney S. Woods of Yuma, Arizona, found Lt. Paul Yeager of Nowata, Oklahoma, a P–38 fighter pilot who had bailed out and had spent two harrowing days only six miles from an advanced American air base.

At Cape Gloucester, a Marine Corps pilot, Albert G. Hoffman, Jr., of Mullica Hill, New Jersey, flew the first Allied airplane—a Cub —off the island of New Britain. He had to equip his newly assembled plane with pontoons because of debris on the captured airstrip. But by the next day Marine Corps engineers had cleared away enough of it to permit Lt. Richard M. Hunt of Washington, D.C., to pilot the second airplane, a Cub, off the island.

Marine Cubs dropped emergency one-meal rations to a forward patrol base fifteen miles inland from Cape Gloucester on the far side of 6,600-foot Mount Talawe in weather that had grounded the birds. They provided the same patrol a communications link with field headquarters when a radio "dead spot" enfogged the area.

Regularly the liaison planes delivered blood plasma for the wounded. The squadron of Marine Corps artillery Cubs was dubbed, affectionately, the "Luftwaffe." When weather grounded all other air support, one Cub was the entire air force for a Marine Corps invasion of the Willaumet peninsula on the island's north coast—its crew tossed hand grenades at the enemy. A Cub sighted a dozen Japanese soldiers trying to escape from an island in two native canoes. Returning to base, the pilot and observer snatched up a machine gun and hand grenades, bombed and strafed the canoes, killed three

AN LST DISGORGING CUB
Lightplanes flew blood plasma to the wounded.

of the enemy, and hovered overhead until a PT boat summoned by radio captured the rest.

In the Marianas campaign, liaison planes called down Marine Corps artillery fire on Japanese strong points. In one instance guns on Saipan liquidated a Japanese battery on the north end of Tinian seconds after a lightplane radioed the coordinates. In time, Japanese artillery, like the Germans' in Italy, learned to fall silent when a spotter airplane was aloft.

On Leyte during MacArthur's invasion of the Philippines the first airstrips hacked out by the engineers were for Cubs.

For the Lingayen Gulf landings the airplanes were dismantled and stowed, wings included, aboard amphibious "Ducks." These in turn were loaded into LSM's (Landing Ship Medium). Launched offshore, the Ducks ferried the planes to the beach where they were re-assembled for the Luzon campaign.

The 25th Liaison Squadron of the 71st Tactical Reconnaissance Group, which already had won a Presidential Unit Citation for its performance on Leyte, got a call for help in December 1944 from the 11th Airborne Division. It had outrun its supply lines and was rapidly being surrounded by the enemy. For almost a month Cubs, Stinson L-5's, and a single C-47, the military version of the air-

THE BRODIE DEVICE
Wire-launched Cubs poured artillery fire on Okinawa.

lines' Douglas DC–3 transport, supplied the division with food, ammunition, and medicine. On one day alone the Grasshoppers airdropped nearly eighteen tons.

It was at the invasion of Okinawa, which had to be neutralized to permit the use of the air forces' mightiest bombers on the Japanese home islands, that the virtuosity of the lightplane reached a new high. Back at Fort Sill, Capt. Tony Piper had experimented with as nutty—yet workable—an idea as ever was inflicted on pilots.

Known as the "Brodie Device," and named not for the man who jumped off the Brooklyn Bridge but for an army lieutenant named James Brodie who pushed for it, it was engineered to permit an L–4 to take off from and land on a cable strung between a brace of stanchions. The airplane with a hook at the center of gravity atop the wing was mounted in a heavy nylon sling that dangled from a trolley on the cable. To take off, an L–4 pilot opened his throttle, sped down the cable, and yanked a lanyard to free his hook. Landing, he jockeyed his plane to engage the hook in the sling.

Tony Piper was one of the first to try out the Brodie Device. Curious about what reduction in drag would result from removing the landing gear, he flew off and on the Brodie without wheels— naturally without authority. The risk was not in an accident. It was in all the explaining that he would have to do if he crashed the airplane. The Brodie, happily, worked.

For Okinawa, army artillery had been set up in the adjoining Kerama Retto Islands to shell the Japanese defenses. It needed photography and air observation, but the Keramas had no suitable area for a landing strip. The Brodie Device had been installed on some LSTs. The first such ship, in fact, to be outfitted with it was christened the USS Brodie. The pilots were ready. They had been schooled by Lt. Earl B. Montgomery, a pilot with the 77th Infantry Division Artillery.

Brodie Cubs zeroed-in the rounds from the Keramas onto the Okinawa Japanese. Not a pilot or airplane was lost.

Joe E. Brown, the comic, flew in Cubs to entertain the troops. So did comedian Bob Hope. ("A Cub," wrote Hope in a newspaper column, "is a Mustang [fighter] that wouldn't eat its cereal.") So did Ernie Pyle. He flew off a Brodie to his last assignment, a rendezvous with a sniper's bullet on Ie Shima.

In India in 1943 Allied troops were poised to fight their way back into Burma, from which they had been so ignominiously chased by the Japanese the previous year. The Cub-equipped 71st Liaison Squadron ran messages, did reconnaissance, and pasted the enemy with artillery fire.

Both the L–4 and the L–5 were used by engineers to survey the projected route of the Ledo Road across northern Burma, to join the 1,445-mile Burma Road from Lashio to Kunming, capital of the Chinese Yunnan province, and thus assure a route to supply the Nationalist forces.

In the jungle C–47 transports brought supplies by wholesale to prepared fields, and the small planes dispersed them by retail to advanced outposts.

It became procedure during the offensive against the Japanese in the Northern Hukawng Valley for Chinese-American advance columns to construct lightplane landing strips. The route taken by Brig. Gen. Frank D. Merrill's famous Marauders was marked by a string of such strips.

Lightplanes even flew the Himalayas—the "Hump"—winding through serpentine valleys at only nine thousand feet.

In response to a desperate plea for help from a big British force trapped in the Arakan area of southern Burma, seven lightplanes and nine sergeant pilots in fifteen days evacuated seven hundred casualties—with British Spitfire fighters flying cover.

U.S. Army Air Forces

BAZOOKAS ON AN L–4
They knocked out German tanks.

"Without you men and your aircraft," Maj. Gen. O. C. Wingate told the puddle-jumper aviators, "this campaign could not have hoped to be a success."

In the final campaigns of the war in the European theater, light-planes added some new wrinkles to their versatility.

Their first task was to aim the big guns, and on June 7, 1944, D-Day-plus-one, they were laying down naval fire on German fortifications behind the beaches of Normandy. Three days later they were being deployed for artillery battalions. Scores of L–4's fitted with extra gas tanks were flown across the English Channel. Others, dismantled and reassembled, came by ship. The L–5's, with longer range, needed no extra fuel.

Normandy farm fields posed a new hazard for the air OP's. Retreating, the Germans liberally mined them, and the Grasshopper pilots, suddenly sucked into battles of such quick movement that establishing landing strips was out of the question, quickly learned to put down in pastures where cows were grazing. The cows themselves were a hazard, but they couldn't coexist with mines.

The OP's acquired armament, the same bazookas that Col. John C. L. Adams had tried to install back home. Two California lieutenants, Harley Merrick and Roy Carson, were the first to mount rockets under each wing. A major with the 4th Armored Division, Charles Carpenter of Moline, Illinois, thought so well of the idea that he rigged six rockets on his struts. He was credited with knocking out five tanks. He thought nothing of attacking entrenched enemy infantry. Rocket-firing lightplanes supplemented their OP duties in the breakthrough at Saint Lo.

In the Patton 3rd Division's lightning thrust across France, lightplanes directed traffic for the endless line of supply trucks known as the Red Ball Express. No disabled vehicle clogged a road for long. Grasshoppers spotted it and radioed ordnance repair depots for help.

Lt. Galen L. Curry of Tecumseh, Nebraska, was the first Allied pilot to land in Paris. Putting down on Issy les Monlineaux airport in a Cub, he receipted for Resistance rifle fire. He waved a white handkerchief. A head popped up behind a concrete wall.

"Boche?" asked the man who owned it.

"No."

"British?"

"No, American." The champagne flowed.

At Bastogne in the Battle of the Bulge ("Nuts!" replied Brig. Gen. A. C. McAuliffe of the 101st Airborne Division to the German demand for surrender), a Cub pilot flew in a doctor to tend the wounded—the besieged garrison radioed it had more than five hundred casualties needing first aid. Another, Lt. Kenneth B. Schley of Far Hills, New Jersey, defied darkness, enemy fire, and an order not to take off to deliver a supply of penicillin to Bastogne. To circumvent any order to return while he was en route, he shut off his radio.

Beyond the Moselle River, five Cubs in the absence of artillery delivered dynamite to reduce an enemy strong point, Fort Koenigsmacher.

When Patton spearheaded the attack on the Siegfried Line a Cub landed Maj. Gen. J. W. O'Daniels between his own troops and the German "dragon's teeth" tank obstacles so he could make a personal reconnaissance.

At a point on the Rhine, Lt. Horace E. Watson, liaison pilot for the 8th Armored Division, spotted a reconnaissance outfit held up by a blown bridge. Circling the area, he found another bridge intact. Making a low pass, engine idling, he yelled at the troops, "Follow me!" They did.

At 7:30 A.M. on Sunday, December 7, 1941, Japanese aircraft for the first time fired in anger at an American airplane. It was a Piper Cub lazing over Oahu's Diamond Head with Ray Buduick, a Honolulu attorney, at the controls. Though his plane was riddled with bullets, he dived for the deck and escaped. Robert Tyce, the Cub distributor in Hawaii, was less lucky. Japanese gunfire cut him in two.

Of his Cubs and other lightplanes and the war, William T. Piper, Sr., said at the time, "They will have a place."

When on May 7, 1944, Germany surrendered, and on August 14 Japan, the Grasshoppers had carved for themselves a far bigger place in the annals of armed conflict than a general, or an admiral, or indeed W. T. Piper himself had ever anticipated.

The Well of Innocence

LONG BEFORE THE LAST SHOT HAD BEEN fired in anger in the Pacific, the U.S. aviation manufacturing industry had begun to plan products for its postwar markets. The bull elephants of the business—Boeing, Lockheed, Douglas, Martin, Consolidated, and North American Aviation—who measured income in the billions of dollars, knew that their contracts for military aircraft would be scrapped the moment the hostilities were over. Washington had begun cutting back orders on some types of airplanes, in fact, as early as January 1944. These already were in surplus. When the final blow fell, when the big manufacturers had fabricated more than 300,000 combat aircraft at a cost in excess of $47 billion, they would have to make airplanes for commercial customers. For the most part, that meant transport-type airplanes, and the bulk of these would go to scheduled, certificated airlines both at home and abroad. The market was waiting. During the war, the public had discovered the virtues of air travel. The airplane was swift. It was becoming dependable in anything but the worst of weather conditions. Passengers jammed airports, clamoring for priority space. In only six years the revenue miles flown by domestic airlines had tripled, and the number of passengers carried and the route miles on the airways map had quadrupled.

Those other aircraft manufacturers, the little fellows, were turning out the putt-putts for the war effort, airplanes that could tote only two to four persons. Their contracts too would be scrapped at war's end. These aircraft fabricators too were looking toward an inevitable, peacetime bonanza in sales. That market was waiting. Everyone said so. To begin with, was anyone stupid enough to think that the several million men in the U.S. Army Air Forces and in the U.S. Navy and Marine Corps air arms would be satisfied to be shackled to surface transportation? Each would be in the market for his very own flying machine. And the general public—uncounted hundreds of thousands of good citizens introduced to air transport during the war—would be assembling at the gates of the lightplane factories to purchase their own wings.

A GI Bill was rumored, which would finance trade and professional training for the millions in the armed forces who would be coming back to civilian pursuits. Untold thousands of them would want to get into aviation. That would mean the establishment of hundreds of flying schools. These alone would need thousands of airplanes.

The lightplane industry's belief in its future was as sublime as a child's conviction that the doctor brought babies in his medicine satchel.

By right of their stature in the business, William Thomas Piper and his brood led the optimists in forecasting a boom in postwar personal flying. A company booklet issued in 1944, titled "What Your Town Needs for the Coming Air Age," said: "Flying is the most flexible means of transportation the world has ever seen." Another booklet, "The Piper Cub in War and Peace," published the same year, stated that after the war "lightplanes will . . . dominate the air just as popular-priced automobiles dominate the road. . . . Thousands of Uncle Sam's pilots will always consider flying the best means of transportation. . . . We can look forward to a great air age after the war."

Appearing on March 20, 1945, before the U.S. Senate's commerce committee as president of his own corporation and a member of the executive committee of the Personal Aircraft Council of the Aeronautical Chamber of Commerce of America, W. T. Piper testified: "The need . . . is for legislation that will permit the construction of the largest number of landing facilities possible quickly, cheaply, and in convenient or accessible locations. . . . Every community (in the land)—all 16,752 of them—should be encouraged to provide a convenient and economical landing facility immediately." His pitch was for "airparks, flightstops, and air harbors." The airpark would be a full-facility airport for personal aircraft, offering hangar space, gas, oil, and repairs. Flightstops would be landing strips in the tens of thousands alongside the nation's major highways to serve as havens for itinerant pilots. Neither airparks nor flightstops would require paved runways. Air harbors would be to float airplanes what airparks were to wheeled aircraft.

He had a point. In all the 3.6 million square miles of continental United States, there were only 2,364 prepared places that qualified as airports for aircraft. For the itinerant lightplane pilot there were in addition 2,126 "landing fields"—largely privately owned, converted pastures, now and then opened to cows or sheep to spare the owner the toil of cutting the grass and weeds, and embellished by a makeshift hangar.

SKY COUPE
Not a bad airplane, just not a good one.

William, Sr., traveled endlessly on speaking dates.

There were words of caution from some longheads. In *Wings after War,* a book published in 1944, S. Paul Johnston, a respected journalist, warned that military pilots would not be returned to mufti to buy personal aircraft wholesale. Reginald M. Cleveland and Leslie E. Neville, equally respected, in another volume, *The Coming Air Age,* stated in the same year, "Predictions are that we shall have between 300,000 and 500,000 private planes in the sky by 1950"— as against fifty million private automobiles. (The exact figure for all nonmilitary aircraft, including commercial transports, turned out to be 92,809.)

Even W. T. Piper rebuked the unredeemed dreamers. "Visions of an airplane in most garages," he warned in February 1945, "are unfounded. But lightplanes will be big business."

In anticipation of peace, William, Sr., had been doing some off-in-the-corner tinkering. So had his staff. There had been the Sky Coupe, a two-place pusher-propeller airplane with twin booms on either side running back to the tail surfaces. It wasn't a bad airplane. It just wasn't a good one. The fenced-in propeller was a safety factor, and a tricycle landing gear made the plane compliant on the ground in crosswinds, but it didn't fly very well. There was the Skycycle. This was a single-place airplane with a fuselage fashioned from a big, droppable wing fuel tank made of a plastic reinforced with sisal fibers and used on a navy Corsair fighter-bomber. Someone at Piper,

THE SKY SEDAN
It could have made the difference between profit and disaster.

glimpsing a sketch of the contraption, exclaimed, "Gee, we could sell a million of those things." So they attached wings on the droppable fuel tank and cut a hole in the top of it for a cockpit, enclosed it in a bubble canopy, bolted an engine to the nose, put a fin, tailplane, rudder, and elevator on the other end, and flew it. Everything went dandy until the bubble blew off. That destroyed the air-flow over the tail surfaces and the thing became almost unmanageable. But, more important, Mr. Piper decided that basically the machine wasn't stable enough to be trusted to an inexperienced pilot.

And then there was the Sky Sedan. This was a four-place machine —for a pilot and three passengers—with a low wing in place of the lightplane's traditional high wing, a retractable landing gear, air-oil shock absorbers, and a single, six-cylinder Continental "flat" engine of 165 horsepower that could supply a commendable cruising speed at sea level of 160 miles an hour. The Sky Sedan, or PWA (post-war airplane)-6 as it was dubbed by the factory, could climb to eighteen thousand feet. Dave Long, young and imaginative, whom Jamouneau had named chief design engineer, was largely responsible for the Sky Sedan.

None of these new-idea airplanes ever made it to the production line. The anxiety to get going on current model civilian aircraft infused the entire company. It had been under wraps ever since Pearl

Harbor, delivering a skimpy 5,673 liaison-observation planes to the army when it could have manufactured 20,000. The factory had its jigs and tools from 1941 ready to supply the civilian market. Like the automobile industry, it would resume manufacture with almost the selfsame products that it was making when the war began. These would be the J–3 trainer and the Cruiser. The Coupe had been dropped. Updating could come later when the pressure of consumer demand eased a little.

Piper Aircraft's income and outgo was in the black, but just. It wound up its fiscal year on September 30, 1945, with a gross take of $7,700,000 and a net operating profit of $229,000, or 2.9 as a percent of sales. That should have flipped up a warning flag. It didn't.

The rest of the lightplane industry was no less impatient. Little by little, the government was releasing stockpiled, strategic materials to factories of all descriptions and, receipting for their share, the lightplane makers put on double shifts of engineers to fashion vehicles for the aerial highways to be aborning. Piper, of course, would lead the way to Utopia. But other manufacturers were girding themselves to offer competition. Strictly in the small plane field, Piper was joined by Aeronca and Taylorcraft, the latter now firmly controlled by the Fairchild Aviation Corporation, as the chief producers. A winsome little machine called the Ercoupe (for the Engineering and Research Corporation of Riverdale, Maryland), designed before the war, promised to capture a share of the market. Crafted by a gifted engineer, Fred Weick, it was a two-place aircraft without rudder pedals for simplified control; cables integrated the movements of ailerons and rudder. Its tricycle gear and low-wing configuration were sassy. Stinson, in a Detroit suburb, could easily convert its L–5 observation plane into a fine, four-place civilian version. At Inglewood, California, North American Aviation already was test flying a high-performance, four-place airplane named the Navion. At Bethpage, Long Island, the Grumman Aircraft Engineering Corporation had another fine, four-place, all-metal machine. The Republic Aviation Corporation at Farmingdale, Long Island, had a pusher amphibian, the Seabee, ready for production. Luscombe would be back in the civilian market with a line of sleek, metal fuselage, high-wing airplanes. There were others: Waco, Bellanca, Meyers, and even a potential entry from one of the big west coast transport builders that rumor identified as Douglas, the creator of that workhorse of the airlines, the DC–3, and the four-engine wartime transport, the DC–4. Counting the imperishable shoestring companies financed by hope and tooled only with a slide rule and a pair of metal-cutting shears, two and a half dozen brands of small and smallish consumer-type airplanes were about to burst upon the market. Their authors were too busy preparing their counting boxes to be exalted by their mission. They rationalized any predictions on consumer demand, no matter how extravagant. They were in mass hypnosis, bent on mass suicide.

"Here we go!" remarked Jake Miller, tamping the tobacco in the bowl of his pipe with the heel of a wooden golf tee, when the news was broadcast that the Superfortress Enola Gay had dropped an atomic bomb on Hiroshima, and in the ensuing months the market for personal aircraft proved to be every bit as large as everybody had been saying it would be. Piper's backlog of orders grew to $11 million. At a distributors' meeting the demands for airplanes became so insistent that rationing had to be instituted.

"We'll have to build sixty airplanes a day at this rate," said Miller.

Cruisers were selling on a black market at prices several hundred dollars beyond that fixed by the factory. As an apparent token of the acceptance of personal airplanes by the public, on October 6, seven weeks after the capitulation of Japan, Piper aircraft were displayed at department stores in Chicago, New York, and Philadelphia. By November production in Lock Haven had been pushed to 15 planes daily and the plant was humming six days a week on three shifts. By the close of the calendar year the company had turned out 938 civil airplanes and the bell on the cash register was playing a symphony.

The pundits of periodical journalism added their voices to the chorus of bravos for lightplane manufacture. A nine-page article in *Fortune* in February 1946, surveying the market for personal aircraft, said in part: "The trend is in the right direction—toward cheaper, safer airplanes, many more air parks, and much less governmental red tape for pilots. The outlook is good."

W. T. Piper was in his element again. Things were turning out as he had hoped. The "Air Age" was indeed here. An assembly operation, a branch plant, was established in Ponca City, Oklahoma, with Hanford Eckman as manager. A number of employes from Lock Haven went out to build Cub trainers. A Super Cruiser was engineered. This was an outgrowth of the prewar Cruiser that had been the apple of W. T. Piper's eye. With a 100-horsepower Lycoming engine on the nose, it did ninety-five miles an hour bearing a pilot and two passengers. It could climb at 650 feet per minute, and had a service ceiling of 16,000 feet. It was a tractable airplane. It had only one real fault, and that a minor one—it tended to "float" when a pilot squared off for a landing.

"It just wants to keep on flying," remarked the president of the company indulgently.

Howard Piper fought a losing battle to get the Sky Sedan produced.

"We ought to produce that airplane," he argued to Walter Jamouneau. "It's the real market." Mr. Piper's youngest son was presently in Jamouneau's engineering department. "Maybe," he said, "we can subcontract the work and assemble here."

He flew off to explore. An outfit in Michigan was willing to build the wing panels. A sailplane company in Elmira, New York, would contract for the fuselages. But no one in Lock Haven had the time even to help coordinate the effort to produce the Sky Sedan.

Everyone agreed that there was need for a third type of airplane on the Piper showroom floor to forestall "conquest" sales by competitors, something in the order of a Buick in the automobile business to add to the Chevrolet (the Piper J–3) and the Pontiac (the Super Cruiser). If the Buick was too heroic an effort for a manufactory badgered by the demands of customers for delivery of its products, then perhaps a simpler airplane design—a Volkswagen—could be purchased from an independent engineer. One such free lance in airplanes was Johnny Thorpe. He knew his business, having knocked around southern California airplane plants for years. Thorpe had a low-wing, side-by-side airplane that he called the Sky Scooter. In performance it was a slight improvement on the Piper Coupe. A modest engine of sixty-five horsepower gave it a cruise of eighty-five miles an hour, but it could get out of a small field with a run of less than 600 feet and could climb at 600 feet a minute. Best of all, it was mechanically uncomplicated. It would be a snap to produce.

Pug Piper and Jamouneau flew to Thorpe's site of operations, Van Nuys airport.

"Do you want to part with the design?" asked young Piper with characteristic bluntness. "What do you want for it?"

Thorpe temporized. Jamouneau and Pug Piper returned to Lock Haven empty handed. Thus the Sky Scooter was added to the Sky Sedan as an airplane that might have broadened the appeal of Piper products in the new, burgeoning Air Age.

There were arguments within the councils of Piper Aircraft on pricing the existing products. The flyaway price of the J–3 at the start of the war had been $1,440. With the addition of such items as a compass, brakes, running lights, a battery, a special paint job, and wheel pants (reviving memories of the early days in automobiles when bumpers and a spare tire came extra), the figure could go as high as $1,636. Allowing for the drop in the purchasing value of the dollar during the war years, the price on the J–3 went up to $2,195. In 1941 the Cruiser sold for $2,150. After the war this was advanced to $3,205 and presently, with the addition of a radio, battery, and generator, to $3,495.

"That's enough," pronounced W. T. Piper, who precipitated most of the hassles over the tags on his products, "that high and no higher."

Materials were a problem in the postwar manufacture of any type of hardware. Every industry in the United States was fighting for a share of steel, wood, rubber, cloth, and chemicals, not to mention machine tools. At Lock Haven, Wichita, and Middletown and Alliance, Ohio, where the chief fabricators of personal aircraft were being subjected to the same pressures of materials shortages as the makers of cars, refrigerators, and radios, grave decisions were being made. Companies turning out aircraft engines would not talk business unless the customer was willing to sign contracts in bulk— thousands of engines at a time—because in turn they could not obtain their steel and iron except on a bulk-lot basis. Aluminum companies would not deliver wing spar billets except in contract quantities that appalled the airplane manufacturers. Cloth for airplane skins had to be purchased in the tens of thousands of yards, and delivery was by sight draft. Even nuts and bolts were available only in wholesale lots. Storage space at the Lock Haven factory began going at a premium.

"What can you do?" shrugged Mr. Piper.

He wasn't really worried. By now he had almost 2,600 men and women on the payroll, hundreds more than at the peak of his war production, and of these, more than 1,600 were on an hourly basis, turning out the products to make the operation prosperous. He had fifty-two domestic distributors and 1,380 dealers.

Despite booming sales, Piper Aircraft for the fiscal year ending September 30, 1946, looked on a rather bleak balance sheet. It posted a net loss of $26,437 on sales of more than $11 million. The patient's temperature and pulse rate were of only momentary importance. The company's financial health was good. Assets exceeded liabilities by more than $3 million in a ratio of almost two to one. Long years later the Pipers advanced several reasons for the poor showing. The most compelling one was that their products had been underpriced.

"I guess," reminisced William T. Piper, Sr., "that we just didn't charge enough for our airplanes."

"We kept thinking," said Pug Piper, "that volume production would reduce our costs and justify the prices."

Tony and Bill, Jr., both said, "A hundred dollars tacked onto the price of each airplane would have put us solidly in the black." Indeed, it would have. For the calendar year the company wound up with a sale of 7,773 units, and it targeted 10,000 for 1947.

The immediate trouble was something more fundamental. In the frenzy of hiring and training help, committing itself to the purchase of vast amounts of materials, and pushing sales in the face of a growing competition, the company had not established a good cost-accounting system. It had not, in fact, ever had one. Market research? That consisted of wetting a finger and holding it to the wind. The business had outgrown the capabilities of the front office. Policy decisions, such as that on pricing, were strictly the responsibility of the president of the company, and William, Sr., was too involved with his first love, selling, to pay much mind to the colors of the ink used by the bookkeepers.

The long range nub of his problem was partly geographical, partly a product of the company's structure—a lengthened shadow of the man himself.

The community of Lock Haven, cloistered by its hills, was isolated physically from the movers and shakers of a new generation of socioeconomic theorists who had proliferated in government and industry under an umbrella of radical—and to William T. Piper, Sr., frightening—legislation belabored into law during the administration of Franklin Delano Roosevelt. William, Sr., held no truck with these new, fancy-pants philosophical concepts. (On one occasion Gordon Curtis, trying to get the boss on the long distance telephone, had trouble identifying his man to the operator at a Florida hotel. "He's the one who can't stand the president," Curtis said finally. Within minutes William, Sr., was on the other end of the line.) Unlike almost all the other companies in airframe manufacture, Piper Aircraft maintained no lobby in Washington to generate business. The idea not only was foreign to its nature, it was actually abhorrent. If a corporation could not exist without government handouts (airport construction as a public facility excepted), it ought to close its doors. That did not mean Piper would turn down government business; it meant only that the company refused to wine and dine a Washington purchasing agent in order to get it. Such shenanigans if not immoral were at least amoral. The inevitable result of such an attitude translated into policy was that competitors reaped the fruits of peacetime contracts paid for from the public treasury.

In structure, the Piper organization was inbred. It was a family fief and so administered. Its patriarch—who was looking a little less rumpled these days under the domestic ministrations of a second wife, the former Mrs. Clara S. Taber of Plano, Texas, whom he had known in his twenties—sat at the head of the table. If arguments developed within the organization, he listened patiently until, finally, he put his foot down. That ended it. The Piper domain was, in dimension, a vest pocket edition of that built by Henry Ford the elder, with which it was often compared. Members of the board of directors from out of town, and particularly those from New York, were outsiders. Some were covertly mistrusted.

In the late spring of 1946 the crests of even the higher reaches of the gently scalloped Bald Eagle mountains in the valley of the West Branch had yielded the last of their snow patches to a warming sun. Green shoots of jack-in-the-pulpit, soon to adorn themselves with white petals and yellow anthers, sprang from the rich loam of river bottom fields, and the yellow, scarlet, red, and green of the columbine contested for display space on the hillsides with pink lady's slipper and the white and rose of mountain laurel. The bare, enfolding slopes had yielded their nakedness to the fresh, bright green of trees once again come to life. Rooster tails soon would be chasing power boats across the broad, placid bosom of the river at Lock Haven, picnickers would spread their tablecloths on the lush, grassy banks, and fishermen would wet their lines tipped with lures for trout. In this fourth week of May 1946, everyone was walking on the balls of his feet. Winter had gone.

On Saturday the 25th a light rain began falling. Then the drizzle quickened.

"I've heard a report or two about the river coming up," remarked Findley Estlick, the manufacturing superintendent, late in the afternoon, "but it's probably only a scare. Think I'll go home."

Flood scares were a way of life along the West Branch. They were precautionary warnings, mostly. Seldom did the stream leave its banks. Still everybody watched. Since the Great Flood of 1889 when, reported the *Evening Express*, "The once beautiful city of Lock Haven is today completely devastated," there had been ten major floods, four of them disastrous.

By Monday's dawn two inches of rain had drenched the valley. The skies would clear now, or so said the forecast. Still it rained. A river watch would be maintained, and a slight rise in the level of the West Branch could be anticipated, but cooler, drier air was due to move in on the morrow. At one o'clock Monday afternoon the river was up a foot and a half at Lock Haven. Milesburg, twenty miles to the west, reported it four feet above normal.

It was a peculiarity in the terrain that made part of the valley of the West Branch flood prone. The river had its inception near Ebensburg in Cambria County, many miles to the southwest of Lock Haven, and perversely flowed northeast, not south, and then southeast to its confluence with the main branch of the Susquehanna at Sunbury.

Five substantial creeks contributed to the volume of the West Branch above Lock Haven during rainy seasons or snow melts: the Chest, Clearfield, Moshannon, Sinnemahoning, and Kettle. The farthest from the source of the West Branch, the Sinnemahoning, was fifty river-bed miles upstream from Lock Haven. Immediately below Lock Haven, Bald Eagle Creek also fed into the West Branch. It had a nasty habit of backing up water into the southeast section of the town in time of flood.

The bed of the West Branch was fairly steep above the point where it accepted the waters of Sinnemahoning Creek, with an average fall of 10 feet per mile. From that point to its mouth, it fell only 2.4 feet per mile. Thus in times of heavy excess flow the water in effect was partly stoppered on the lower reaches of the river and piled up to burst its banks. Normal flow on the West Branch at Renovo, twenty-eight miles upstream from Lock Haven, was 131 million gallons per hour. At Lock Haven the flow increased by a tenth, or to approximately 144 million gallons. At Williamsport, thirty-one miles downstream, this rose to 235 million. The normal depth of the broad river at Lock Haven, 2 to 3 feet, was boosted by a dam.

The height of a flood, as measured by the U.S. Weather Bureau, was the vertical distance between a purely arbitrary zero reading on a datum pole on a pier of the East Water Street bridge and the surface of the water. A reading of zero flow meant that the actual depth of the water was 8 feet. The West Branch escaped its channel at a datum reading of 22.5 feet. This occurred at a low point on the river's south bank opposite 806 East Water Street, the residence of Dr. W. C. Holter. A datum 23.5-foot flood did not mean an even distribution of 1 foot of water over the entire community—the land sloped off to the southeast, and there, on East Bald Eagle Street at the fringe of town and six blocks from the river, sat the factory of the Piper Aircraft Corporation, just above the point where Bald Eagle Creek entered the West Branch. A flood stage of 23 feet deposited only six inches of water on the eastern end of Main Street, which ran through the center of town, but at the factory, four blocks south, this grew to 6 feet if the river and the creek crested at the same time. Conscious of the flood danger, the previous occupant of the building, the Susquehanna Silk Mill, had built the lower of its two floors 6 feet above ground level. In a progressive expansion since 1937, however, Piper had built its final assembly line eastward from the main building at grade. This sloped 2 feet from its inception to its end.

The worst flood since that of 1889 had occurred the year before the Piper company moved down from Bradford. Measured at 32.3 feet on the datum pole, it had driven hundreds of Lock Haven residents to the sanctuary of the silk mill's second floor by boat. Water stood 9 feet deep in the Texas Restaurant ("Open 24 Hours") in the center of town. Jake Miller had cause to remember that flood. The pressure leveled the rear concrete wall of his hangar at the airport, on the river side, and pitched his airplanes, all five of them, out the doors. The water reached the rafters. William, Sr., had had his experience with a flood in his engineering days on the Ohio River, and already had had one brush with the West Branch. On December 31, 1942, he had walked into New York's Pennsylvania Railroad station and asked for a ticket to Lock Haven.

"Sorry," said the man behind the wicket, "we're not running there."

"But I've been riding that line for five years."

"Not tonight, you're not."

Rail bridges had been washed away by a flood that measured twenty-three datum feet at Lock Haven. William, Sr., denied the route through Harrisburg, had to get home by way of Elmira, in upstate New York, and Williamsport. Water damage at the factory had been minor.

By 7 P.M. of this Monday in 1946 the West Branch's datum reading was 14.15 feet. At 7:30 Hubert F. Parker, Lock Haven's official river-watcher, was advised by L. F. Conover of the U.S. Weather Bureau at Harrisburg to look for a crest of 24 to 25 feet. Rains were heavy over the entire West Branch watershed. Conover had lost communication with Renovo.

Tony Piper, newly mustered out of the army after a short postwar assignment in Korea, was pulling into Lock Haven at this hour after a drive over the mountains along state route 44 to the east. Alerted that the river was coming up, he parked his car on a hill a few blocks west of town and registered at the Fallon Hotel. The Fallon was fairly safe. At the time it was built twenty floods had been of record since the year 1692, and John and Christopher Fallon, those agents for Her Majesty, Queen Maria Christina, had shrewdly specified that the main floor must be beyond the reach of the West Branch. Findley Estlick, by now concerned, but with little experience with the capriciousness of the river, elected to stay in the factory all night with an emergency crew of forty men. It was now too late to fly sixty finished airplanes, parked on the airport, to safety. The two Williams, Sr. and Jr., were away on a trip. Pug Piper, like Tony newly out of uniform, was in Bradford with his wife awaiting the completion of construction of a new house in Lock Haven.

In their initial stages West Branch floods were not a melee of turbulent, surging, white-plumed waters. They rose quietly, invincibly, inch by inch, gurgling around the trunks of great trees along the banks until they abraded the soil to expose the roots, seeping relentlessly into hollow and crevice, spilling over curb and furrow, fingering the texture of what they were about to engulf. They advanced remorselessly until they crested. The waters were dirty, brown with the mud scoured from channel bottom and stream bank.

At 6:30 A.M. Tuesday the West Branch was lapping at Dr. Holter's stoop, rising at a rate of a foot an hour. Four and a half hours later it had reached its crest—26.85 datum feet. At that moment the river was flowing at a rate of 3.9 billion gallons per hour, twenty-seven times its normal volume. Bald Eagle Creek had been over its banks for hours.

Two-thirds of Lock Haven was affected in major or lesser degree by the flood. Water filled the basements of 770 homes and invaded hundreds of first floors. Some 5,500 men, women, and children were rescued by boat, canoe, or raft, or given precautionary evacuation by car. Gas for cooking was shut off to obviate the danger of fire. Water Street, east and west, was submerged for its length. The entire southeast section of town was a lake, the product of the river and creek. The lower floors of two paper mills were flooded. The Roxy and Garden theaters on Main Street were inundated. So was the basement of Montgomery Ward's on the opposite side of the street. Water had just reached the porch of the Fallon Hotel. It was two feet deep inside the Texas Restaurant. The *Lock Haven Express,* an old hand at floods, had removed its paper stock and the electric motor on its press from its basement before it filled with water, and in the best traditions of journalistic effort was on the street with a mimeographed edition on Tuesday afternoon.

Only one man in the immediate area lost his life. Charles Gilmore, a coal dealer in nearby Mill Hall, was swept to his death when he was struck by a log.

Residents of other parts of central Pennsylvania were less fortunate. Floods claimed fourteen lives. The weather bureau at Harrisburg had lost contact with Renovo because a sixty-ton landslide not only had severed telephone lines but stopped highway and rail traffic as well.

An airplane factory without a usable airport was like a railroad without tracks. Pug Piper and his wife flew down from Bradford, cruised over their troubled community, and flew back.

Piper Aircraft (reported the *Express*) was the hardest hit of the several local industrial establishments. Estlick could testify to that. He and his crew had worked all night and into the morning to remove materiel and airplanes in the process of manufacture in final assembly to the main floor of the plant, untouched by the flood. They had been only partly successful. Jamouneau, living downtown eight blocks from the factory on a piece of ground that escaped the water, had a canoe in his backyard. Toward noon, with an assistant chief

132

A TYPICAL LOCK HAVEN FLOOD
Dr. Holter's stoop was the first thing engulfed.

engineer, Richard Hoy, he portaged the canoe a half block to the
flood waters on Main Street and launched it. The two men paddled
to the plant and through the doors of final assembly just below the
rafters. Taking soundings with their paddles, they concluded that
the water depth was at least six and perhaps seven feet. (It was eight.)
Estlick had had to shut off all the electricity, and Jamouneau and
Hoy poked around in a funereal half gloom. A chill damp soaked
through their bones. Tails of airplanes that Estlick's crew had been
unable to move thrust up through the brown water. Hundreds of
aircraft instruments were down there on the floor in a bath that
would ruin most of them. Upholstery and wing fabrics no doubt
had been damaged beyond salvage. Submerged engines would have
to be sent back to factories of origin for disassembly and cleaning.

"Well," said Jamouneau with a sigh when he had located Estlick, "we certainly know what our biggest problem is."

"Yes," agreed Estlick, "it's mud."

It took ten days to clean up the mess. Sixty-eight finished airplanes at the delivery end of the production line and on the airport had been submerged. The steel tubing that served as the skeleton of the aircraft had to be drilled, drained, and flushed with hot linseed oil to insure it against rust. The elegant Sky Sedan, ignored in the melee of postwar production but still a viable, promising flying machine, had been jacked up to escape the water.

As though contrite over its sins, the West Branch receded faster than it had risen. Estlick had no need to pump out. Nature and gravity disposed of the water. But there was a trick to the use of the fire hoses to wash the factory walls, floors, jigs, and fixtures. As fast as the water level dropped, strong streams from the hoses flushed away the mud before it got a chance to dry. Even so, for months afterward a patina of light tan powder, the river's calling card, clung to everything. Reams of dripping production line records on paper were run through a laundry mangle and hung out on a fence to dry.

William T. Piper, Sr., and his cohorts at this moment in 1946 took the vagaries of the West Branch in stride. They had another kind of flood to contend with—orders for airplanes that they couldn't fill.

The Kidney Puncher

IN THE SECOND WEEK OF MARCH 1947,
the roof fell in on a tiny segment of the American business community known as lightplane manufacture. There was no warning. For eighteen months since the close of the war the industry had been straining to fill its orders, adding shifts of workers, badgering suppliers to hurry deliveries, and pleading with dealers and distributors to please fly away their aircraft promptly so as not to clog the available parking space on the airports. In calendar 1946 the factories had fabricated upwards of thirty-two thousand units. Still the backlogs of orders piled up. On September 30 of that year Piper's was twelve thousand aircraft valued at $26 million. If there was to be a softening in the demand for airplanes by the ultimate consumer, it was nowhere in sight. It was quite true that in the low-cost lines of airplanes, trainers were outselling other types in a ratio of four to one, and this gave pause to some of the more conservative heads. A solid business could not be built on students orbiting airports. W. T. Piper recognized this, and his concern was compounded by another factor. Since 1938 and the start of the Civilian Pilot Training program he had been annoyed that so much of his income had been largess from the United States treasury. It had been only federal monies that had kept his enterprise, like tens of thousands of others, alive during the war. Even now, in a civilian economy, he had not escaped his dilemma. A substantial amount of his income was from exactly the same source, as dealers stocked up on training airplanes to teach ex-soldiers to fly under the GI Bill.

As late as October 1946 he said publicly that the private flying boom under way was largely a product of government-sponsored war veterans' training and an enthusiasm for flying generated by the war. A statement in December that a production of six hundred units a month of his Super Cruiser would not meet the demand was his way of saying that he still had faith in a lightplane market that did not depend wholly on flying schools for survival. As another token of his confidence, he ordered the capacity of the Cruiser expanded to

134

four persons including the pilot, and production of this machine, the Family Cruiser, began in March 1947.

In January and February thirty airplanes a day rolled off the assembly line. They had been sold, every one of them, before a welder's torch had begun fashioning the frame.

In that second week of March, sales plummeted to three and four airplanes a day. Piper was not alone. The lightplane industry was suddenly plunged into a depression. It was incredible, but there it was, staring everybody in the face. The cause had to be the bitter weather—it was too cold to be jouncing around the sky in airplanes that supplied only marginal cabin heat. It had to be a pause among dealers and distributors for stocktaking. Maybe it was a tight credit situation, though that didn't seem to be affecting other lines of business. By mid-April, when the annual pickup in sales in anticipation of warm weather flying did not appear, the industry, and William, Sr., in particular, reluctantly began to read the signs aright: the market was saturated. The second ersatz flying boom in twenty years was over. Flying for everybody was kaput. In a market for hardware items that still belonged to the seller for products of any and all descriptions, from A-for-automobiles to Z-for-zippers, and the presence of spiraling airline traffic, this was an anomaly.

The head of Piper Aircraft, whatever his faults, was not afflicted with naivete in marketing, his specialty, when finally he sat down to sort out the reasons for the slump. To start with, the schools were full-up with training planes. Then, since September 1945 the government's War Assets Administration had been dumping airplanes on the civilian market at ridiculously low prices. Some thirty-five thousand of these surplus wartime aircraft had helped glut the market. Lightplanes that had been manufactured prewar were still around to satisfy the needs of pilots who were loath to lay out money for new ones. Foreign markets, up to then never a major factor in total sales, were being satisfied in part with refurbished lightplanes that the army simply had abandoned where they sat when the peace was made. For its part, the industry had vastly overproduced. Many buyers, ordering in duplicate and triplicate—placing an order for a single airplane with two or three companies and taking the first one available—had given the manufacturers a false notion of the size of the market.

All those were secondary reasons for the collapse. The stark, single biggest reason, on which all else impinged, was that the product had not changed in sixteen years. The fabric-skinned lightplanes coming out the factory doors were, essentially, fair weather machines suited only for around-the-airport flying.

"We wouldn't be where we are," remarked Pug Piper with some bitterness as the depression deepened, "if we had begun producing the Sky Sedan."

Where the company was, made for some lugubrious reading. By July 1 three hundred finished airplanes were immobile on the Lock Haven airport, tied down with ropes. The inventory came to $2,930,-000. At the close of the 1947 fiscal year Piper's net operating loss ran to $563,000. The unpaid tab for suppliers was $631,000. A bank loan ran to a quarter of a million. For a small company, all this added up to a lot of money.

If the one-man, backyard projects were counted, thirty aircraft companies closed their doors in the next two years. Some just quit, some went into bankruptcy. The shakeout was pitiless.

Taylorcraft, one of Piper's competitors for the consumer's airplane dollar, sank, never again to surface. Aeronca, in trouble, managed to survive. North American Aviation and its Navion got into and out of the personal airplane business without pausing for breath. Headed by J. H. "Dutch" Kindelberger, a brusque, hardheaded man, the company had good credentials. Among its airplanes that helped win the war was the Mustang, the only Allied land-based fighter that could match the performance of the British Spitfire. The four-place, 150-mile-an-hour Navion, a lineal descendant of the Mustang, was priced at $12,000. Nobody wanted it.

"Dutch," an old friend asked Kindelberger one day when the man who had guessed wrong was in the throes of trying to offload his design, jigs, and fixtures on anybody who would buy them, "can you let me have a Navion at cost?"

"Gladly!" snapped Dutch. On low volume, he was losing $2,000 on each airplane he produced.

The Republic Aviation Corporation, another wartime producer of fighter aircraft, tagged its amphibian Seabee, accommodating four persons, at $3,995. With scanty power and capable of a cruise speed of only one hundred miles an hour, the Seabee appeared in mid-1946 and lay down and died as a production line item in October 1947.

In Wichita, which had once billed itself as "The Air Capital of the World," Beech was relatively untouched by the debacle of 1947. Headed by a World War I pilot, the company had an impressive record. It was a Beech-made airplane, the Woolaroc Travel Air, that won a $25,000 prize in an Oakland–Hawaii race in 1927 with Art Goebel and William Davis at the controls. Beech was in a different league from the manufacturers of putt-putts.

Beech emerged from the war with a high hole card and a woman on its Mahogany Row who was gradually assuming more and more authority in the management of the company. Her husband, Walter

MR. PIPER, OLIVE ANN BEECH, DWANE WALLACE
Customers who couldn't drop $10,000 at dice without contemplating suicide didn't interest her.

Beech, was ailing and Mrs. Beech, a woman of no mean physical proportions, was more than merely competent in a business she had grown up in. Olive Ann Beech in 1945 was having no part of the low-cost airplane business. She had no interest in customers who couldn't drop $10,000 at cage dice in Las Vegas without contemplating suicide. Her hole card was a twin-engine airplane, the Model 18, that Beech had begun producing eight years before. By the spring of 1946 Beech was ready for the postwar market with a re-worked version of the Model 18 priced at $63,000. A year later it produced a four-place, single-engine personal airplane, the Bonanza, and put it on the market at a flyaway price of $6,995. Beech planned to produce 2,000 the first year. The slump hit. It sold 350.

As for Cessna, it did get hurt in the lightplane industry's arti-ficial depression, but the wounds were far from mortal. Despite an ambitious advertising campaign on a "Family Car of the Air," the company had not been taken seriously as a competitor in the civilian market. It had never achieved volume production in private air-planes, and its products were priced out of the Piper-Aeronca-Taylor-craft bracket. At war's end Dwane Leon Wallace, he of the craggy features and brush haircut, did enter the lightplane market. His offerings were facsimiles of a sprightly, metal-fuselage airplane, the Luscombe. He had two models, both high-wing and all-metal except for fabric-covered wings, the 120 and 140. They were priced somewhat higher than the Piper J–3 but were considered competitive for GI training. When the crunch occurred, a group of New York financiers dispatched Gordon Curtis, Mr. Piper's close friend and adviser, to Wichita under the impression that Cessna was hurting. The financiers thought to use the company as a tax writeoff. Would Wallace be interested in selling out?

Wallace gave Curtis a humorless smile. "No," he said.

He was prepared for bad weather. He had diversified. Nor did he overlook the cocktails-and-dinner circuit in Washington. Wallace was ready for any direction the ball bounced.

In May, William, Sr., commented to the press on a visit to Detroit, "We are not in the market to sell planes to people who can't use them." Private flying, he said, should be left to persons aged forty-five to fifty "who have established themselves and found that they have the money, time, and ability to fly a lightplane."

On July 10 William T. Piper, Jr., secretary of the company and assistant treasurer, announced that the directors had voted to postpone action on a preferred dividend because of an "extremely restricted cash position."

In August in Wichita Mr. Piper conceded that the aviation industry was "sick."

"We've had all the government 'help' we can stomach," he said. "They lift you out of the pond by the seat of your pants and hold your head under the water. All that the industry needs is time to age and season."

By mid-April, the alarm spreading through the corridors of the Piper company led to cutbacks in both hourly paid and salaried personnel. It was hard for Mr. Piper to furlough employes, especially those he regarded as personal friends. In May he called a meeting of the production line workmen.

"Some of you," he said, "no doubt have been wondering why we are cutting back on production and furloughing employes. We are overinventoried. Sales are not what we expected. This will pass. I'm sorry that this has come about."

The Manufacturers Trust Company in New York dispatched a vice president to Lock Haven to speed up the cost cutting. He laid down an ultimatum: the payroll had to be slashed more. Department managers combed their files and fired the people who were most dispensable. The bank wasn't satisfied. Another round of separations from the payroll began. Now the company began cutting off men who, in Mr. Piper's opinion, were not dispensable. Wholesale firings were not getting at the cause of the company's ailment. They were only nibbling at it.

"We've got to cut back more," William, Jr., said to his father. "But I don't see how we can go on this way."

At the height of production in February the payroll had numbered 2,607. By the end of June this had been reduced by two-thirds.

Piper stock closed on the New York curb exchange on August 27, 1946, at eight dollars. On the same date one year later it closed at two and five-eighths.

William, Sr., called in Dolan. Manufacturers Trust, the bank to which he was indebted, had just made another of its demanding telephone calls. Dolan enjoyed the confidence of the key banks, of Joe Swan, of J. E. Swan and Company, a member of the Piper board, and of Lee Morey, of Chadbourne, Parke, Whiteside, and Wolf, Piper's legal counsel.

"They've decided they don't want any of their money in the airplane business," W. T. Piper told Dolan. "Is there something you can do?"

As he had in the minor crisis in 1941, Dolan got on the telephone to New York. "These people have got all kinds of assets," he said, "but they're frozen. They've got materials, they've got airplanes. I'd recommend that you go along with them over a two-year period. They'll go along with you to the extent that you can send in your own man to manage things . . ." He turned to William, Sr., "Right?" The president of the company nodded, ". . . until the notes are cleaned up."

Dolan hung up. "His name will be Shriver," he announced.

"A man named Shriver will be coming," Mr. Piper told his eldest son.

"A Mr. Shriver will be arriving," he said to Jake Miller, the assistant sales manager, "to take things over and get some bills paid."

"I think," he told Tony Piper, "we'd better prepare for a change in things around here."

Nobody knew much about Shriver. Dolan said he lived on a farm near Huntington, Indiana, and was a professional troubleshooter for companies in financial pain. The job just previous to the one he was about to embark on at Piper had been to bail out a bakery in Baltimore that had been using horses and wagons to make door-to-door deliveries in an age of gasoline.

"There's this thing about Shriver," added Dolan, "his personality."

William Craig Shriver arrived late in June. Of less than medium height, square-built, sandy-complexioned, freckled, and redheaded, he appeared to be in his middle fifties. He had deceptively mild eyes.

He cultivated few friends. Indeed, he discouraged such innocent intimacies as given-name salutations. He brooked no argument over his decisions. Shriver was not a man with a fan club among subordinates in companies to which he ministered. Walter Jamouneau, the phrase-maker, promptly nicknamed Shriver "the Kidney Puncher."

William Shriver ostensibly was at best a boor, at worst an ogre, perhaps both.

He checked into the Fallon Hotel and for three days cased the town and the Piper Aircraft Corporation. He looked at the books without expression. He tramped through the factory and paced the airport, taking inventory. He walked swiftly, at a half trot. His hours were precise: 9 A.M. to 5 P.M.

"Selling any airplanes?" he asked W. T. Piper.

"Some." That was true. The company just wasn't selling nearly enough.

"Well," said Shriver finally, still expressionless, "I don't find any fingers in the till."

His first official act was to close down the plant. Not a wheel moved. His second was to order that all pencils were to be worn down to a stub and then turned in. He introduced himself to Ted Weld, vice president and general manager, with the announcement, "You've got to cut down the sales department."

It was inevitable that Shriver would cross swords with the least pliable—and, pushed into a corner, the most bellicose—of the Piper clan, Howard. Pug sensed that Bill, Jr., was coming under fire in his role as assistant treasurer. He sought him out. Bill, Jr.'s head was bowed.

"He's going to let me go," he said of Shriver.

"Cheer up," said Pug, not at all sure that his brother wasn't right, "I don't think so." He went to Shriver.

"About my brother Bill," said Pug, "he's not to blame for our financial condition."

"He's the assistant treasurer."

"He's been involved in the day-to-day financial picture," argued Pug, "not in policy. You're unfair. No one person is responsible for the situation. We're all responsible, including my dad. Circumstances fooled everybody in the industry."

"All right, all right. Your brother didn't keep the bank advised of your situation." Shriver was adamant. Bill, Jr., would be relieved of his duties. For good measure, Shriver transferred his attack to William, Sr. "Your father's so honest, he thinks everyone else is honest."

Shriver called in the eldest of the Piper sons. "I want you out on the road selling," he said, adding, "in California."

"It's a sort of relief," remarked William, Jr., to Tony. "I was getting the impression that he was going to fire all the Pipers."

A few mornings later Ted Weld walked into Jamouneau's office looking pained. "What do you think happened?" said Weld. "Shriver told me that I had to fire St. John." Weld and Walter St. John, the sales manager, had been close personal friends for years.

That same day, after lunch, Shriver called in Jamouneau. He smiled faintly. "I've just fired Ted Weld," he said.

Firing accelerated. Odds were laid as to whose head would land in the basket next. Weld's brother Paul, purchasing agent, vanished overnight. So did Max Book, assistant secretary and controller. The finance department was reduced to one person, the payroll clerk. Out on the road, Jake Miller kept getting reports on the erosion in the sales staff. Wally Smith, who had just joined the company—and years later was hired back to become director of both domestic and foreign sales—was separated in Memphis by telephone. Miller wondered how Shriver expected to sell airplanes without anyone to peddle them. Presently only Bill, Jr., and he were left to beat the bushes for business.

Shriver closed the Ponca City assembly plant. That lopped off the payroll the monosyllabic Swede, Hanford Eckman.

Within weeks the payroll, including both salaried and hourly workers, had been cut to 157.

To W. T. Piper, Shriver said, "I'll take your office." Sitting down in the president's chair, he proceeded to put his own paraphernalia on the desk. The first item was a bottle of aspirin. "There must be someplace," he went on, "in the hangar across the airport for you." As though mildly apologetic, he added, "I'll only be here a year and a half."

Thus banished, the man who had founded the company sixteen years before relinquished his reins of authority.

Shriver consulted Gordon Curtis.

"You're going to need the resignation," Curtis said, "of every officer and director of the company."

"I just reached that conclusion."

"Okay, here's mine."

That left the two W. T. Pipers, Howard Piper, Ted Weld, Joe Swan, and Franklin Field on the board. Weld, while no longer an officer, could not be removed by anyone but the stockholders if he chose to make a fight of it. But he saw no hope for saving the company. He submitted his resignation and sold his stock. So did Curtis. Of the five remaining men, four were asked for, and submitted, their resignations. Shriver did not ask for the resignation of Mr. Piper.

He instituted a board of his own choosing. He had taken a liking to Jamouneau.

"Do you want to serve on the board?" asked Shriver of Jamouneau with characteristic abruptness.

"Sure." He too could see no future for the company, but he was fascinated by Shriver's operation.

"Will you serve as an officer?"

Jamouneau became not only a board member but secretary and assistant treasurer as well.

The stockholders posed no problem, especially since a third of the shares were held by the Pipers. Shriver rounded up the proxies to add Lee Morey, the legal counsel, and himself to the directorate. With Mr. Piper, that made a tidy four. Shriver didn't need a board. He was only satisfying the laws of the Commonwealth of Pennsylvania. He alone would make all the decisions from now on.

He made a deal with the bank. The entire company inventory was pledged to satisfy the loan. It was put in trust to a nationally known concern, the Lawrence Warehousing Company, and NO TRESPASSING signs were posted around the materials. A Lawrence manager was put in residence. Every nut and bolt withdrawn for airplane manufacture had to be accounted for in writing.

What William Shriver was up to at this point would not be evaluated dispassionately for some months after he departed the premises of Piper Aircraft.

His first self-assigned goal was to reduce the outgo of money, in the presence of meager income, from a flood to a trickle. His only target for that was a drastic reduction in hourly pay and salaries for those he hadn't fired, and he moved in on this murderously. At the same time he had to demonstrate dramatically that no one in the Piper family now had a voice in running the company. The almost new directorate would quiet the creditors. Mr. Piper's membership on it did not count. He was outvoted. Shriver's lodgment of the eldest Piper in a small, nondescript office in the hangar and the dispatch of Bill, Jr., to the west coast were symbolic. Tony Piper, only recently returned from his army duties, had not had time to become involved in policy matters. Despite the fact that he had sat on the board, Pug Piper at 29 was too young to have been inducted into management.

For political reasons Shriver had to censure somebody in authority for the company's malaise, and he hung that black eye not on the head of the establishment but on Bill, Jr. To have done that to Mr. Piper would have had repercussions in the aircraft business community and indeed beyond it to the New York mart where Piper shares were traded. It could have destroyed W. T. Piper and with suppliers clamoring to be paid, the company as well. That, Shriver did not want. When he was done, the Piper Aircraft Corporation and its titular head man, its respected founder, had to be alive and kicking, ready to resume his role as the Henry Ford of Aviation. Otherwise he, Shriver, would be given bad marks on his stewardship. That would not help his own business—mounting rescue parties with Saint Bernards and kegs of brandy for those engulfed in financial landslides.

The rest of the Shriver plan was more obvious. The changing of the guard was completed by lopping off the heads of the second echelon personnel, Jamouneau excepted. Shriver had other plans for Jamouneau.

W. T. Piper took all this with self-restraint and even good humor.

"He's got a job to do," he said of Shriver to William, Jr., on the eve of the latter's departure for the west coast. "The least we can do is give him a free hand."

It was a legitimate suspicion that Mr. Piper made some shrewd guesses on the meanings of Shriver's moves. At the nadir of his fortunes he paid a visit to his daughter Elizabeth and her husband Tom Harford in Spring Lake, New Jersey. In the privacy of their bedroom the Harfords talked over what had to be the sad state of the morale of the Piper clan's chieftain. He must be worrying himself sick, they concluded, down there in the living room where they had left him. They tiptoed in. Mr. Piper was sound asleep on the sofa.

"He was snoring, too," was Tony Piper's account of the incident.

Once he had the bank under sedation and the Piper Aircraft table of organization restructured, Shriver tackled the task of keeping the creditors outside the fence while he disposed of unsold airplanes and somehow created a market for others, to be manufactured from the mountain of raw materials in escrow to the bank.

He had to move fast. A group headed by Continental Motors, from which Piper had ordered some ten thousand engines, wanted the company thrown into involuntary bankruptcy and its assets liquidated. A creditors' committee was organized. Shriver and Harlan Van Bortel, who had been an understudy to Ted Weld, flew to Cleveland to fight a delaying action. This was Shriver's forte.

"You'll get your money," he told the committee, as cool and cocksure as though he were holding aces and kings back to back, "and with interest. If you're interested in less than a hundred cents on the dollar, go ahead and pitch us into bankruptcy. Otherwise, take our notes."

The committee decided to hold its fire.

Still some of the creditors simmered. A second meeting was held

in New York at Lee Morey's office. That one lasted the better part
of a night. In the end Shriver got his way. The creditors, by and
large, would hold off. He, Shriver, would come to see them indi-
vidually and discuss the terms of payment, or he would delegate a
man with authority to represent him. That was where Walter
Jamouneau came in. Van Bortel would take similar assignments.

"I'll tackle the big ones," Shriver said.

With Jamouneau he went to Pittsburgh to stare down executives of the Aluminum Company of America. The two flew to Akron,
and came away with the promise of the Goodyear Tire and Rubber
Company to accept notes in lieu of cash. With that limited tutelage,
Jamouneau was sent off on his own. Going to see a creditor who
was convinced that the company had no hope for survival, Jamouneau
discovered, was not the happiest chore in the world. His way with
words helped.

He visited the "factor" for a New York fabrics company, supplier
of cloth for airplane skins. The factor, a sort of commercial bank for
the yardgoods business, had a fishy eye for the representative of the
Lock Haven factory. The special pleaders for a couple of dozen other
airplane companies had been there before him. The man wanted
his money.

"Can't the fabric we've got be used for men's shirts?" asked
Jamouneau.

"It's not the right kind."

"For bed sheets, maybe?"

"No."

Jamouneau had memorized his speech down to the last comma.
"Taking our note," he said, "is the only way you'll get your money."

The factor looked the courtly but persistent Jamouneau up and
down. Finally, as though in despair, he managed a half smile. "Okay,"
he said, "I'll take your note, and I'll put it here in the vault, but I've
got an idea that it'll never be worth a damn. So," he shrugged, "I'll
toss it out."

Four months later Shriver and Jamouneau walked into the man's
office on Third Avenue and laid down a check for everything that was
owed him.

Another creditor with a Milquetoast husband, a woman whom
Jamouneau characterized as a "dreadnaught with a skiff in its wake,"
charged into Lock Haven with a bloodshot eye. Having by now
borrowed some of Shriver's serene self-confidence, Jamouneau soft-
talked her into taking a note.

Van Bortel assumed some of the jobs of anesthetizing creditors,
but the main chore given him by Shriver was a dirty one—separating
people from the payroll. Van Bortel's popularity soon ran off the
bottom of the graph.

To begin generating income, Shriver contacted Piper's South American export agent, the Jonas Arms Company in New York, on the disposal of the Cubs and Super Cruisers tied down on the airport. Out in the weather, the airplanes had begun to moult. Jonas sold almost the entire lot in Brazil at cost. Here Shriver stubbed his toe. He made Jonas the agent for all export sales except those to New Zealand, Australia, Great Britain, and South Africa. Jonas could not do the job without a big outlay of cash for a sales organization. That much cash it had not.

Shriver called in Jamouneau. "How long," he asked, "will it take you to design a cheap airplane?"

"What kind of an airplane?"

"A two-seater, side-by-side. Remember, cheap."

That eliminated anything in the tandem Cub trainer field. With an engineer's conversatism, Jamouneau said, "Six months."

Shriver called in Tony Piper and repeated the question.

"Six weeks," said Tony.

"Cheap," emphasized Shriver. "All right, you and your brother Howard get going on it."

Pug Piper, still smarting over the company's failure to produce the Sky Sedan, told Shriver, "If you want this design convertible later to a four-place, we can put an extra bay in the fuselage."

Shriver nodded. "For now a two-place. Cheap."

On September 15, six weeks and two days later, the two younger Pipers had the design in blueprint. Dave Long, chief design engineer, had worked with them. On October 29 they flew the prototype.

At a flyaway price of $1,990, the machine was cheap—indeed a bargain—and it would use up the stockpiled material. Lycoming at Williamsport, downriver, a major creditor, had scads of parts on the shelves to assemble the sixty-five-horsepower engines for this rump-born flying machine named the Vagabond.

As a product of what had been the world's most prestigious lightplane factory, the Vagabond was a pretty sad airplane. A conventional high-wing, it had a gear with no springs, not even the Cub trainer's rubber shock cord, to absorb landing impacts. Taxiing it over rough ground was enough to cause a man to swallow his cud of Spearmint. It did perform rather creditably on its little sixty-five-horsepower engine; trimmed right, it would go ninety miles an hour. Its authors had achieved this by using the Cub trainer wing and razoring three feet off each tip to reduce drag. The Vagabond came in one color, yellow. Its fuselage carried no decorative stripe, and immediately Jake Miller, already unhappy with the churlishness of the new regime, launched into an argument over this with Shriver.

"The plane looks like hell," he said, "without a stripe."

Aerial Photography, Pacific Air Industries

THE VAGABOND

"Remember," emphasized William Shriver, "cheap."

"No stripe," snapped Shriver.

"It would only cost pennies."

"No stripe."

Like Pug Piper, not overawed by Shriver, Miller began campaigning to make the Vagabond a four-place even before it was put into production. Miller knew wherein one of the company's problems had lain when sales had begun to toboggan. "When are we going to get a bigger airplane?" he asked.

Shriver shook his head. Miller was becoming annoying. He challenged orders.

"We've got what we've got," said Shriver, "and that's what you've got to sell."

Privately Mr. Piper counseled Miller, "You keep that up about a bigger airplane, and he's going to fire you sure as shootin'."

Miller was a fellow outcast of William, Sr.'s in Siberia. In their shabby hangar office they were allowed secretaries, Madelyn Blesh and Virginia Hungiville. In the Shriver context of operating policies, this was opulence. Miller would not be shushed. He kept it up. The Family Cruiser, he knew, was not the answer to a salable airplane. The passenger compartment was narrow and cramped and the headroom and legroom were poor.

Something else was eating on Miller. In taking orders from Shriver, he had convinced himself that he was being disloyal to William, Sr. To him, the founder of the company was still the boss.

Perversely, it appeared, Shriver sought out Miller of an evening to gabble over policy, consuming Miller's martinis in Miller's living room.

"As a matter of fact," recalled Jake, "Shriver was not a bad guy outside office hours."

But their respective attitudes were polarized, and Miller could see the beginning of the end of his employment.

"I can't run with the ball," he said firmly, "without a line in front of me. How do you expect me to sell airplanes?"

Yet Shriver, again perversely, kept picking Miller for tough jobs.

"Get a commitment from each distributor," he ordered, "to take a given number of airplanes."

Miller managed to do pretty well in convincing distributors that they ought to help the manufactory out of its dilemma. He did one selling job in a hospital. Clyde Shockley, the distributor in Muncie, Indiana, had just broken a leg in an automobile accident.

"If you'll just take a monthly quota—" urged Miller.

"Sorry." Shockley shook his head. Sitting beside his bed, Miller recited the whole story of the crisis and painted the future in less somber colors. He must have been eloquent. "Okay," said Shockley finally.

"How'd you do in Muncie?" asked Shriver.

"Seventy-five thousand dollars."

That didn't resolve the problem of Miller's relations with Shriver.

"What was getting at me," Miller related later, "was Shriver's attitude. He gave me the impression that Van Bortel was walking at his right heel, and if I cooperated I could walk at his left. That was not for me."

Presently Jake Miller got a telephone call from Claude Ryan, the president of Ryan Aeronautical. Ryan, who had a profitable factory, had just bought the Navion from Dutch Kindelberger. Miller went on the Ryan payroll. He knew that William, Sr., and Claude Ryan were friends, and he suspected that there had been some telephoning going on from the hangar on the Lock Haven airport. To the end, his boss never admitted it.

Shriver's ploys were working. The creditors were quiet. The stockpile of materials was melting, if slowly. Money was coming in, if slowly. Now he needed several hundred thousand dollars to convert the remainder of the surplus material into money, and fast. The Vagabond could be put into production to that end.

Piper Aircraft had tried in vain prior to Shriver's arrival to borrow money from the Reconstruction Finance Corporation (RFC), a government agency born in the Great Depression and still in operation. Shriver missed no tricks. In cultivating the acquaintance of John W. Guibord, an official of the Lycoming Division, he chanced on an interesting coincidence. Victor Emanuel, board chairman of the vast and wealthy Aviation Corporation (AVCO), was not unknown to the Democratic party, currently in power in Washington. As one of Piper's larger creditors, AVCO certainly didn't want to see Piper Aircraft go down the drain.

Shriver and Jamouneau flew to the national capital to keep a date with Guibord at the Washington Hotel. With a suite at the hotel was George Allen, a poker-playing friend of Harry Truman and once characterized by Drew Pearson, newspaper columnist, as a "court jester to presidents." Allen evidently was far more. Guibord, Shriver, and Jamouneau went to Allen's suite. The conversation was polite, casual, and vague.

"Oh," remarked Allen of Shriver's current business, "lightplane manufacture! That's a nice thing to have in this country. What's your problem?" Guibord and Shriver mentioned money. "That will be taken care of," said Allen, and, excusing himself, went to a luncheon in the next room.

The whole interview had consumed five minutes.

Two days later Jamouneau drove to Philadelphia and picked up a representative of the RFC. Together, they returned to Lock Haven. So did a government check for $390,000.

It was not until January 5, 1948, that Shriver was ready to resume the production of airplanes, specifically the Vagabond. He began hiring back production line workers, and by June 27 had put 459 on the payroll.

"We won't make much money on that airplane," he said in one of the rare instances that he deigned to impart information to his handpicked board, "but we'll use up materials."

Surprisingly enough, in 1947 the company managed to dispose of 3,492 airplanes, though it racked up a loss of $222,000. In the next twelve months the sale of aircraft units dropped to 1,470, but the loss was only $75,000, and the bleak figures told only a pittance of the story. The bank had been paid off. The Reconstruction Finance Corporation had its money back. Practically all the suppliers had been satisfied. As for the stockpile of materials, the company had to go into the market for more before the Vagabond production was closed out. In 1948 the sales staff got rid of 514 of the uncomfortable airplanes.

William Shriver's record for near-infallibility was, in the end, blemished by his insistence on production of the two-place Vagabond. For the short term he was justified. He got the company out of the mire, and that was exactly what he had been hired for. But, as Pug Piper had suggested in designing an extra bay into the air-

THE ACQUIRED STINSON
No money changed hands.

plane, the market no longer wanted a skimpy flying machine toting two persons. What Shriver gained in eating away at accumulated steel tubing, he sacrificed in sales.

On December 1, 1948, he committed another error. Through Tom Dolan he arranged for the purchase of the assets of the Stinson Division of the Consolidated-Vultee Corporation in San Diego. Stinson's parent company, controlled by Floyd Odlum, the financier (and husband of Jackie Cochran, the hell-for-leather, record-smashing flier), wanted to get rid of a dead property. The Stinson airplane, named for Eddie Stinson, a pioneer in the aircraft business, was a good airplane as its record in liaison work in the war had attested. But the Stinson had a fabric skin in a new day of metal personal aircraft. Eddie Stinson's business heirs had no experience in the Piper-Cessna field, and the machine was soon a corpse.

No money changed hands in Piper's purchase of the Stinson Division. Piper simply increased its number of common shares by one hundred thousand and handed them over for the acquisition. Shriver saw a chance of liquidating Stinson at a profit. His stated reason for acquiring Stinson was that it would give dealers and distributors an additional type of airplane to sell and produce revenue for them and the company. Two hundred finished aircraft went with the deal.

As Piper emerged from its doldrums under William Shriver's guidance, additions to the board were made, and among those re-admitted to the sanctuary was Joe Swan. Swan was the champion of the Stinson deal.

"Stinson's a fine name," he kept repeating.

W. T. Piper, Sr., opposed the Stinson purchase but on grounds other than the type of skin fabrication. Swan was an "outsider." He was identified with New York, with the New York banks.

"I'm entirely opposed to this purchase," Pug Piper told Swan tartly, adding with sarcasm that he did not attempt to veil, "but of course I'm a member of the Piper family."

Jamouneau backed him up. Shriver ignored all the gabble.

With the Stinson sale and stock transfer went another addition to the directorate. He was William C. Rockefeller, assistant to the chairman of the Consolidated-Vultee board. William Rockefeller's family and that of the oil-rich John D. Rockefeller were separated by seven generations. Shriver's purchase of Stinson was perhaps not a mistake per se. But, as he could have foreseen, it led to fissures on the directorate. Possibly at that point he was beyond caring. Rockefeller and Swan teamed up to represent the opposition interest to the Piper family on the board.

"Why not," suggested Rockefeller, "rename the company the Stinson-Piper Aircraft Corporation?"

For the Pipers, this was tantamount to spiking the runner on the instep as he rounded third base.

"No," said Mr. Piper and made it stick.

The suspicion grew that Swan, aided and abetted by Rockefeller, was trying to ease the Pipers out of the company. If it were true, he was going about it in the wrong way. Outstanding by now were 843,000 shares. To obtain a working control through stock purchases even at a price of two dollars a share, it would have cost him well in excess of a half million dollars to top Mr. Piper's holdings. Perhaps he couldn't raise that. But he remained a question mark.

"I'm not sure of Swan's motives," even Shriver remarked to Jamouneau.

William Shriver quit short of the year and a half that he said he would be in Lock Haven. Plainly he had lost interest in his job. Only companies in dire financial straits stimulated him, and while Piper Aircraft still had some distance to go to invest in black ink for the books, it was out of the woods. He kept no regular office hours. Restlessly, with no apparent interest, he watched the squabble starting to develop on the Piper board of directors. This was not his dish. He packed his bags and, in that funny little half trot of his, departed before the month of December was out. Van Bortel, apparently having misread Shriver's mission in Lock Haven and cast his lot with him, left at the same time after investing ten years of his life in the company. He had no choice.

Some months after Shriver left, W. T. Piper, Sr., received a letter of inquiry from a big New York trucking concern that was considerably in arrears on its preferred stock dividends. What did he know about William Shriver?

"Mr. Shriver," replied Mr. Piper, who had been booted out of his office and ignominiously banished to a hangar, "was pretty hard to take when he was here, but if he hadn't been here, we wouldn't be here now."

Of the Irishman Tom Dolan, who talked the language of the mighty in New York and drafted Shriver to do the job, W. T. Piper remarked to friends at a Fort Lauderdale Rotary Club meeting as late as 1968, "He's the man who saved the company for us."

The Assault on the Castle

W. T. PIPER STILL HAD NOT REGAINED
mastery of his castle. For the post-Shriver period of recovery, yet
another man was sent in to run things.

The memory of those who charged the Pipers with mismanagement
was long. It was reflected in opposition on the board of directors.
The composition of that was changed on the heels of Shriver's
departure. William K. Jacobs, Jr., was added to the membership.
Jacobs represented a number of wealthy investors including some
with money in Sears, Roebuck. Joe Swan sponsored Jacobs. For a
time Jacobs' credentials were in question. He was on the directorate
of National Airlines; and the federal Civil Aeronautics Board (CAB),
which ran such things, had a conflict-of-interest rule on directors
of corporations who wore twin hats in both air transport and aircraft
manufacture. In its ultimate wisdom, the CAB decided that the airline,
transporting passengers in forty-ton airplanes, probably could
not make use of Piper Cubs, weighing less than a ton, in its operations.
It was a landmark decision in the annals of a government
bureaucracy.

Jacobs' presence suited Swan's purposes. While he lacked a
nominal majority on the board, to his advantage was the fact that
Lee Morey, the legal counsel, tried to play a neutral role. Morey was
in a spot. He was a friend and admirer of Mr. Piper, but he also
enjoyed the use of a private telephone to Swan's office at Hayden,
Stone and Company.

With Jacobs on the board, Swan pushed through the employment
of Shriver's successor, August Esenwein, as executive vice president
and general manager of Piper Aircraft. He was to lead the
way back to prosperity despite Piper family interference in policy
matters.

Esenwein was a medium-statured man who was hardly prepossessing
but, like Shriver, had strong convictions. Like Shriver, he
exhibited a profound belief in his own judgment. An engineer, he
came from a well-to-do family. His facade was one of calmness, but

he tired in conferences, and the impression grew among his associates that he was torn by inner tensions. The first idea that he proposed upon taking command was to institute a Piper aircraft modification center, and on a hangar on the north side of the airport a sign was erected: "AIRCRAFT MAINTENANCE AND OVERHAUL." From here on, Piper would invite contracts to alter the configuration, power, and instrumentation of airplanes for personal or corporate owners. This carried the faint implication that the company ultimately would abandon aircraft manufacture.

"I don't think he believes in our products," remarked Tony Piper of Esenwein.

He was partly right. Esenwein didn't believe in lightplanes of the Piper categories.

The executive personnel whom he put on the payroll kept growing. Most of them appeared to be old friends—retired officers of the military services. The resentment among the old hands in the establishment grew. The payroll was getting top-heavy in management salaries. One man hired by Esenwein was reputed to be an expert on sales to the U.S. Government, and gossip at the hallway water cooler interpreted this as a move to change the nature of the company markets. If that proved to be true, it meant a rebuke to Mr. Piper. All the idle talk encouraged a corporate neurosis.

Esenwein was a great man for paper. He drew up a table of organization. He wrote endless memoranda. He wrote a procedure manual (which was promptly put by those executives, Piper-oriented, in the lower righthand drawer of the desk under the telephone book).

Whether by design or the vagaries of fortune, the man Esenwein fought a losing battle from the start. He was caught in a revolving door. He selected targets for criticism from among men who had years of service with the company. One of them was Jamouneau. In addition to being chief engineer and secretary of the company, Jamouneau was assistant treasurer, wearing two and a half hats. Esenwein was not empowered to fire an officer of the company, but he could fire the chief engineer, and did.

Meantime, the Piper product department had not been marking time. Even under Shriver, some drawing board doodling had been going on to make the Vagabond a little more respectable. Shock cord was put on the landing gear. For landings and ground handling it made all the difference between an airplane that was a dog and one that a pilot ceased complaining about. An 85-horsepower engine was substituted for the anemic 65-horsepower job, and presently this was boosted to one of 115 horsepower.

MR. PIPER AND CUB MODEL
It was his bread and butter.

Egan Photo Service

To disassociate the refurbished machine from the Vagbond, it was given a new name—the Clipper—and merchandised as a fine private owner and training airplane that could double for charter work. Presently attorneys for Pan American Airways, behemoth of U.S. transoceanic commercial airline operation, formally notified the Piper Aircraft Corporation that the word "Clipper" had been copyrighted. Pan Am's big airplanes were, indeed, called Clippers. The airline was having nightmares. It could see Piper Clippers strewn over the countryside by thickheaded private pilots, with an immediate association of name with its own aircraft. Piper was to cease and desist.

"We could fight this to a standstill," counseled Lee Morey. "The word 'clipper' was used a hundred years ago on sailing ships. It's in the dictionary, uncapitalized. But would it be worth it?"

So the Piper Clipper became the Pacer. The Clipper, like the Vagabond, had carried a dozen gallons of gas up front behind the firewall and engine. The Pacer had its fuel tanks in the wings, and dual wheel, instead of stick, controls. It acquired a plushy interior, wheel "pants," and fairings on the struts. For its 115 horsepower it had no mean performance: a cruise of 112 mph, a range on a lean

carburetor of 500 miles, and a service ceiling of 13,500 feet. Its price
was $3,295.

When William Shriver departed Lock Haven and the original
Vagabond had contributed its share toward the erasure of the Piper
indebtedness, the production line again was idled. The payroll
dropped to 132 persons, the lowest number since 1936. Now as Esenwein's broom began sweeping through the property on East Bald
Eagle Street, the welding torch, riveting hammer, and dope sprayer
reappeared. W. T. Piper had not forgotten his first love, the tandem-
seat Cub, his bread-and-butter airplane. He prevailed on the board
to produce a Super Cub. The J–3 was phased out. Almost twenty
thousand Cubs and almost identical L–4's, the army version, had
rolled off the Piper production line. Reconstituted, it had a far longer
life than Henry Ford's Model T. Driven by a Lycoming 108-horse-
power engine, the Super Cub attained a cruise of 105 miles an hour.
But speed was not the airplane's claim to fame. As it went up in
horsepower over a period of years to 150, the Super Cub was nicknamed the "Poor Man's Helicopter." It got off the ground with a
run of less than three hundred feet—the length of a city block—and
its landing roll was just a bit more than that. It was versatile. It
ranged frontier country like the Canadian bush and the Australian
Outback. Daily it patrolled cross-country oil and gas pipelines looking for breaks. It adapted easily to skis or floats. In Switzerland it

SKI-EQUIPPED CUB IN SWITZERLAND
Saving mountain climbers from their own folly.

rescued mountain climbers from the results of their own folly. It was ideal for aerial photography, spotting forest fires, and mountain rescue work. It was used by ranchers to check on their herds; by farmers; and by government naturalists to get counts of elk and deer on national preserves.

August Esenwein decided about the time of the spring crocuses in 1949 that Piper Aircraft ought to launch into the production of twin-engine aircraft. This was no new idea in Lock Haven. It had been discussed from time to time in the councils of the company with no great seriousness, ever since the midpoint of the war years, and from time to time legitimate objections had been raised to it. To begin with, twin engines encompassed a state of the art of airplane manufacture that Piper had not achieved. Mounting engines on the wings—the conventional method of using two power plants driving propellers—and providing for the contingency of asymmetrical thrust with the loss of one of them was, for Piper, an engineering venture of no small proportions. That was only one of many factors. Wing structures would require extensive revision. Fuel lines no longer could be gravity fed. The design of tail control surfaces would be a complete area of study by itself. Where a few hundred factory tools sufficed to produce an aircraft with a single engine, and that on the nose, a twin-engine machine would require thousands. The investment in production machinery and in the retraining of workmen would run the price of such an airplane to manyfold that on any Piper airplane ever produced. Now, only two years after the factory had escaped catastrophe by the slimmest of margins, the notion for a twin-engine flying machine was being advanced by an "outsider" lodged in the seat of authority by those people in New York.

To save the time that would be required to start a design from scratch, Esenwein looked over two prototypes available. One was a high-wing known as the Smith Twin, designed by Ted Smith, a former engineer for Douglas Aircraft in Santa Monica. Years later it became the Aero Commander. Just as the first of the Boeing four-engine commercial landplanes resembled the Flying Fortresses that the company previously had manufactured for the army, so the Smith Twin looked like a Douglas attack bomber grown pregnant. Besides Piper Aircraft, Claude Ryan was looking at Smith's airplane in one of his on-again, off-again flirtations with General Aviation manufacture.

Esenwein also cast an appraising, and increasingly covetous, eye over a twin-engine plane known as the Bauman Brigadier. The Brigadier, like the Smith Twin, put together in California, differed from the other airplane in two important respects. Whereas the Smith had some money behind it, the Brigadier had been built from parts scrounged from aeronautical junkyards. And its engines were installed backwards. That is, the propellers were on the trailing instead of the leading edge of the wing. They pushed instead of pulled. The Brigadier, also a high-wing, was all-metal and carried four persons. It was a big airplane for its carrying capacity, and a heavy one, and slow. For inspection by the Piper board of directors, it was flown from California to Lock Haven in a trip that had to have been scripted by Odysseus in returning to Ithaca after the siege of Troy. It landed a couple of dozen times en route because the engines kept cutting out.

Esenwein decided the Brigadier would be just the airplane to launch Piper into twin-engine manufacture. He was called before the board in August. Haggling ensued. A pusher had several strikes against it. Rear-mounted engines provided no prop-wash over the leading edge of the wing for added lift, and therefore the airplane was less efficient than one with tractor propellers. The propellers were downstream of the airflow and therefore, of themselves, contributed less to cooling the engines. Working in turbulent air, they produced less thrust than tractors. The engine installation necessitated extra-length shafts for propeller mounting, and that encouraged shaft whip. If anything fell off a cowling, it could go through and damage the prop. Finally, pushers were noisier than tractors.

"If we're going to build this airplane," stated Jamouneau, "it ought to be a tractor."

Reluctantly Esenwein acceded. The change would require a reengineering of the wing and a study of balance and load factors.

"How much money will this take?" asked Joe Swan.

"Forty thousand dollars," responded Esenwein. That did not include the biggest expense, tooling.

"How long will it take?"

"Six months."

"For what?"

"To start production."

"How was that again?" asked Jamouneau, incredulous.

"For production," repeated Esenwein stubbornly.

"What will the plane retail for?"

"A cost analysis would indicate about $22,500."

W. T. Piper's jaw dropped. "I am opposed," he said, "to this project."

August Esenwein was dangling before him, just out of reach, the keys to his kingdom.

For the first time in the history of the company, a market research study was launched. Distributors were interviewed. Would a twin sell? The sum of their verdict was, it might if it were not ex-

158

pensive to buy and maintain. Anything beyond $3,500 was beyond the company's experience in pricing its own products. Disregarding Esenwein's guess, a twin would have to retail for perhaps five times $3,500 if it was to be profitable.

Five men participated in the market research on the proposed twin: Mr. Piper, Bill, Jr., Jamouneau, Pug, and Tony. Esenwein was not consulted. The "greenhouse"—the passenger-pilot compartment—would have to accommodate no less than four persons, preferably more. The airplane would have a fixed, not retractable, landing gear. The propellers would have a fixed pitch. The fuselage would be tubular steel, like all the fabric airplanes that had come off the production line up to now. This was in deference to Mr. Piper's insistence that it be skinned with cloth, the Stinson notwithstanding. That would keep the fabricating cost low. The wing, however, would be skinned at least in part with aluminum alloy. It would carry fuel tanks, and metal would be a safety factor. The first target price mentioned was $13,300. That was iffy. If the company could market two hundred units a year, the total investment in tools and jigs would be $826,500. That figure, too, was iffy.

In the community of Lock Haven things began taking on a spurious appearance of normalcy. The Lawrence Warehouse signs came down. The West Branch in high spirits burst its banks and shut down the factory for eight days. William Thomas Piper, Jr., returned from his enforced hibernation on the west coast. Fully in character, he bore nobody a grudge. He was just glad to be home. So was his wife, the former Margaret "Pud" Bush. She enjoyed traveling but, a native of Lock Haven, she missed Main Street. With Esenwein's approval, Mr. Piper telephoned Jake Miller in San Diego to ask if he would like to head the sales department.

Miller was frustrated in peddling the Navion. In his two years at it, Claude Ryan, addicted to government contracts, couldn't make up his mind what to do with the airplane. His engineering department puttered.

"Yes," Jake Miller told W. T. Piper, "I'll come back. What's Esenwein like?"

"He's going to build a twin."

Miller withheld judgment. One of his problems at Ryan had impinged on endless doodling to make a twin out of the Navion.

Ferment was growing under the apparent calm at Piper. In converting the Brigadier, Esenwein was having to do without the genius of Dave Long. The company's chief design engineer, a restless spirit who loved to race, had built himself a midget Mustang in his spare time. Men who fashion their own aircraft are imbued with a sublime disbelief that their mounts, turned savage, could ever kill them. On a sunny day en route to a race the midget Mustang had plummeted from the welkin. Fred Strickland, chief stress engineer, replaced him.

August Esenwein was fidgeting because no one had proposed him for membership on the board. Jamouneau opposed him, and it was a fair conclusion that Mr. Piper would have voted against him. Jamouneau would have been less than human if, after Swan's boy Esenwein had used every resource at his command to divorce him from the company, he had not encouraged the engineers to dawdle on the conversion of the Brigadier to tractor engines. Chief engineer or no, he still exercised authority in that department.

When Esenwein arrived, he had had a heart-to-heart talk with Pug Piper.

"There won't be any change in your status," he assured Pug. "You go right ahead doing what you're doing."

Pug and Tony Piper were working on airplane design. As autumn speckled the hillsides with scarlet and gold, Esenwein changed his mind.

"I want you out selling airplanes," he told Pug.

Pug looked at Esenwein and saw Ananias. "How am I going to believe anything you tell me?" he snapped.

He was shunted off to Myrtle Beach, South Carolina, as southeastern sales representative. William, Jr., wasn't enjoying the favor of the executive vice president either. Slated for a job in advertising and sales promotion, he was passed over. A man from New York was put in the slot. On November 25 Pug wrote his brother from Pulaski, Virginia:

"I have felt right along that Esenwein's actions have been more or less a breach of confidence, if not ethics, and I regret that I haven't been in a position to steer [his] actions, at least to some extent. . . .

"In any event, I doubt that he [Esenwein] will be with us long."

The backfire that Esenwein unwittingly had touched off was growing. Jake Miller made it no secret that of the two twins that had been considered, he favored the Smith. He considered the Brigadier a disaster.

"I think," Jamouneau remarked to Mr. Piper, "we're headed for a showdown, and we'd better get prepared for it."

W. T. Piper *had* been preparing. Two years before, he had purchased an additional block of preferred stock convertible to common, and now he was investing all the cash he could lay his hands on in additional common. This was a replacement move. At the height of the 1947 crisis he had been forced to unload some of his holdings to stay afloat.

January 10, 1950, a Tuesday, was fixed for the next board meeting. It would be held in New York at the offices of Hayden, Stone. The "outsiders" preferred New York for meetings, the Pipers suspected, because William, Sr., enjoyed a psychological advantage on his home grounds. For a man with an engineering background, August Esenwein had made an incredibly bad forecast for conversion of the Brigadier. Even without Jamouneau's foot-dragging, the six-month deadline to start production could not have been met. Esenwein had spent his $40,000, and he wanted more. He estimated that it would take "6,000 to 7,000 more engineering hours to bring the plane to the flight test stage." That meant from 750 to 875 man-days of work. Ten engineers would eat up two and a half more months on the job.

At 9:30 A.M. on the day of the board meeting William, Sr., and Jamouneau paused at the intersection of Broad and Wall streets in lower Manhattan before proceeding to the Hayden, Stone offices. For January it was a surprisingly mild day, with the temperature in the forties. The two men had their coat collars up. Rain squalls were sweeping the city.

"This is going to be a rough one," remarked Mr. Piper. "There may be some skulduggery."

"We've still got an out."

William, Sr., had consulted Lee Morey.

"If anything really amiss occurs in the meeting," said Morey, "you can call a special meeting of shareholders to straighten things out."

With considerably less than majority control, a management was only as good as its performance, and the Piper performance of 1946–47 had been something less than brilliant. "That's a risk," said W. T. Piper.

"Of course."

"All right, if I have to, I'll do it."

The meeting was called to order at 10 A.M. William Thomas Piper's assault to regain control began. The battlements of his domain had been in the hands of others since July 1947. He presided. A majority of the voting shares was represented.

In attendance besides W. T. Piper and Walter Jamouneau were Jacobs, Rockefeller, Swan, and Morey. Esenwein was permitted to appear. He asked for authorization to spend $25,000 more on the Brigadier.

"It's not a productive project," protested Mr. Piper.

"The money is wholly inadequate," said Jamouneau.

The motion to grant the money was put and seconded. Morey was uncomfortable. He abstained. The motion carried three to two.

Now, by prearrangement, Tom Dolan appeared. To Swan, Rockefeller, and Jacobs, the auditor was a surprise witness. He carried with him a memorandum, running to three single-spaced typewritten pages, reviewing Esenwein's stewardship. It was Dolan's product, composed after extensive interviews with William, Sr., Jamouneau, the three Piper sons, and other selected personnel at Lock Haven. It tore the hide off the executive vice president.

Tempers rose. Everyone in the room would have been cooler in a sauna bath. Noon came and went. At 1 P.M. Swan sent out for some ham-on-rye sandwiches and coffee. By asking questions, William, Sr., and Jamouneau kept taking the pulse of the other four men, looking for an ally. If Morey, feigning neutrality, abstained on a crucial motion, one vote would do it.

Jacobs moved that Jamouneau be removed as company secretary. Swan seconded. Morey voted no for a three-three tie.

"Jamouneau can't vote on a motion affecting himself," said Swan.

The question was referred to Morey. Morey temporized.

"I don't see any problem here," put in Jamouneau with ostensible generosity. "Let's say that I'm no longer secretary. That'll settle it."

Suddenly Jacobs called for pen and paper. Disgusted, he wrote out his resignation on the spot, in his haste dating it January 10, 1949. He stalked from the room. That knocked out the props from under Swan.

"I move," he said, "that Jacobs' resignation be tabled." He had no second.

Morey offered a motion to accept the resignation. Mr. Piper seconded. It was the key vote, adopted three to two. William Thomas Piper was back in business.

Five hours had elapsed between the start of the meeting and the adjournment.

Soon after, Rockefeller resigned from the board. Esenwein resigned as executive vice president. No doubt he deserved better. He was not a man without talent. From Lock Haven he went to a responsible post at Consolidated-Vultee, and for a time headed the aircraft manufacturers' trade association. Where he had erred was in underestimating the patriarch of the Piper clan.

W. T. Piper had a rare gift for generating loyalty in his subordinates. He had encouraged, or had not discouraged, opposition to Esenwein because the money crisis was over, and Esenwein, apart from following policies with which Mr. Piper sharply disagreed, stood in the way of his regaining control.

For all his battered hats and unpressed suits, the head of the clan had proved himself a rather adroit politician.

At a board meeting the following April the directors went through the motions of reelecting themselves with shareholders' votes present and proxy-represented. Swan did not attend. He was not on the slate.

The corpse of the Brigadier wound up in an aviation trades school in Williamsport, to which Piper Aircraft sold it for a song, for dissection.

In a sense, the disaster that overtook the lightplane industry in 1947 had been good. It forced a soul searching, a reassessment. If the age of wings-for-everyone that the manufacturers had been trumpeting did not exist, then where lay the markets for their products? Indeed, was there a market at all? If the lightplane was to fill a niche in the spectrum of transportation, it would have to undergo major change. It would have to be fast. It must have range. It would have to offer the buyer an alternative to the commercial airliner. It would have to take off with a reasonable assurance of getting where it was going, the weather almost notwithstanding. It could not carry Mickey Mouse instrumentation.

Esenwein's idea for a twin had been valid. Only the execution was wrong.

"The market," concluded W. T. Piper, "will have to be made, and we'll have to do the making."

"That's a job for the industry as a whole," observed Jake Miller.

"We've had no experience in designing and building twins," the conservative Tony Piper pointed out.

"We can get it," said Pug Piper, impatient as always to get started.

The atmosphere in the company headquarters changed overnight after the January 10 meeting. Gone was Shriver. Gone was Esenwein. Gone were the "outsiders," particularly those who lived among the spires and minarets of New York. The relief among the administrative personnel was enough to drive a man to the bottle, and the evening consumption of spirits rose proportionately. A man returned home at night without that cutting edge on the greeting to his wife that provoked arguments. The kids could ignore bedtime without getting their tails tanned.

In Lock Haven a reassessment other than that on the nature of the market was in incubus. It was subtler in complexion. The corporation began looking at itself in a mirror. As a flesh-and-blood structure, whither had it drifted? Shriver had left it in political chaos, Esenwein in bewilderment. Unlike those models of crisp industrial efficiency, General Motors and International Business Machines, it was not departmentalized with precise chains of command that reached down to a little black box in the far lefthand corner of the table of organization.

"Titles didn't mean much," said Tony Piper. "We just sort of divided up the duties."

No next-in-line man was being groomed for a key job. If W. T. Piper could be credited with any forward planning in personnel, it had to be in producing three sons. No executives with lists of academic accreditations after their names adorned the management roster. Except for Dolan's ministrations, money management consisted of thumbing through the bills and counting the cash in the till.

All this, a legacy of Mr. Piper's formative business years when an oil well successfully spudded-in meant the difference between spaghetti and steak on the table, was about to change. The transformation would be gradual. It would begin under the most conservative of the Piper sons, Thomas Francis, now short of his thirty-sixth birthday. His communication with his father was extrasensory. The idea of expansion was anathema to Tony.

"I'd rather be small and vigorous," he said.

He was a past master at paring costs, and woe betide the salesman who entered ten bucks on an expense account under Miscellaneous.

"To Tony," commented a member of the sales staff, "that was the equivalent of charging the company for bordellos and overcoats."

On April 1, 1950, Tony Piper was made vice president and general manager. While it was not so stated, he was chief executive officer. A decade of efficient, often severe, company management began.

Birds with Wings on the Bottom

WHILE THE LIGHTPLANE MANUFACTURING industry was going through the pains of coming of age following the debacle that closed the decade of the 1940s, something extraordinary was happening to systems of transport in the United States.

Getting people and goods from one place to another overland had experienced three major revolutions in technology in a little more than a hundred years, the second and third of them in the last fifty. The first was on rails. By the time two gold and silver spikes were driven into a tie of polished laurel wood at Promontory Summit, Utah, on May 10, 1869, to link the Atlantic and Pacific oceans by steam locomotive, railroads had established themselves as the basic means of land transport. The second revolution was on rubber tires. The personal automobile arrived at the turn of the century, accompanied presently by the truck and later the mammoth truck-trailer. Self-propelled wheels transformed a static Main Street society into a nation of nomads.

Then a third revolution in the transport of people and goods occurred in the fading years of the 1920s. Stuart G. Tipton, president of the Air Transport Association of America, a trade group of U.S. scheduled airlines, later called it "the longest and most significant . . . in modern industrial history." The third revolution was on wings.

The lightplane in 1950 was on the threshold of participating in it.

After the donnybrook that opened the establishment to Shriver and Esenwein, Piper Aircraft at this point needed the ministrations of Thomas Francis Piper, W. T. Piper's second male issue. While he concentrated on running the company at the engineering and production levels, he strictly budgeted each department. That didn't encourage growth. He didn't intend it to. He wanted efficiency and profits. He pared the production control force. He refused to resur-

TONY
"Pop," he announced, "I'm through."

rect a plant newspaper that began during the halcyon postwar days and fell victim to Shriver's knife, and he frowned on the revival of an employe credit union that had gone through the same phases. It took monumental persuasion to convince him that the plant had to have a new piece of equipment. Department heads learned early not to say, "I've got to have so-and-so."

"You don't got to have anything," he answered. "Name me your alternatives."

He did give more money to Engineering. If that twin-engine airplane they were talking about were undertaken, Jamouneau and Strickland would need men expert with slide rules and drawing pencils. He had his hand in everything going on in the factory on East Bald Eagle Street—production, labor negotiations, and salary and hourly-wage decisions. He was austere and introverted, traits complementary to his frugality. He came to work with a lunch pail and ate with the men in the experimental department.

He could break up under emotional stress. On one bleak day,

BILL, JR.
A master of the soft sell.

a week before Christmas, he met with a union committee representing the production line workers to announce that he had to furlough a substantial number of men. He got only halfway through his remarks when, getting up from a table where the conference was taking place, he walked to a window to check his tears. Findley Estlick, the general superintendent, had to finish for him. Oddly enough, Tony never developed ulcers.

With his assumption of power, the pecking order on the top administrative level of the company became fixed. W. T. Piper made the major critical decisions. Bill, Jr., having recovered the epaulets that William Shriver had so brusquely stripped from him, was sitting in for his father with increasing frequency on day-to-day matters. The restless Howard Piper—Pug—was deep in product research and facility planning for production.

The twin-engine airplane project still awaited a green light. W. T. Piper was thinking about it. If it broke new ground in product design—opened up markets that no one else in the industry had really explored—it might do something else too: change the company's image.

"We've got to get away from the Cub idea," said Pug.

Another factor was nudging Piper toward an affirmative decision on a twin. That was more sophisticated instrumentation, a fancy name for giving a pilot confidence at night and in poor weather, that was becoming available. The airlines had the money to buy high-priced artificial horizons and navigation gadgets and landing aids.

Piper customers had not been able to pay the price. But now, as a result of intensive research in World War II and government surpluses, cockpit appurtenances cost less. For the important ones, this meant gyroscopes first of all for a pilot's attitude recognition. Then omnirange navigation had appeared. It converted a butter-fingered navigator into an expert. For twenty years airmen had struggled with a system known as "radio ranges" that the Department of Commerce had installed on the nation's airways. The signal that the ranges generated was aural, and a man in a crowded cockpit fighting a crosswind under dismal weather conditions in the presence of low-frequency radio static was hard put to stay on course. If he tuned to the wrong radio range and failed to catch the periodic station identification signal in his earphones, he was in trouble.

Bad crashes resulted, many of them on the airlines. The radio ranges also had a bad habit of shifting courses several degrees and had to be monitored constantly. Carole Lombard, a movie star married to another celluloid celebrity, Clark Gable, crashed to her death on January 16, 1942, against a mountain in Utah, along with a planeload of other airline passengers, because of just such a shift in signal.

The new omnirange emitted a static-free signal that was converted to a visual reading on the instrument panel.

Pending a decision on the twin, Piper began making up optional combination units of omnirange radio receivers, radio direction finders, gyro instruments—including an artificial horizon—and a complement of communication radios for its current aircraft. For a price

PUG
He did his homework.

of $6,475, the private flier and charter operator could buy an airplane to make him as secure as the pilot of an airliner even in weather that discouraged the birds. Piper's "Super Custom" package was so priced that presently more than eight out of ten Pacers turned out were equipped for instrument flight.

Mr. Piper called a meeting. For a man of his equanimity, he seemed tart-tongued that day. "We've done the market research on a twin," he said. "Do you think we can build one?" The head of the company had made up his mind.

Howard Piper was elated. "Yes," he said.

"It'll take a lot of money," said Tony.

"I'm not talking about financing," said Mr. Piper. "I'm talking about our ability to design and manufacture airplanes with two engines," He looked at Jamouneau.

"Yes," said Jamouneau.

"We'll have to have a whole new marketing setup," put in Bill, Jr.

Miller nodded. "Amen. Our distributors and dealers don't think in terms of those prices."

So the decision was formalized. Once again W. T. Piper, the curious combination of plunger and conservative businessman, would gamble. Piper Aircraft would go for broke. Now he posed the second and prickliest question: What price would this flying machine retail for?

"Seventeen thousand," suggested Howard Piper. Miller nodded agreement.

To W. T. Piper the figure equated with the national debt. "For a steel tubing airplane in fabric?" he exclaimed. He was still clinging to the concept of a soft-skinned airplane.

"It depends," said Miller soothingly. "How many can we turn out? How many can we sell? The volume is going to have a lot to do with the price tag."

Mr. Piper shook his head. "All right," he said reluctantly, "but we'll have to shave that figure, you'll see."

The engineering department had its green light. "Nobody," Jamouneau recalled twenty years later, "was very brave about it."

Once committed, W. T. Piper began thinking in no small terms. Up to the tooling stage, a half-million dollars would be allocated to the airplane. A loan of $400,000 (subsequently boosted to $500,000) could see them through to model announcement time. A time cushion was put on the vehicle's appearance to prevent any buildup of anxiety. A prototype twin was going to take probably three years and maybe four.

In design it would be a low-wing, a radical departure from the Piper tradition, and would incorporate a tricycle landing gear. Meantime, the Pacer was fitted with tricycle gear to cure its tendency to ground-loop. It became the Tri-Pacer and an instant success. The Pacer had done well. Through calendar 1951 more than 800 had been sold. The Tri-Pacer began pouring even more money into the company coffers. In its first two years it racked up sales of more than 900, and before the line was closed out twelve years later 7,668 had found buyers.

Cessna, too, was busy on a low-wing twin, its first for the commercial market. Dwane Wallace's product promised to be a sleek, all-metal airplane with a pointed nose, tapered wings, and well-cowled, husky Continental flat engines. Drummers for aircraft manufacturing suppliers regularly called at Lock Haven, and at other centers of plane fabrication with order books in hand, retailing industry gossip and contributing opinions, asked for or not, on the worth of designs taking shape on the drawing board. One, from Continental, was especially profligate with his judgments on Piper's new venture.

Carefully skirting any mention of the new Cessna design, Wallace's model 310, he told the brood of Pipers, "You haven't got enough power, no performance. Besides, what're you doing fiddling with low wings? Whoever saw a bird with wings on the bottom?"

Despite his seventy-one years, W. T. Piper was as much a peregrinator as ever. He demanded and got his personal Tri-Pacer with his name on the side. He voyaged everywhere, often alone. When, now and then, he had a fellow pilot aboard, he relinquished the controls and napped. The newfangled instruments were dandy, but give him a map any day. That was the way he had learned to find his way cross-country. Waking up, he would look over the side and announce, "That's Slippery Rock. We'll hit Youngstown in fifteen minutes."

While the company's energies were directed at bringing the twin to fruition—all else except current profit was subordinate—the contracts department under Bill, Jr., began taking up the slack in production occasioned by limited sales by doing subcontract work for companies turning out materiel for the Korean War. The army bought some Super Cubs for liaison duty in Korea to supplement some surplus L-4's. Washington bought Cubs in limited numbers for distribution to Turkey, Greece, and other NATO countries as trainers.

The twin began getting teething pains while it was still on the drawing board. Jamouneau and Strickland not only were scouting unfamiliar terrain, they were fettered as well by Mr. Piper's ukase that the product must carry a low price. They were fenced in on a decent cruising speed by his demand that the machine must get in and out of small fields without paved runways with a full load of four persons and their luggage. It was quite an order. Then there was a problem of low power.

"If we stick to four cylinders," W. T. Piper said, "the maintenance will be cheap. That's important." For the twentieth time he added, "And the thing's got to be easy to fly."

The airplane was a cut-and-try product. At one point Jamouneau ordered two engine nacelles brought into his office and, sitting at his desk, positioned them at each side. A pilot had to be able to see over the cowlings. "About there," he concluded as his staff moved the nacelles in and out with relation to the fuselage, his desk.

Jamouneau flinched each time he surveyed the blueprints. The landing gear was fixed, nonretractable. The budget allowed for nothing more. Yet some money would have to be spent on that. A twin would be too heavy for gear held together by rubber bands. The Sky Sedan, fabricated at the close of the war—the airplane that could have made the difference between success and crisis in 1947— had been Jamouneau's baby, his own creation. Now the Sedan's landing gear was adapted to the twin. While the Sedan had been a tail-wheel airplane, its main gear had been of the air-oil type, designed expressly for Piper by a Los Angeles engineering firm.

By March 1952 a mockup of the proposed airplane had been hammered together. It looked like something that had come out of a conference committee on box cars. All angles and projections, it was neither fish nor fowl, not a fabric airplane, not a metal one. A fabric-skinned airplane required a strong steel-tube structure, and this one had it in full measure. The wing was metal clad only near the engines. Control surfaces were metal. For directional control a long tailplane was adorned with two vertical stabilizers and two rudders. That underscored the boxiness of the whole.

Jamouneau could have been suspected of creating a monster in order to destroy it.

In July 1953 a test airplane was ready to be airborne. Jay Myers, a local boy whose grandfather had owned the farm that was now the Lock Haven airport, drew the test-flying assignment. Everybody, including the clerical help in the administrative offices and production line workers, watched. Myers came unstuck easily after a run of a few hundred feet. He climbed into a sky filled with great towers of alabaster clouds. Thirty minutes later he returned, settling gently onto the runway, engines ticking over.

"It's got the shakes," he reported as he climbed out. Vibration was no novelty in prototype aircraft when components of the same resonance frequency slipped by the engineers.

"At what speed?" asked Jamouneau.

"In landing, near the stall speed."

In Experimental they went over the airplane checking resonances. Nothing matched. A power-off phenomenon unassociated with normal engine-propeller vibration, the trouble was mystifying. Myers flew the twin again, and again he reported the shakes. Jamouneau imported a veteran test pilot, Hank Kurt, from Grumman on Long Island for consultation. Kurt dismounted after a flight looking puzzled.

"It's just the nature of the thing," he said, "like a dog shaking the water off after a swim. I don't know what's wrong."

"Maybe it's the tail," suggested Pug Piper. "The tail doesn't do anything for the looks anyway."

Again, the Sky Sedan served as a stand-in for the twin. Its empennage was duplicated and affixed to the stern. With a modification of the fin, it worked like a charm, and it noticeably improved the appearance of the airplane. But it didn't cure the shakes.

The search for a solution was running up the development cost of the machine. At their wit's end, Piper engineers built a one-tenth scale model and trucked it to a wind tunnel in the mechanical engineering department of Pennsylvania State University. To read the flow of air around the model, the engineers fed smoke, produced by burning cigar clippings soaked in paraffin, into the tunnel situated on the second floor of a building that had classrooms on the first and third floors. The smoke leaked. It permeated the classrooms. The building was no place for a man trying to give up tobacco. Professors paid calls on the Piper crew, threatening bodily expulsion. The aircraft engineers stopped generating smoke. The tests proved nothing.

A Piper engineer decided to try tuft studies. These normally employ short strands of yarn attached to parts of a model to determine air flow. Instead of attachments, he tied a piece of silk thread two feet long to a stick and held it in front of the wing at the inboard side of one of the engine cowlings as the propeller generating air velocity revolved slowly to simulate landing speed. At the junction of the cowling and the wing's upper surface near the trailing edge he discovered a vortex that carried on back to the tail and struck the face of the horizontal stabilizer. The turbulent air shook the tail, and the vibration was transmitted to the entire model. With clay, the engineer and his fellow workers fashioned a triangular filleting, tapering from the engine cowling on one side and from the fuselage on the other, to the leading edge of the wing. That did it. The vortex disappeared. So did the shakes.

Only one other incident marred the flight test syllabus of the twin. Strickland was having some difficulty in engine cooling in single-engine operation.

Myers took off on a temperature flight one chill December night. The company was scheduling flights night and day to accelerate the licensing. Jamouneau and Strickland were monitoring the communication radio. Suddenly Myers' voice was strident.

"I'm at fifty feet," he reported. "My engine is getting awfully rough. The plane's shaking."

"Can you start your other engine?" asked Jamouneau.

"It's stone cold."

"Try."

"I *am* trying. I can't steady my hand enough to punch the starter button."

That was all. Myers had his hands too full of airplane to say more.

A minute later he swooped onto the runway, his airplane intact. By dint of wild effort, he had managed to start the dead engine and shut down the ailing one. Luck had been with him. An examination of the sick engine disclosed that the electric starting motor had fallen from its bracket, and its gears had jammed the starting ring gear.

The head of the Piper clan slowly began accepting the inevitable—his new twin-engine airplane would have to be modified considerably if it were to sell. To start with there was that fabric fuselage. Perhaps he was influenced by his primary customers, the distributors. The reactions of many of them as work progressed summed up to uh-huh. Pug Piper was dropping remarks in the family councils. He wanted a performance airplane that was at the same time a pleasure to look at.

"All right," W. T. Piper announced one day, "we'll make the whole thing of metal, if that's what you want." If there was a trace of resignation in his tone, no one detected it.

It was too late to do much about the steel tube structure. Without it, months more would be expended to engineer the cabin portion of the airplane to carry the loads imposed by flight and landing impacts. So Engineering proceeded to amputate everything behind the passenger cabin and redesign from there. Now the airplane looked less like a box and more like a flying machine.

Engine power was boosted from 125 to 150 in each nacelle, and the word was adroitly planted at strategic points in the company that constant-speed propellers would give the airplane a lot more performance. With such propellers a pilot selected his engine revolutions per minute, and a governor varied the blade pitch to hold them to that value. It resulted in maximum thrust for the power expended. Props like that were costly.

"All right," said William, Sr., when he got the message.

Then there was the fixed landing gear hanging down in the airstream and gobbling up fuel. Power-retracted gear would increase the top and cruise speeds, save gasoline, and raise the service and absolute ceilings to which the airplane could aspire. Besides, wheels that tucked up into the wings and fuselage made an airplane a thing of beauty in flight. *They* were expensive.

"All right," said W. T. Piper.

"We really ought to have a stylist," remarked Strickland to Jamouneau.

"Now," said Jamouneau to Mr. Piper, "about styling. . . ."

"All right," said Mr. Piper.

Howard Piper came up with a name for the twin—the Apache.

"It can be the start of a whole series of Indian names," said Jake Miller approvingly.

As a production item, the Apache was hard to fault. It was docile, easy to fly. It was eager. It throbbed when the engines were fired up, and the exhaust pipes emitted pure Mendelssohn. It could get in and out of short strips with a full load. But no one was anxious to talk about price. Already price had become a sore subject. Division of opinion was shaping up on the decision echelon.

"Suddenly," recalled Tony Piper, "we were looking at a tag of $30,000 for the new twin."

A fresh personality on the command level had begun affecting the corporation's posture toward money. Charles W. Pool had been made treasurer. He was a bland-faced man who rode shotgun on the company strongbox and sat in on policy decisions. A business school graduate who kept an electric printing calculator on his desk, Pool had been in the accounts payable department at the time of the 1947 debacle. He had served as chief of property accounting in the Air Force Materiel Air Service Command at the Miami Air Depot. He looked at red ink with the distaste of a garment manufacturer for a nudist cult. His cost analysis studies were thorough to the third decimal point. He was blunt on pricing for profit. The automobile industry was content with sales reports each ten days. Pool demanded a daily report. That covered the state of the inventory, production, and income.

At a session of the management committee on October 26, 1953, called to put a price on the Apache, Pool came loaded with statistics. He talked in terms of profit. Jamouneau supported him.

"What we're dealing with here," said the chief engineer, "is profit but something besides. It's prestige. Which would you rather wear—a forty-five-dollar suit off a pipe rack or one for eighty dollars with a Hart, Shaffner and Marx label?"

Pug Piper said, "A good price could help us get away from the Cub image."

"All right," said W. T. Piper, "what's the figure?"

"With the discount to the distributor," submitted Pool, " we can gross $23,400 on each unit."

"That's a retail price of what?" asked Mr. Piper. He was too sharp at mental arithmetic not to know. He just wanted to hear it said.

"Thirty-two five."

"You're just hogs!" exclaimed Tony Piper, looking at Pool and Jamouneau. "You're trying to push us into the price brackets of our competitors."

"If we're hogs," said Jamouneau, "it's in the interest of a sound, solvent company."

"Sure," argued Tony, "but there comes a point where you begin losing customers on price."

W. T. Piper had confidence in Pool. "You're for it?" he asked the treasurer.

"Yes."

That much was settled. Jake Miller's sales organization would have to live with the figure.

Six months before the first Apache was due off the assembly line, Miller called a general meeting of distributors in Lock Haven. Mr. Piper, Miller, and other company functionaries made their pitch. They fielded questions from the floor. One of the key distributors, Roy Neal of Lubbock, Texas, sought out Miller after the meeting.

"Can't I sell Piper airplanes," he asked, "without handling this one? Personally, I don't see a market for the Apache at that price."

"Don't make a decision now," said Miller. "It's going to be months before you get a demonstrator anyway."

A month before the airplane was due, Miller called Neal. The man in Lubbock was still chary.

"What would you do," he asked, "if you were in my position?"

"I'd take the airplane and demonstrate it. I know you're going to sell *one*."

The first production airplane came off the line on December 21, 1953. On February 2, 1954, a certificate of airworthiness was presented by a Civil Aeronautics Authority official to W. T. Piper in suitable ceremonies at the factory. Apaches one and two, bearing the registration designations N1000 and N1001, were assigned to the sales department as demonstrators. Apache 1002 went to Ed Brockenbrough, the distributor in Charlotte, North Carolina. A month later he wrote the factory:

"I can't sell it, not at the price you're asking."

He did, though, and others.

Ken Dewitt, the Maine distributor, and Neal in Lubbock accepted their Apaches, sold them, and ordered others. Cliff Hyde, in Houston, exuberantly said he wanted to order a hundred. Roscoe Turner, a flamboyant scarf-and-goggles pilot who strolled the streets with a pet lion named Gilmore on a leash, bought an Apache. So did Charles F. ("Boss Ket") Kettering, one of the giants of the General Motors hierarchy.

Jake Miller revived the discussion of five years before on the problem of merchandising an airplane costing a small fortune as compared with the Cub.

"I've had a feeling all along," he told the management committee, "that the field organization will have to undergo some changes if we're going to market this airplane. It takes a different kind of man from the fellow who is used to selling Cubs."

He set out to comb through his list. With some distributors he used persuasion. He let some talk themselves out of selling Piper products. Sucking on a dead pipe, he expressed sympathetic agreement—selling Apaches was just too big a job. He sought, and found, replacements for the faint of heart. He staged demonstration trips.

Apache sales took off. Demand for the airplane fast outpaced the supply. Production was slow. It was not until September that the factory was able to produce 1 a day. By the close of the fiscal year on September 30 Piper had sold 59 of the aircraft. By the end of the calendar year the company had sold 101 and was 200 units behind in its orders.

The reason was clear. Despite a price that was almost twice the one originally targeted, W. T. Piper had what he wanted—the world's least expensive twin-engine airplane. Beech's Twin Bonanza, brought out in 1949 as the T-50, a military version, and employed in the Korean War, had assumed civilian garb in 1952 bearing a tag of almost $70,000. Cessna's 310 model retailed for just short of $50,000.

Each company had designed for its own market. Piper wanted volume, Beech wanted class leadership, Cessna wanted performance per horsepower. The Twin Bonanza and the 310 were roomier than the Apache and provided adequately for luggage; the Apache did not. The Apache was shy by other yardsticks. It was not nearly as fast as the other two machines. At 60 percent power at an altitude of 10,000 feet it cruised at 170 mph. compared with 203 for the Twin Bonanza and 205 for the Cessna 310. The Apache did not have their rate of climb. It lacked their range of operation. Squeezing a fifth seat into the Apache, as was done now and then, made for a bit too much togetherness.

But virtues had been built into the Apache where they counted. Its four-cylinder engines required less maintenance than the competitive sixes. Its wing loading—the amount of weight each square foot of wing area must carry at full gross—was only 17.2 pounds as against 22.7 for the Twin Bonanza and a whopping 26.2 for the Cessna. A landing speed of fifty-two miles an hour was actually below the maximum speed permitted automobiles on the open road by almost all states, and a rollout of 670 feet after touchdown was scarcely more than a city block. As compared with the Cessna, the Apache had short-field capability. The Lock Haven engineering staff had adhered to the dictum of W. T. Piper: the more small airports that the Apache could get into and out of, the greater its utility.

The Apache did compare favorably with the Twin Bonanza on power loading, the number of pounds of gross weight that each engine horsepower had to tote—11.6 and 11.5, respectively—but it was far above the Cessna at 9.6.

In June, Alfred W. "Scorchy" Munro, a Piper test pilot, began giving W. T. Piper instruction in the new twin. Mr. Piper made the airplane. He sold it. It bore his name. And he was obstinately determined to master it. At the age of seventy-three, the president of the company, perfectly at home in a single-engine airplane, had to learn the techniques of flying twin-engine aircraft that frustrated many a man his junior by fifty years. He wasn't ready for solo until he had twenty hours of dual time.

"Okay," said Munro, who doubled as a government examiner, early on the morning of July 21, 1954.

The Piper family was watching. The chief of the clan climbed aboard an Apache alone, taxied to the downwind lip of the runway, opened his throttles, and soared aloft in a plane that bore as much resemblance to his original flying machine as a Ford Thunderbird to a Model T. He circled the field, squared away for his approach, flared for his touchdown, and settled onto the asphalt strip with the aplomb of an airline pilot. Back at the flight line, he dismounted, grinning.

"Anybody can fly that thing," said he.

"All right, Pop," said Tony, "now you've got your twin-engine rating. Let the younger guys fly you around."

It was Mr. Piper's first and last solo flight in a twin. Three years later he was induced, finally, to quit solo flying altogether.

"It would be a hell of an advertisement, Pop," Tony pointed out to him, "if you wound up killing yourself, wouldn't it?" That was something that W. T. Piper, the salesman, understood.

Max Conrad, of Winona, Minnesota, and Prescott, Arizona, a pilot with ten children, who in the ensuing years became known as

BILL, JR., AND PUG ABOUT TO FLY THE SOUTH ATLANTIC
A taxi driver in Belem overcharged them.

the Flying Grandfather, had flown a Piper Pacer from Minneapolis to Rome and back in 1950 with stops in New York, Labrador, Greenland, Iceland, and England. In 1952 he set a world distance record for that type of aircraft with a nonstop flight from Los Angeles to New York. Now, carrying extra fuel, he contributed to the Apache's exposure to public view with a flight from New York to Paris, the first nonstop solo performance eastbound between the two cities since Charles A. Lindbergh's in 1927. Bill, Jr., and Howard Piper delivered an Apache to South Africa in March 1955, bridging the South Atlantic with an insouciance that made headlines.

"Any incidents?" Pug was asked on their return.

"Yeah," he reported, "a taxi driver in Belem overcharged us."

The response of the stockbrokers to Piper Aircraft's new affluence born of hitting the jackpot with a new kind of twin-engine machine was prompt. On June 13, 1950, Piper common closed on the curb exchange at 1 7/8. In 1954 the brokers began peddling. On June 13, 1956, the stock closed at 16, and was still going up.

The company began sitting back and looking at its products. Profits there were aplenty, but there were holes in the spectrum of aircraft being offered the consumer. It was a result of Tony Piper's austerity policy in all things that cost money and did not offer an immediate return, and this included market research. The high-wing Tri-Pacer was becoming dated. Piper had toyed with the idea of a four-seat, low-wing, single-engine machine for several years.

As early as 1952 it proposed buying a design by Al Mooney, the shoestring manufacturer. Mooney was a clever man with a pencil and slide rule. The aviation manufacturing community also said that he was afflicted with tinkeritis—once he got a flying machine off the ground, he refused to let it alone. Yet he had racked up an imposing list of credits. One of his designs, the Bellanca Flash, was sold in the 1930s to the government of Spain as a fighter. He was responsible for much of the Monocoupe, a fast pilot's airplane manufactured by Claire Bunch in Moline, Illinois.

Pug Piper wanted the Mooney design as a test bed for the proposed single-engine low-wing. Buying it outright would save engineering hours and the expense of prototype construction. Jamouneau opposed the deal. The Mooney had a wood-structured wing covered with plywood, and this was no time to fiddle with materials requiring fresh techniques. Moreover, the Mooney cockpit was cramped.

Mooney temporized. In the end he refused to sell, but not before he agreed that his cockpit could stand expansion. He drew up the specifications for that, stuffed them in a file drawer in his office at Wichita, and left on a business trip to Washington. There he broke a leg. Flat on his back for weeks, he telephoned his staff in Kansas to go ahead with the production of his airplane. The staff didn't know about the new cockpit drawings. Mooney didn't know that the staff didn't know about them. His engineers went ahead with the cramped-cockpit version. Mooney was stuck with it.

Piper again looked at Johnny Thorpe's Sky Scooter in its search for a new single-engine airplane and backed off. In 1955 the project of a Piper-designed four-seater was revived. The sketches were dusted off for review with a proposed "lead time" of three years between concept and manufacture. The airplane would be a relatively inexpensive substitute for the Apache in cross-country flying. Its market would be the businessman and the fixed-base operator running charters. The target price was $12,000. It would not be pretentious. Its interior was laid out to be plain and functional.

Tony Piper and his father fought a losing battle to retain simplicity in the machine, named "Comanche." They were opposed by Pug Piper and the sales department, now convinced that a bargain basement airplane had no appeal for potential customers.

For Piper, the Comanche introduced an innovation, a movable tailplane called a stabilator. In conventional construction the tailplane was fixed, and to it was hinged the elevator. The stabilator eliminated the elevator. The tailplane itself was the elevator, moving to make the airplane climb or descend in response to movements of the cockpit control stick or yoke. A Lockheed patent of Johnny Thorpe, the stabilator made for a cleaner empennage configuration and a more positive response to cockpit commands. The Comanche

incorporated something else brand-new in a small, private airplane—
a swept tailfin used by U.S. Air Force fighters and commercial jets.
Other manufacturers, including Beech and Cessna, copied it.

When the Comanche made its debut in 1958, it was something
more than the factory originally bargained for. It retailed for $14,500
with a 180-horsepower engine and for $17,900 with one of 250 horse-
power. In its huskier version it cruised four persons at 171 miles an
hour, climbed 1,400 feet a minute, had a service ceiling of 20,000 feet,
and a range of 705 miles, and it was pretty.

Besides the Comanche, Piper needed a new training airplane.
Jake Miller kept talking about "student inputs." The trainer was the
vehicle to get novices aloft. When they learned to fly, they became
potential aircraft purchasers. The Super Cub, for all its fresh horsepower, was as passe for training as a skirted bathing suit for women.
The Tri-Pacer did not qualify. Not only was it dated, it was too big.
Cessna was proselyting Piper business with a couple of metal airplanes that bespoke Dwane Wallace's acumen in assessing the market.
As with the Comanche, the Piper engineering and sales departments
searched outside the company for something already in being to buy
time for the development of a trainer. The Ercoupe, the tidy, low-
wing, two-control—but only two-seat—airplane that had been swallowed up in the gloom of 1947 and ever since had been handed
around like an aging mistress, was in distress in Greeley, Colorado.
Miller went to investigate it. So did a team headed by Pug Piper.
The tools could be bought for $275,000.

"What will it cost," asked W. T. Piper, "to put the thing in production?"

"About the same amount again," answered Pug.

For the first time in the memory of anyone in the establishment,
the president of the company brought his fist down on the table.
"No!" said he. "We'll build our own airplane."

"That will take time," Bill, Jr., quietly pointed out.

"The answer's still no."

He didn't want to be pushed. His memory of unsold two-place
aircraft multiplying on the airport was too recent and too vivid. A
decision on a new trainer was put off.

Pug Piper was giving his reluctant brother Tony a hard time.
Tony did accede to the expenditure of enough money to modify the
Super Cub as an agricultural sprayer and duster, a new market for
the company.

Pug unleashed a new campaign. He wanted the company to invest in a combination research-production center somewhere outside
Lock Haven. He enlisted allies. He had a natural one in Jake Miller

who recognized the need for an expanded line of aircraft in which an owner could "move up" as his income grew. Pug got his elder brother on his side, and between them they began to win over their father. Pug's arguments were valid:

"The best way to go broke is to sit here and stagnate. We've got to grow. We've used up the labor supply in Lock Haven. We've got to have a place that offers better weather to people like research engineers."

"Where?" asked his father.

Pug had done his homework. "Florida."

For Mr. Piper, that was the clincher. If the company was going to expand, it had best be in a state with a "right-to-work" law—where a man did not have to belong to a union to hold a job. And Florida offered year-around flying.

As early as 1956 Bill, Jr., Pug, and their wives flew to Florida to look for a site. The peninsula had been a favorite haunt for the Pipers for more than a quarter century. They wanted a small community. Mr. Piper's distrust of big ones continued endemic. That ruled out anything as far south as Palm Beach, where the megalopolis began that stretched beyond Miami. They wanted warm winter weather, which ruled out anything as far north as Jacksonville. They preferred the east coast, but would settle for a town on the Gulf if it offered enough enticements. When the adding-up was done, the choice came down to two places, Vero Beach (pop. 8,800) on the Atlantic, fifty-five miles south by southeast of Cape Canaveral (later Cape Kennedy), and Venice (pop. 3,500) on the scalloped Gulf coast, fifteen miles south of Sarasota, the Ringling Circus winter quarters.

It was a toss-up between the two communities until some letters began arriving from the good citizens of Venice. Venice, they said, essentially was a residential town. Bringing in an aircraft factory would increase the population. Increasing the population would increase the birth rate. Increasing the birth rate would necessitate more schools. More schools would mean higher taxes. That hadn't happened in Lock Haven, but the good burghers of Venice were self-convinced.

Pug managed to extract enough money from the till to get started at Vero Beach. Here the replacement for the Tri-Pacer would be born. He already had a name for it: the Cherokee. On the company records it was designated the PA–28. The engineering on the basic configuration was farmed out to that genius for simplicity, Johnny Thorpe.

With a staff of thirty, the director and chief engineer of the newly founded Piper Engineering Center moved onto an old naval air station at Vero in 1957. He was Fred E. Weick, no novice at airplane design. He had spent ten years with the National Advisory Committee for Aeronautics, precursor of the National Aeronautics and Space Administration. He had fashioned the Ercoupe, and at Texas A. and M., an agricultural airplane.

As the decade of the 1950s neared its close, W. T. Piper and his brood had few frets. While their unit share of the lightplane market had dropped five points to a shade more than 33 percent, largely due to a preoccupation with filling orders and a lack of sufficient engineering to expand their line of products, they had produced and sold no less than $100 million worth of aircraft in a brief three years. Piper Aircraft on February 11, 1957, moved from the curb exchange to the big board, the New York Stock Exchange.

Nor did General Aviation have many complaints. That bastard offspring of flying had persisted obstinately for thirty years largely without benefit of billions of dollars sunk into military aeronautics and spun off into transport designs for the airlines. It had found its place. It was thriving, an element firmly fixed in the U.S. spectrum of transportation.

Thomas Francis Piper, the short-spoken, pragmatic loner who had led the company out of its wilderness and into a land of milk and honey, was wishing that his compendium of problems would go away. Pressures were building up under him. The demands for business expansion grew ever more strident. His stewardship, reflected in the bookkeeping, could not be faulted except for the sums that he had denied for forward planning, and right now, with competition eating into the company's share of the market, that had become a sore point.

"I guess," he commented later, wholly without bitterness, "I held the lid on too long."

Late in May 1960, Tony walked into the office of his father and announced, "Pop, I'm through." On June 6 he made it formal. Tony's elder brother, Bill, for the first time assumed the helm of the Piper Aircraft Corporation, his decisions subject to the advice and consent of W. T. Piper.

The Organization Men

WILLIAM THOMAS PIPER, JR., FORTY-NINE
years old, the new executive vice president, was a fisherman of monumental patience, a sharp man with a card in high-low-jack, a golfer with a six handicap, a bowler who averaged 180, a student of the changing business climate in the United States, and a master of the soft sell.

"Been watching General Motors stock lately?" he remarked offhand to one of his constant cronies with rod and reel as they wet their flies.

"No."

That closed the conversation on the stock market. It was not until several days later that Bill, Jr.'s friend realized GM had advanced several points since his question. Thereafter he kept his ears open when the man who had become the executive administrative officer of Piper Aircraft engaged in small talk.

The contrast between W. T. Piper's first and second sons was stark. It was almost instantly apparent when Bill, Jr., took over. He soft-sold his program by suggestion, implication, and understatement. He reorganized the administrative apparatus of the company. He delegated authority. He insisted that department heads make their own decisions and be prepared to back them up.

He was a people man. He walked the production line to talk with the hourly-wage employes. He thought nothing of devoting an hour to composing doggerel to be read at a party for some little old lady in tennis shoes whom he had known since his boyhood.

Like his father, he knew the value of a dollar. In the 1934–36 period, when he was paid a salary of $15 a week, he banked every third paycheck. Cruising over his territory in a Cub with a Rand McNally highway map on his knees, he sniffed out weekend air shows to hop passengers at $1.50 a head. It had been no novelty for him to bed down in a corner of a hangar to save the price of a hotel room. He was blind to social strata. He bowled and played basketball with production line employes. Long years later, become wealthy, he had difficulty recognizing his affluence. Thumbing through a book titled *The Rich and Super Rich,* he remarked, "What do *they* do with their money?"

He did not communicate his personal or business problems to friends or even to his immediate family except as they were affected by them. If the factory was in bad straits, Pud, his wife, had to learn about it from others. He did share one trait with Tony—if he was troubled over a decision, he resolved it in front of his shaving mirror. He had a phobia about imposing on anyone. Once, with a kidney infection that sent his temperature soaring to 103 degrees in the middle of the night, he refused to let his wife call a doctor.

"Wait until morning," he said. "How'd you like to be routed out of bed at this hour?"

He had an abiding respect for his father. As Mr. Piper relinquished more and more of the president's duties to him, he never failed to keep the head of the clan advised of decisions about to be taken. Outside the family councils he always referred to his father as "Mr. Piper." Asked to speak at a banquet after his father, he got up to deliver eight words: "I couldn't top him. I wouldn't try to."

While he was tolerant of an antipathy by his father and brother Tony toward labor unions, he recognized that the company must live in a new national climate of labor-employer relations.

"How many people have you got working here?" Becky Gross of the *Lock Haven Express* once said Mr. Piper was asked by a visitor to the factory. His tart answer, reported Becky, was, "About half."

Speaking at Vero Beach, Mr. Piper, referring to the International Association of Machinists (later, Lock Haven local 734 of the Aerospace Workers), told an audience of businessmen, "Ever since we began, we've been hounded by this union. The politicians are so scared, they've given the unions everything."

1941 STRIKE
"How many people have you got working here?" Mr. Piper was asked. "About half," he said.

The union had moved in in 1939. It emerged from a one-week strike with an open shop and no dues checkoff. In the next fifteen years it idled the production line a half-dozen times for from two to five days. In 1954 it struck for three weeks following a two-week vacation shutdown. In 1959 it struck for two weeks. One of W. T. Piper's few voiced complaints about William Shriver was that he had granted the workers a union shop to keep the plant running.

Now in 1960 Bill, Jr., saw public attacks on union labor as a blot on the company image. Periodic dialogue on labor-employer differences had to be, but they had best occur behind closed doors. It was better business.

While Bill, Jr., rated no elocution prizes, he was a better speaker than Tony.

He knew the ins and outs of cost control, but unlike Tony, he was philosophical about vagaries of annual unit sales.

"You make your estimate and set your price," he told a business magazine reporter in one of his rare interviews, "and you're stuck with it. Suppose business slows down. You've got an organization of good men who have been hard to come by. What do you do?"

He answered his own rhetorical question. "The worst thing you can do is furlough your good men. You'll lose them. Then what are you going to do when business picks up?"

His belief in expansion, shared with Pug, was evident at the start of the new administration. Within limits dictated by fiscal responsibility, the lid was off. A complete line of airplanes would be produced. Sales were the key to a healthy till, and to that end Jake Miller was given a new assignment. He had been in charge of marketing and sales. Domestic and foreign sales had been lumped into one department. Marketing, for which Miller was now made responsible, meant overall product planning. Selling—reaping profits—was only a function of marketing, as was promotion. Two sales departments were established, one for the domestic market, the other for the foreign market. The foreign market sales setup, accounting for one income dollar in every four, was showing stress at the seams. Bill, Jr., dispatched Miller to Switzerland to establish Piper International, staffed by men on the Lock Haven payroll.

A corporate planning group for interdepartmental coordination was set up. Everything was computerized. Studies proliferated.

"For a while there," Jack Miller drily opined, "I think we got ourselves overorganized."

Mr. Piper, at heart still a door-to-door salesman, reacted predictably to all this: "Good lord, how can a busy man read all that stuff?"

Bill, Jr., his phalanxes of Xerox-equipped organization men notwithstanding, hated paper work too. He was all too aware that his corporate restructuring up to then was about all that the shocked older heads could ingest.

THE PAWNEE
For the farmer, ecologist, entomologist.

As for Mr. Piper himself, at the age of eighty he displayed a marked aversion to being left out of anything. In 1961 he accompanied Charles Bockstahler of the sales staff and George D. Rodgers, a company pilot—later executive vice president of ATCO, a distributor of aircraft parts and accessories based in San Jose, California—to a sales promotion shindig in Reno. At day's end the two younger men became painfully aware that Mr. Piper expected them to eat and go to bed. They saw him to his hotel room, yawned in counterfeit fatigue, said their goodnights, and promptly went out on a town of showgirls and roulette wheels. Returning at 3:30 A.M., they found the boss sitting in the lobby waiting for them.

A new trainer airplane that Jake Miller wanted for boosting the number of "student inputs" could not be materialized out of thin air. The company improvised. The engineers ripped the two rear seats out of the Tri-Pacer and named the result the Colt to differentiate anything so gauche from the breed of Indian-name products. The Cherokee, the machine that the Comanche started out to be, was in prototype. A four-place low-wing with fixed landing gear and fixed-pitch propeller, it had even fewer structural components than the Tri-Pacer, making use of plastic moldings, glass fiber, and other lightweight materials. That kept the retail price down to $8,500. While Johnny Thorpe had sketched the basic Cherokee, the design was largely Fred Weick's. The tailplane was Thorpe's stabilator. With a 150-horse engine, it cruised at better than 130 miles an hour on 75 percent power, took off in 800 feet in still air, and stalled in at 54 miles per hour with a rollout run of only 535 feet. It went 735 miles between refuelings. Presently, in one version, converted to a two-seater, the Cherokee became the trainer that Jake Miller so devoutly wanted.

By mid-1960 the company had thrown up enough factory space at Vero Beach to put another line of aircraft in production, and by the following January Cherokees began rolling out the door.

Weick's agricultural airplane, named the Pawnee, was one of Pug Piper's prime projects. Put into production at Lock Haven, it was perhaps the ugliest flying machine—man-made, that is, which excluded the pterodactyl of the Mesozoic era—ever to be socked into fabric and metal. Humpbacked like a camel, it was strictly functional, a bench mark in specialized aircraft design. It had a virtue possessed by no other airplane ever used in agriculture. Its components were put together for progressive collapse, starting at the nose, in a crash. It could turn over without crushing the cockpit. A rounded aluminum cushion above the instrument panel kept a pilot from bopping his head on dials, knobs, and buttons. A rear rest protected his head and spine from whiplash. Shoulder straps kept him in his seat. Rudder pedals had no protrusions. A pilot had emergency window releases, and he could abandon ship from either side of the cockpit. The humpback had a purpose—it raised the cockpit floor ten inches above the bottom of the fuselage for flat-crash impact absorption. The pilot sat aft. Engine, fuel tanks, and hopper load buffered him in collision. Longerons, the fuselage longitudinal forming members, were bowed slightly to buckle outward.

This was a new concept in agricultural aircraft. In the previous seven years the five thousand U.S. agricultural planes had had one accident for each twenty-six hundred hours of flying. One man had been killed for each twenty thousand hours. The Pawnee slashed these figures to one accident in each five thousand hours and one fatality for each ninety thousand hours. Its wings were a throwback in Piper design—they came straight from a J-3 Cub. The tail design and part of the landing gear were borrowed from the Super Cub.

Reducing the hazards of AG flying, the Pawnee cut costs. For the farmer, the ecologist, and the entomologist, the Pawnee was tailor-made. It protected livestock and poultry from ticks and mites. It was used to forestall plagues and epidemics. It saved crops. It restocked streams and lakes with fish. It banished mosquitoes. It kept roads free of ice in winter by dispersing salt compounds. It deiced airport runways. In Ghana it doubled the yield of cocoa crops. In Australia and New Zealand it seeded and fertilized thousands of acres of marginal land, converting it to rich pasture. In Florida it suppressed pests to make the peninsula a corn producer for the first time in history. In Colorado it restored the bounty of burned-over forest lands with reseeding. For the United States alone, the Department of Agriculture estimated that AG airplanes were saving the farmer from losses of three and a half billion dollars a year.

Promptly copied by competitors, the Pawnee commanded a mar-

AZTEC PRODUCTION LINE
It was the aristocrat of the Piper stable.

ket of six of every ten AG airplanes sold in the United States. In
the next five years it was exported to ninety-one countries.

The Apache had been perfect for 1954 and for the next half
dozen years, but Pug Piper recognized that it was becoming outdated
by the demands of business and industry for faster, more commodious
transportation. Its second generation replacement was the Aztec, an
elegant airplane described at the time as the aristocrat of the Piper
line. It had the same lines as the Apache but seated five comfortably.
Two hundred more horsepower gave the Aztec a cruise speed of 210
miles an hour and a range of a thousand miles. Presently, modified
Lycoming turbo-boosted engines increased the cruise to 250 miles
per hour at an altitude of twenty-four thousand feet, at that time
the maximum operational height of the propeller-driven commercial
airliners. A "stretched" fuselage in another version accomodated six

ARROW PRODUCTION LINE
The landing gear came down automatically.

persons, and compartments both in front of and behind the green-house accepted luggage in copious quantities. The price was in the $50,000 range.

The Comanche was put under review.

"We've abandoned the $30,000 market," Tony Piper pointed out.

So the Comanche was double-breasted to create a low-priced twin. Four models were added to the original Cherokee, accommodating from two to seven persons and cruising as high as 168 miles per hour. The star Cherokee was the Arrow.

"Of all accidents in retractable-gear airplanes," Pug Piper remarked one day to Fred Weick, "30 to 35 percent are caused because a pilot fails to get his gear down. Why can't we have gear that comes down automatically?"

Weick took on the job. Automatic retractables were nothing new but they were optional at extra cost. Beech had had one. Pug specified that self-lowering wheels be standard equipment on the Arrow. The airplane became the world's best selling low-wing, single-engine, retractable-gear aircraft.

Still another airplane, the Navajo, seating six to nine persons, was added to the Piper line. It was luxurious and expensive, designed for the executive trade, charter work, and "third-level" airlines. In its turbocharged engine version it cruised at 247 miles per hour at an altitude of 23,500 feet.

Options were offered. The single-engine and Twin Comanche and the Aztec were purchasable with turbo-boost engines for added speed and higher operational ceilings. The Navajo was pressurized to maintain a cabin altitude of ten thousand feet when flown at twenty-nine thousand under additional boost.

In conventional twins with propellers turning in the same direction, the thrust vector for the left engine was inboard, for the right engine outboard. The Twin Comanche got counter-rotating engines to equalize propeller thrust. The prototype of another twin, the Pocono, the biggest airplane that Piper had ever proposed to produce, was built. Mr. Piper himself pushed it as competition for Beech's fifteen-passenger turboprop model 99. He and Pug listed the requirements. It would be a workhorse for passengers (sixteen) and/ or freight, cruising at 216 miles per hour for a range of 800 miles. Mr. Piper insisted on gasoline-fed piston engines.

"There are lots of places in the world," he pointed out, "where you can't buy aviation kerosene." For his export trade he wanted no gas turbine engines, which were expensive anyway, driving propellers.

Even for the lowest-cost line of aircraft in the world, Piper's prices began to reflect the growth of General Aviation's contribution to air transport. Yesteryear's airport plaything had become a national —indeed, an international—instrument of communication. Fully equipped, the Navajo's retail price was more than two hundred times

TURBO COMANCHE "C" COCKPIT PANEL
Instrumentation made a pilot secure in weather that discouraged the birds.

THE POCONO
Davis, Parsons, and Strohmeier
A workhorse for passengers and/or freight.

that of the original Taylor Cub. Concerned over its rising prices and anxious to retain its niche in the low-cost twin-engine market, the company in 1971 introduced the Seneca, a spacious airplane seating six to seven persons. It was the lowest-cost machine of its type in the world. In terms of 1954 dollars it bore a lower price tag than the original Apache. Counter-rotating propellers obviated asymmetrical thrust.

On the huskier Piper products automatic pilots became a regularly ordered option. A coupler between the autopilot and the

THE SENECA
The world's lowest-priced, multi-seat twin.

THE $5 RIDE

Chester E. Pancoast

Student inputs were the key to airplane sales.

omnirange receiver flew an airplane to a selected station while the
man in the cockpit sat with his hands in his lap, monitoring. Optional DME (Distance Measuring Equipment) told him visually and
progressively how far he was from the station, just as certainly as
road signs told a motorist he was fifty or twenty or ten miles from
Sunbury or San Antonio or Salinas. For safety in the presence of
heavy air traffic in thick weather, an optional transponder "squawked"
the identification of his airplane to airway and airport flight controllers.

Borrowing a leaf from automobile industry merchandising, the
company designed posh interiors. If Pontiac could have a Bonneville
model, Piper could accord its products the Palm Beach treatment.

Who was buying the output of the lightplane factories at a rate
of twelve to fifteen thousand a year? The answer to that lay at the
learner level. Jake Miller had a salesman's practical analysis of airplane marketing:

"For the random prospect, flying looks as though it might be
fun. He doesn't say, 'This would be useful in my business.' He
doesn't know flying or airplanes well enough, despite our advertis-

ing. So he signs up for lessons, and he learns and becomes a potential airplane purchaser."

All through the decade of the 1950s the annual "student input" in nonairline, nonmilitary U.S. flying sat between fifty and sixty thousand. In 1961 Piper inaugurated a new idea—an introductory lesson for five dollars. Anyone could walk into a Piper dealer's, plank down that amount of money, and be taken aloft. He could handle the controls himself, with the instructor following his moves to keep him out of trouble. If he was in dungarees, he was back on the ground in a few minutes. If he wore a business suit and looked interested, his flight might last an hour. Two years after Piper began advertising its five-dollar ride Cessna's promotion department called one day from Wichita. Did Piper mind if they used the five-dollar ride idea?

"We wish the whole industry would use it," said Jake Miller.

Cessna blossomed out with an advertising campaign pegged on the line, "If I can fly, you can fly."

The experts with the graphs reported that for every thousand five-dollar introductory lessons, roughly four hundred persons would sign up for a full course of instruction. The dropout rate was 50 percent. Half went on to qualify for private licenses. Of the two hundred certificated, 1.2 percent bought new airplanes, and 2.8 percent, used ones, within a year. In ten years, 12 percent of the two hundred would own their own airplanes.

PUBLICITY SHOT
The cheesecake proliferated.

HUBERT HUMPHREY, MAX CONRAD, AND HARMON TROPHY
An award for 7,878 miles nonstop.

As part of the sales promotion effort, publicity photos flowed out of Lock Haven to the publishing media in a steady stream. Cheese-cake shots proliferated. Record flights, fixtures of the earlier days of the company, had been instituted again. Piper footed a substantial part of the bills. This time, the ventures had a different tincture. Formerly, many were stunts, pure and simple, dreamed up by characters after personal publicity. It was a newsworthy event after the Second World War when Clifford Evans and George Truman flew

CONRAD CONTROLLED CRASH
Something went wrong with his fuel system.

around the world in a brace of Super Cruisers. So was a world altitude record for "category II" aircraft—a rating based on weight—set by Caro Bayley at 30,203 feet with a Super Cub at Miami. Max Conrad's round trip to Rome and record nonstop from Los Angeles to New York, in Pacers, plus his New York–Paris flight in an Apache, were only openers for a new day of headline making. The format and purpose of record flights had changed. The goal no longer was anything-for-publicity. It was to expose the versatility and dependability of the product.

Max Conrad was stage center. On June 2, 1959, he took off from Cazes Airport, Casablanca, Morocco, in a strictly stock Comanche—except for extra fuel tanks—on a nonstop flight scheduled to El Paso. Flying at treetop level over the island of Trinidad's Piarco International Airport to be identified by officials of the Federation Aeronautique Internationale (FAI), world supervisory organization, he was clocked at twenty-six hours, and thirty-nine minutes out of Casablanca. Crossing Corpus Christi, he was picked up by aircraft posted a hundred miles southeast of El Paso. Now he altered his plan. In deference to a reception committee at El Paso, he made a low pass over the airport. He flew on west, in the company of several Apaches judiciously supplied by Piper to carry cameramen and reporters.

When Conrad touched down he had reached Los Angeles. He had been aloft 58.6 hours and was credited with a distance of 7,668 miles, 812 beyond the previous record for Class IV aircraft.

He racked up other records in Pipers. In November he did fly from Casablanca to El Paso, 6,967 miles, in a lighter, 180-horsepower Comanche for a new and 2,000-miles-greater Class III record. He landed with enough reserve fuel for ten more hours of flight. He tackled the closed-course Class III record of a Czech pilot, Jire Kunc, 3,084 miles. Flying a triangular circuit from Minneapolis to Chicago to Des Moines and back to Minneapolis eight times, he covered 6,921 miles. He made a thirteen-stop circuit of the world—25,946.5 miles—in an Aztec in a total elapsed time of eight days, eighteen hours, thirty-five minutes, fifty-seven seconds. This established not one new international mark but two—for piston-powered aircraft regardless of size, and for aircraft weighing between 3,858 and 6,613 pounds. Conrad's average speed was 123.2 miles per hour. Over the 1964 Christmas weekend he flew a Twin Comanche nonstop from Capetown, South Africa, to Saint Petersburg, Florida, a distance of 7,878 miles, to establish the first mark in the FAI Class V category for aircraft weighing between 6,614 and 13,227 pounds (3,000–6,000 kg). For that flight he was awarded the Harmon Trophy for the outstanding feat of individual pilotage in the calendar year.

Seldom did his luck desert him. Once he walked away from a controlled crash when something went wrong with his fuel system.

MARIO ANDRETTI, INDIANAPOLIS "500" WINNER
The owners' roster contained famous names.

Other fliers rode Piper airplanes to fame. Sheila Scott, England's most celebrated private pilot, captured the Harmon Trophy by flying a Comanche around the world between May 18 and June 20, 1966. Betty Miller of the United States won it by being the first of her sex to span the Pacific, California to Australia. Her mount was an Apache. In 1969 Mara Culp of Newport Beach, California, won the annual All-Woman Transcontinental Air Race (commonly known as the Powder Puff Derby) by flying from San Diego to Washington, D.C., at a speed of 210.4 miles per hour. Pilots of Pipers made off with four of the top five places in that race, and with eleven of the top fifteen.

Over a period of years, the roster of current and former Piper aircraft owners contained some notable names. A few: Clarence Chamberlain, transatlantic flier; Edgar Bergen, ventriloquist; Graham Hill, Bobby Unser, and Mario Andretti, automobile racing drivers; Senator Barry Goldwater, of Arizona; Thomas J. Watson, Jr., chairman of International Business Machines; Paul Hahn, international trick golfer; John Wayne, Jackie Cooper, and Robert Cummings, actors; Mel Torme, singer; Colin Chapman, managing director of England's Lotus Motors; John Volpe, secretary of transportation in the Nixon administration; Walter Taylor of the Taylor Wine Company; and Dr. Guenther Neugang, publisher of the Deutscher Aerokurier.

As a footnote to history, a national magazine in 1961 asked a panel of five judges headed by Jimmy Doolittle of World War II fame, to choose the twelve most famous aircraft from among the thousands that had been designed and built since the beginnings of powered flight. The C. G. Taylor–W. T. Piper Cub was one of them. Vintage Cubs were on display at the Smithsonian Institution in Washington, D.C., along with the Wright Brothers' first airplane, another of the twelve machines named by the panel; at the Henry Ford Museum in Dearborn, Michigan; and at the Pennsylvania Museum of Industry in Harrisburg.

As the decade of the 1960s aged, Bill, Jr., resumed his sophistication of the Piper organization. The five-dollar introductory ride led to another creation, "Piper Flite Centers," a national system of flight training run by franchised company dealers and flying schools. A thirty-step curriculum reduced licensing time by almost 20 percent. The centers went international, to Europe, South America, the United Kingdom, Australia, and the West Indies.

Less related to immediate profit—and more, indeed, to a broad social effort in academe—was Miller's establishment of an Air Science Education Department, working with the factory-level organization, distributors, and dealers to support programs in public and private educational institutions. The goals: to create a public understanding of the social, economic, and technological implications of General Aviation as an integral part of the U.S. transportation system, to stimulate educational curricula in aviation, to insure a pool of trained personnel to fill the manpower requirements of the aviation industry, to expand the market for General Aviation aircraft and related dealer services, and to foster a working relationship between the nation's educational apparatus and General Aviation on local, state, and national levels.

The Department of Commerce was the authority for the estimate that while the growth of the gross national product between 1965 and 1970 was in the area of 8 percent, and transportation of all descriptions was at 8.5 percent, air transportation was racking up a growth of 35 percent.

The Piper Aircraft Corporation was closing the decade with impressive resources. Its net worth was $54 million. At peak production, it had 4,800 employes. Annual wages and salaries were $29,445,000. Piper's manufacturing facilities comprised 1,234,000 square feet, equal to the area of 825 three-bedroom houses. To the Lock Haven and Vero Beach factories were added plants at Quehanna and Renovo, Pennsylvania, respectively sixty and twenty-eight miles upriver. Quehanna produced small sheet metal parts and assembled tail surfaces. Renovo made fiberglass components. A new factory was abuilding in Lakeland, Florida. The new satellite factories had to be, for at both Lock Haven and Vero Beach the company had ex-

UP GO THE PRODUCTION FIGURES
Lightplanes flew as many people as the airlines.

NEW ADMINISTRATION BUILDING
Built on stilts against the exuberances of the West Branch.

hausted its labor supply. A new engineering building had gone up at Lock Haven in 1961, only to be soaked to desk-top level by a West Branch flood a year later. This time completed airplanes and those in fabrication escaped. They were trundled in advance to a raised airport parking lot that W. T. Piper had ordered built.

On June 5, 1968, a new million-dollar administration building, constructed on stilts five feet above grade in deference to the periodic ecstasies of the river, was dedicated. Elegant, ultramodern, its tiered three stories had a canopied entrance over a reflecting pool and a big paved area in front to park visitors' airplanes. The exterior was a royal blue. The decor of the lobby was built around another pool—sunken—flanked by white marble. The carpeting was a lively orange, the walls were paneled, and the chairs and benches richly padded.

"When a man spends $100,000 for an airplane," commented Mr. Piper, "he's entitled to a free cup of coffee in pleasant surroundings."

On the third floor were the main administrative offices.

"You could cut my place in two," he said as he looked over his plushy quarters, "and still have plenty of space for a man to work."

The drinks at the luncheon on the third-floor terrace that followed the dedication were as soft as sea-spume.

On February 6 Bill, Jr., had been elected president and Pug, executive vice president. Tony retained a vice presidency. Mr. Piper remained chairman.

On one of his annual Christmas trips to enterain U.S. troops abroad, Bob Hope, the comedian, reported: "We're flying in a C–141 (a 150-ton Lockheed military transport), and it's really huge. To give you an idea, they have a Piper Cub flying the food in from the galley."

Despite Pug Piper's efforts at upgrading his company's product image, the generic noun "cub" persisted. In some areas of aviation and politics, it was becoming a dirty word.

The Storm Breaks

THE LIGHTPLANE WAS CONFOUNDING THE
most outrageous forecasts of its potential versatility made by its
partisans at the close of the Second World War. In a speech before
the Newcomen Society, William T. Piper, Jr., described the stunning
variety of General Aviation flying in the third great transportation
revolution. The term encompassed all nonmilitary, nonscheduled
flying.

Each morning a Navajo and an Aztec owned by Safair Flying
Service of Teterboro, New Jersey, took off from Rochester, New
York, with film processed in a Kodak laboratory during the night
destined for dozens of retail photo shops in Philadelphia and Allen-
town, Pennsylvania; Washington, D.C.; New Haven, Connecticut;
Providence, Rhode Island; and Boston. In the afternoon the airplanes returned to Rochester with undeveloped film collected at
the ports of call. Safair's air express carried fourteen thousand rolls
of film daily. A photo shop customer who left his exposed film in
the morning had it back the second afternoon. Eastman Kodak had
similar air taxi schedules all over the United States.

At Muskogee, Oklahoma, each evening a Beechcraft identified as
"Stage 22" took off with a load of mail. It dropped off sacks at Tulsa
and Oklahoma City and picked up others. Landing in Wichita at
midnight, the Beech offloaded its mail cargo into a truck for local
delivery and into four Piper Aztecs for hops to eight Kansas communities: Colby, Dodge City, Hays, Salina, Emporia, Topeka, Independence, and Fort Scott. Mail that the Pipers had hauled into
Wichita from those points was, in turn, put aboard Stage 22 as it
continued its flight to Joplin, Kansas City, and Springfield, Missouri.
Mail posted at 5 P.M. in Muskogee was home-delivered the next
morning, six days of the week, in the cities served by the five airplanes.

Super Cubs, Cherokees, and Pawnees flew daily on federal fish
and game missions and patrolled the borders to intercept narcotics
smugglers.

Gordon Vincent, Lock Haven, Pa.

NEW MEXICO STATE PLANE WITH SMOKEY THE BEAR
All that, and intercepting narcotics smugglers at the border to boot.

Abroad, Aeronaves Alimentadoras flew commuter services from Mexico City to forty-five towns between there and the nation's northern border, to the Mexican west coast and to Lower California. Heart of the operation was a fleet of turbo Navajos.

Cessnas, Pipers, and Beechcrafts opened up areas in Central and South America that had been reachable only by mule team or Indian dugout canoe. In Colombia, the hoppers of Pawnees flew coffee beans to market. In the lonely Mato Grosso region of Brazil, cattle ranchers radioed Cessna air taxi firms to bring in supplies or to fly the ranchers themselves to Sao Paulo or Rio de Janeiro.

Saudi Arabian Airlines used Apaches for pilot training. In Canada and Alaska, Pipers explored landscapes as bleak as the moon's.

Aztecs linked the islets of the New Hebrides, southeast of the Solomons, in the seas where Piper Grasshoppers in olive drab flew in World War II.

Australian "outbackers" no longer had to live on a diet of meat and tinned foods. To the isolated communities of Cobar, Bourke, Brewarrina, and Goodoga in the bush country went daily shipments

SUPER CUB IN ALASKA
Flying over landscapes as bleak as the moon's.

of chicken, ice cream, fish, vegetables, apple pie, and sponge cake, all frozen at a plant at Orange, in central-western New South Wales, for daily transport by a Cherokee SIX.

Piper twins spanned the Rift Valley between Nairobi and Keekorok in East Africa's great Masai Mara game preserve to slash a dusty, four-hour journey by car to one of three-quarters of an hour. They carried live game, on one occasion a frightened baby elephant.

At Tokyo, Navajos trained the flight crews of All Nippon Airways; and at Brown Field, an old military airport halfway between San Diego and the Mexican tourist city of Tijuana, students of Germany's Lufthansa and Japan Air Lines won their wings in Comanches and Aztecs.

At Rotterdam, Pawnees were dismantled and loaded aboard an airline freighter for transport to Tunisia to crisscross flood-ravaged Karouan Province, sowing cereal seeds to forestall famine.

The movement of mail by General Aviation charter operators was helping underscore a growing financial plight of the railroads. E. V. Rickenbacker, World War I fighter pilot hero and, later, head of a highly successful airline, had campaigned for years to get the post office to send all first class mail by air. He could have saved his breath. The answer lay not in politics but in economics. The curtailment of rail service was shocking. In 1930, 10,000 mail-toting passenger trains were on the rails daily. By 1969 there were only 425. For distances of 250 miles and more, the mail had to move by air. An even dozen class one railroads had dropped all passenger service in the previous nine years. Among them, the Kansas City Southern—Kansas City to New Orleans—discontinued passenger (and therefore all mail transfer) service. The Penn Central, created by the marriage of the Pennsylvania and New York Central railroads, said it wanted no part of passenger service west of Buffalo and Harrisburg. On its last run, December 2, 1967, the Twentieth Century Limited, by now grown seedy, was nine hours late into Chicago. Airline jets, spanning the distance from New York to Chicago in an hour and three-quarters, had made a caricature of the train's fleet

Friedlich, Fearon, and Strohmeier

LOADING FREIGHT IN KENYA
Slashing an hours-long journey by car to forty-five minutes.

SUPER CUB UNDER BROW OF MT. KILIMANJARO
Flying explorers up the Amazon and missionaries up the Congo.

sixteen-hour schedule. The Chicago & Northwestern Railway notified the Interstate Commerce Commission that it was discontinuing the last of its passenger train service, that between Chicago and Clinton, Iowa. Northern New England was without any passenger train service whatever except for one Canadian Pacific run. Passenger train schedules in the American southwest and in the states of North Dakota, South Dakota, Minnesota, Wisconsin, and Michigan had been halved.

"I think the long distance intercity passenger train," said Louis W. Menk, president of the newly consolidated Burlington Northern Railroad, "should be allowed to die an honorable death."

Davis, Parsons, and Strohmeier

ALL NIPPON AIRWAYS NAVAJO TRAINER
A stunning variety of flying in the third great transportation revolution.

TWIN COMANCHE OVER RIO DE JANEIRO
Opening up areas that had been accessible only by mule team or canoe.

The Interstate Commerce Commission reported on June 25, 1968, that private cars were carrying 88 percent of all intercity passengers, the railroads, 1.4 percent. Domestic air travel had expanded ninefold since 1950, it noted, and now was twice the combined intercity passenger traffic by rail, bus, and water. The miles of roadbed operated by the railroads in intercity passenger service had declined from 104,969 to 67,035 since 1959.

So the long- and medium-distance first class mail was carried by the airlines, the shorter-distance mail by bus. The air taxi routes, of which Stage 22 was one, were intermediate. Two hundred such routes commissioned by the Post Office Department were serving 382 of the 552 sectional mail centers in the United States, and the efficiency of their operations held promise of a steady expansion.

The railroads were not the only common carriers in ferment. It was an irony that the scheduled airlines, picking up the burden of the mail and taking up part of the slack in the intercity carriage of persons and goods, should themselves be in convulsion. As their jet airliners grew ever larger, the major carriers—the "trunks"—deleted stops. Airports that had been on their schedules either lacked sufficient runway length for the thundering new generation of machines, or the cities they abutted did not offer enough passenger and cargo business to warrant service. In three years they removed 285 cities from their timetables. They now served only 186.

E. V. RICKENBACKER AND MR. PIPER
Captain Rickenbacker could have saved his breath.

The regional, short-haul carriers operating on schedules followed suit. They were outgrowing their short pants, selling off their propeller-driven airplanes, and acquiring jets themselves, and *their* jets, though tailored to their needs and therefore much smaller than those of the trunks, were finding airport runways too short or stops unprofitable. The regionals removed 236 cities from their timetables and now served only 434. That did not mean a total of 521 communities had been stripped of scheduled service—many of those dropped by the trunks were stops for the regionals. It did mean, however, that the communities dropped by the regionals were high and dry unless another type of operation filled the void.

Enter now the third-level airlines. In 1964 there were only 15 of them. Four years later there were 240 operating among 850 communities. This more than made up for the cancellations by the trunks and regionals. In 1968 the third-level airlines carried 3.5

million passengers. Beeches, Cessnas, and Pipers, as well as Douglas DC–3's, Aero Commanders, Grummans, Canadian Twin Otters, and British-made Doves and Herons flew into and out of places like Tifton, Georgia; Jackson, Mississippi; Death Valley, California; and Grand Island, Nebraska. The rural community of Spencer, Iowa, was so anxious for access to big cities by air that it asked Minnesota's Fleet Airlines to bring in regular flights and agreed to make up any losses. "Air West" provided timetable "MiniLiner" service to towns in Oregon, Utah, and California with turbo-boosted Navajos. Davis Airlines linked College Station, Dallas, and Houston, Texas, by Cherokee SIXes. Executive Airlines of Boston, Sun Valley Air of Hailey, Idaho, and Scheduled Skyways of Fayetteville, Arkansas, flew Pipers. No less than thirteen commuter lines, according to a survey by *Flight* magazine published by George E. Haddaway, used Beech aircraft, notably that company's "99" model transport. In service with Trans-Michigan Airlines, the "99" required stewardesses no more than four feet, eleven inches tall so they could stand up in the cabin. Hulman Field Aviation of Terre Haute, Pennsylvania Commuter Airlines of New Cumberland, and Trans-Mo Airlines, of Jefferson City were among the carriers using Cessnas.

Enter now, too, 3,800 General Aviation air taxi services like the Sedalia-Marshall-Boonville Stage Lines, operator of Stage 22 from Muskogee. The air taxis were the missing link in a pattern of U.S. air transport in flux. More than ten thousand airports and landing strips dotted the countryside. Fewer than fifteen hundred of them daily felt the impact of the wheels of scheduled airplanes. The remainder depended for air communication on the on-demand and charter operator and on the airplane which was privately or corporately owned.

A storm began breaking. General Aviation was getting in the way of "scheduled" flights. As early as December 1964, William T. Piper, Jr., began building a backfire against criticism of its operations. In an address before the Pittsburgh Society of Security Analysts, he stated that nonairline, nonmilitary aircraft were the biggest users of the nation's air space. General Aviation, he pointed out, was comprised of a fleet forty times the size of that of the airlines.

Then on March 9, 1967, a propeller-driven twin-engine Beechcraft, with only the pilot aboard, and a Trans World Airlines twin-engine Douglas DC–9 jet bearing twenty-one passengers and a crew of four collided over Urbana, Ohio. No one survived.

On July 19, 1967, a propeller-driven twin-engine Cessna 310 with three persons aboard and a Piedmont Airlines three-engine

THE LIGHTPLANE VS. THE 747
The Cub and its spawn were in trouble.

Boeing 727 jet bearing seventy-four passengers and a crew of five collided over Hendersonville, North Carolina. No one survived.

On September 9, 1969, a Piper Cherokee, with only a student pilot aboard, and an Allegheny Airlines DC–9 bearing seventy-eight passengers and a crew of four collided near Indianapolis. No one survived.

Only days later a congressman, Benjamin S. Rosenthal, whose district included La Guardia Airport—one of the three major airports in the New York metropolitan area—plus Flushing Airport, a nearby private field, told a news conference, "Something is wrong with a system which permits a private pilot with only thirty-eight hours of experience to be in the same air space where an airliner is descending for a landing."

Some weeks later a hearing into mid-air collisions was convened in Washington, D.C., by the National Transportation Safety Board, an independent federal government agency. Bitter words were exchanged between those who would ban General Aviation aircraft from the vicinity of big airports and those who challenged anyone's right to do so. Two Cincinnati housewives formed a Citizens for Aviation Safety Committee, an airline passenger pressure group. The *New York Times* editorialized, "The commercial airlines are public carriers, regulated by law, open to all. . . . They are a vital part of the national transportation system. Where limited airport

facilities necessitate a choice, common carriers should have preference over private planes. Delay in making that choice is an invitation to disaster." The *Washington Star* said, "Measures like a priority system for passenger jets are vital." Donald Bain, writer and former airline publicist, published a book, *The Case Again Private Aviation,* an impressively documented work that was flawed by a dust jacket blurb stating that a half million noncommercial aircraft were now using U.S. airways. The General Aviation fleet numbered only a fourth of that as of January 1, 1969, a total of 124,237. The Safety Board publicly acknowledged the existence of a problem in the pilot who imbibed and flew. The spokesman for a sister government agency said that as many as 200 of the 692 fatal accidents in private aircraft in 1968 had been caused by pilots numbed by the effects of alcohol. *Time* magazine referred to the third-level airlines as "the white-knuckle carriers" and said their safety standards often were third rate. A study directed by Ralph Nader, an advocate of consumer causes, said that manufacturers of small airplanes were turning out "the most lethal of the major forms of transportation in the U.S." It was a harsh indictment, supported largely by a tenuous charge of nonfeasance in safety design. A national Sunday supplement magazine, *Parade,* ran an article brutally critical of private flying. Capt. John Harkin of Allegheny Airlines commented: "I blame the manufacturers and salesmen (of light aircraft) for causing

209

a false impression that flying is an easy, casual hobby." The *New York Times Sunday Magazine* published an article with a picture showing a TWA 342-passenger Boeing 747 jet airliner waiting for a runway to take off—a five-seat Piper Aztec was ahead of it in line. The headline read: "THE PIPER CUB VS. THE 747."

The Cub and its spawn, and all of General Aviation, were in trouble.

Twenty-eight domestic mid-air collisions occurred among aircraft of all descriptions in calendar 1969. Four involved lightplanes and airline transports. In one of those, a lightplane pilot was killed. In two of the four collisions no one was killed or injured. Of those four, the sole disastrous one was that between the DC–9 and the Cherokee at Indianapolis. Of the other twenty-four collisions, twenty-two occurred between lightplanes, one between a lightplane and a navy fighter, and one between a lightplane and a helicopter. Thirty-six persons died in the twenty-four collisons.

Author Bain supplied a hair-raising statistic. Pilots had always been reluctant to report a near-miss—aircraft passing each other too close for safety—for fear of disciplinary action for their part in the incident. In January 1968, the Federal Aviation Administration granted immunity to pilots reporting near-misses. In 1967 the near-misses reported were slightly more than 500. For 1968 they came to 2,230.

As compared with that of the domestic airlines, the accident record of General Aviation was not good. In 1969 the airlines accident rate for every million aircraft miles flown was 0.024, that of General Aviation 1.31. The airlines' fatality rate for each million aircraft miles was 0.059, that of General Aviation 0.173. In the number of passengers killed, the airlines were down from 326 in calendar 1960 to 132 in 1969. General Aviation had gone up in the same period from 787 to 1,388. As in all statistical studies, the numbers were deceptive without analysis. The airlines' fatality rate had vastly improved. In those nine years they had tripled the number of passengers carried annually. The number of General Aviation aircraft miles flown was up from 1,768,704,000 to 3,773,000,000 during the nine years.

In assessing the meaning of the General Aircraft record, the number of airplane movements had to be taken into account. Every takeoff, like every initial pressure on an accelerator pedal by a motorist, exposed pilot and passengers to the hazard of accident. To transport 1,000 persons in airplanes seating 6 persons each, required movement of 166 aircraft. Only 10 aircraft movements were required in airplanes seating 100. Skills and individual judgment, whether by a pilot in an airline cockpit or one in a private airplane, or by the driver of a car, varied widely. The variation among those of General Aviation pilots was embossed on the record. It availed nothing to argue that limited skills and judgment cost the lives of 56,400 persons in land-borne motor vehicle accidents, more than 40 times the number killed in nonairline flying, in 1969. Everyone drove a car. Personal flying was esoteric and therefore suspect. General Aviation didn't even come out well in the fatality record on a vehicle population basis. The airplane figure was one death for every 91 vehicles, the highway toll one for every 1,844.

Another way of looking at it, however, showed that the number of General Aviation deaths in 1940 was 359 for 264 million miles flown. In 1968 less than four times that number occurred for 3,740 million—fourteen times the number of miles.

Piper Aircraft itself looked on the General Aviation record with dismay and some mystification. At its factory sites it had had a fine safety record for four decades. In tens of thousands of takeoffs and landings, Piper had experienced one mid-air collision. One accident was too close to home. Dan, one of Howard Piper's sons, was killed in 1961 flying alone from Cambridge, where he had just been accepted for the fall term at Harvard, to Lock Haven. His airplane struck a mountain in the Catskills near Otisville, New York, in level flight on a clear day. No one ever knew what happened. He was seventeen.

The total number of deaths in General Aviation was not the figure that counted in the public response and in the fevered world of politics. It was the number of innocent airline passengers who had perished in collisions between airliners and General Aviation aircraft like those at Urbana, Hendersonville, and Indianapolis. What in hell were the lightplanes doing in those particular air spaces anyway?

Nobody except those in General Aviation paid much heed when the National Transportation Safety Board issued its reports on the tragic Urbana, Hendersonville, and Indianapolis collisions. At Urbana at impact, it said, the airline DC–9 was exceeding a federal air regulation restricting an arriving aircraft to a speed of 288 miles an hour within 30 miles of its destination airport and when under ten thousand feet of altitude. The airplane was descending at about 370 miles per hour. The report concluded, "The board determines the probable cause of this accident was the failure of the DC–9 crew to see and avoid the Beechcraft."

The safety board ascribed the probable cause of the Hendersonville collision to the deviation of the Cessna from the flight path it was to have followed under an instrument flight rule clearance and added that "minimum control procedures" by the Federal Aviation Administration in handling the smaller airplane had been a contributing cause.

The probable cause of the collision near Indianapolis, said the safety board, was the "deficiencies in the collision avoidance capability of Air Traffic Control (ATC) system of the Federal Aviation Administration in a terminal area wherein there were mixed Instrument Flight Rules (IFR) and Visual Flight Rules (VFR) traffic. The deficiencies included the inadequacy of the 'see-and-avoid' concept under the circumstances of this case; the technical limitations of radar in detecting all aircraft; and the absence of Federal Aviation Regulations which would provide a system of adequate separation of mixed VFR and IFR traffic in terminal areas."

The chief industrial organization opposed to General Aviation was the Air Transport Association of America, airline trade group.

General Aviation had no spokesman of that strength. It was fragmented by thirty-three different self-seeking organizations speaking in as many voices. Some were emotionally irresponsible. The periodical press oriented toward the private and corporate airplane spat at its critics. Congressman Rosenthal, Ralph Nader, Donald Bain, and the newspapers evoked quick and often savage response from the defenders of General Aviation.

The most outspoken of the proponents of General Aviation was a man with the fingers of a fine pianist (which he was), the face of a pugilist (which he was not), and the stance of a trial lawyer. His name was Max Karant. A born propagandist, he was tough; he gave no quarter. He was obdurate on a strict interpretation of Section 104 of the Federal Aviation Act of 1958. It read: "There is hereby recognized and declared to exist in behalf of any citizen of the United States a public right to freedom of transit in air commerce through the navigable air space of the United States." Karant fueled the fires of controversy. Vice president of the Aircraft Owners and Pilots Association—biggest organization of its kind in the world—editor of its magazine, the *AOPA Pilot,* and an excellent flier himself, he wouldn't budge an inch from his insistence that a private pilot had as much right to land at a major airport as the captain of an airline transport, provided he observed the rules and his airplane was properly equipped. The airports were built with the taxpayers' money.

Elements in the lightplane manufacturing industry and in user associations more given to compromise issued explanatory, humorless, and—beleaguered as they were—defensive monographs. R. Dixon Speas Associates, management consultants, prepared for the Utility Aircraft Council of the Aerospace Industries Association, a trade group, a *Fact Book on the Magnitude and Economic Impact of General Aviation.* The council was composed of lightplane manufacturers and their suppliers. One of the Speas conclusions scared the pants off opponents of General Aviation: the fleet of nonairline, nonmilitary aircraft would grow from 122,200 (as of 1967) to 260,000 in 1980.

The Federal Aviation Administration issued its own forecast, and this one, to opponents of General Aviation, was even more unnerving than the Speas study. The 691,695 pilots (encompassing students and those certificated as private, commercial, airline transport, helicopter, and glider airmen) of record in 1969, said the FAA, would grow to 1,440,500 by 1980. It was plausible. In 1968 "student starts" were pushing 150,000 a year. The forecast was for at least 300,000 by 1975.

The National Business Aircraft Association (NBAA), with a purpose implicit in its name, issued a monograph quoting *Fortune* magazine as saying that nearly 375 of the 500 leading industrial companies in the United States operated their own aircraft. The NBAA estimated the business fleet as of January 1, 1969, at 22,482.

Piper Aircraft itself issued a study prepared by Arthur D. Little, Incorporated, another research group, designed to bring the charge of overcrowded skies into focus. Bill, Jr., and Jake Miller wrote prefaces. Among the points emphasized were—

(1) "As many people use General Aviation each year as are carried on all the airlines." (2) "Access to any airport must be based upon reasonable requirements of aircraft and pilot capability. . . . No priority treatment should be given to any class of aviation." (3) General Aviation airplanes acted as feeders to the scheduled airline fleets.

The Arthur Little study devoted much space to the insufficiency of airway facilities and the scanty number of airports. W. T. Piper had been saying that for three decades. In 1939 a congressional committee looking into the matter reported that the U.S. airport situation was a mess. Thirty years later it was still a mess. The mess went beyond that. It encompassed airport and airway traffic control. The reasons were twofold: the federal administrative bureaucracy was inert, and Congress consistently refused to pony up enough money to galvanize a program.

A start had been made toward improvement during the presidency of John F. Kennedy. A special presidential task force in November 1961 advised him that updating the airway-airport system would cost a half-billion dollars.

In the intervening years some expansion in the air space reserved for airplanes controlled from the ground did occur. A beginning was made on automatic plane-to-ground reporting of aircraft altitude. By the late 1960s only $176 million of the $500 million needed to boost flying safety had been appropriated by Congress.

General Aviation admitted to air traffic congestion—overcrowded skies—and the danger of collisions, but with reservations. It contended that congestion occurred only at a few major air terminals. Of these, three in the New York metropolitan area—Kennedy, La Guardia, and Newark—Chicago's O'Hare, and Washington's National were the worst. It contended that congestion took place only late in the afternoon and early evening, from 5 to 8 P.M., and that the commercial airlines bore a responsibility for it—five of them would schedule flights from the same airport to the same destination, such as New York to Chicago, at exactly the same time, and schedule arrivals *from* Chicago at the self-same airport at the self-same time. The congestion didn't get bad except in times of poor weather when traffic had to be slowed down in the interest of safety. On top of that, the controllers lacked the proper equipment to do their job.

General Aviation had a case. All it said was true. How good a case it had for using major terminals jointly with the airlines depended on the prejudices of the listener.

While the diverse elements of General Aviation manufacture and flying were subjecting themselves to couch analysis as an answer to criticism, three events intervened to bring everything to a head. The controllers revolted, the FAA began making noises about rationing airplane movements at airports, and Congress started consideration of legislation to modernize the nation's creaky air transport control system.

The controllers began "going by the book," meticulously applying the rules to every aircraft movement. They had been in the habit of bending the rules—providing less time-distance separation of aircraft, for example, than was specified—in order to boost the amount of traffic handled.

In instrument flying weather the slowdown produced chaos. Traffic backed up. A pilot a thousand miles from Chicago's O'Hare or some other airport of destination could not be given a takeoff clearance until he had been assigned a landing slot. Tens of thousands of airline passengers chafed at the delays. At New York's Kennedy alone, twenty thousand passengers on two hundred flights sat ground-borne in a single day. In Europe, westbound international flights were immobilized at their points of origin or diverted to U.S. terminals far from their intended ports of entry.

The FAA promptly got itself into hot water with the airlines and General Aviation alike by proposing stringent quotas for the more heavily burdened airports under IFR conditions. The number of outgoing and incoming flights handled would be cut. At Kennedy, the hours of 5 to 8 P.M. would be restricted to airline flights. Non-airline flying at La Guardia, Newark, O'Hare, and Washington National between those hours would be restricted. General Aviation aircraft accommodated had to be able to maintain an approach pattern speed of 150 knots and be equipped with a radar transponder giving their identities.

To further discourage small airplanes from using its three big airports, the Port of New York Authority imposed a twenty-five dollar minimum landing fee during peak hours of traffic.

The National Business Aircraft Association reacted. Testifying at a Department of Transportation hearing on the proposed rules, Robert B. Ward, executive vice president, suggested forty-one steps that could be taken without banning General Aviation airplanes from major, high-density airports. His organization, he said, opposed capacity allocations which denied business-owned and private aircraft access to the airports. The proposed rules, he said, were arbitrary and unfair.

Max Karant exploded at the FAA proposal. He issued a "Special Action Bulletin" to his members: "AOPA has warned that new restrictions to reduce air travel congestion and delay could cripple your flying. The FAA has now proposed such restrictions. . . . Time is limited. YOU SHOULD ACT NOW!"

The "action" he wanted constituted flooding the FAA offices in Washington, and those of congressmen and senators, with protests. He ran display advertisements in newspapers, attacking the FAA.

Nothing came of it. The FAA sat on its hands. Momentarily the controllers relented. Then again at the start of the vacation air travel season in 1969, they decided they had had a bellyful. They staged "sickouts." They were too ill to work. Again chaos ensued at the air terminals.

"We are at the eleventh hour," John H. Shaffer, administrator of the FAA, told Washington's National Press Club.

And again the controllers relented, abandoning their sickout.

The FAA ignored the NBAA's recommendations. In November 1969 under the prod of the Department of Transportation, it blueprinted another idea—establishing twenty-one "terminal control areas" in which traffic would be cut at the expense of nonairline aircraft. *Flight* magazine termed the proposal "about as popular as a dead mouse in a punch bowl." Meantime the FAA published a rule restricting nonairline aircraft operations at the five high-density airports in New York, Chicago, and Washington. On January 10, 1969, the NBAA filed a brief in the U.S. Court of Appeals for the District of Columbia seeking a review and stay of the rule. The rule, it said, was "arbitrary and capricious." The court upheld the FAA.

In 1968 Congress had begun hearings on an "Airport Development Act." They were long overdue. William T. Piper, Jr., observed it was time to turn up the wick.

"We can't solve our problems by arguing," he said as he tied flies at his home on Lock Haven's West Water Street for a fishing trip. "What's needed is money—money for airports and airway facilities. We need money for instrument landing systems at a lot more airports. It's not going to come from Congress unless the aviation community itself provides it." He conceded that any form of added taxation on General Aviation would not be readily accepted, much less popular.

At long last, some elements of U.S. aviation that had spoken from the Tower of Babel began drawing together in common cause. Bill, Jr., became chairman of an ad hoc "Aviation Progress Committee" composed of organizations that were the principal manufacturers of General Aviation aircraft, their power plants, electronic communications and navigation equipment, airframe construction materials, and distributor and service companies. It took a long time for Joseph Geuting, Jr., head of the Utility Aircraft Council, to put together the committee to offer testimony in Washington.

Prominent among other organizations heard were the airlines through their Air Transport Association, the National Business Aircraft Association, the Aircraft Owners and Pilots Association, and the National Air Transportation Conferences (NATC). Headed by Thomas S. Miles, the NATC was a mother hen to three groups: the Commuter Air Carrier Conference, composed of noncertificated airlines operating on schedules; the Air Taxi Conference, the airplane-charter group, and the Cargo/Mail Conference, composed of mail and cargo carriers.

Testifying on the proposed legislation, Alan S. Boyd, federal secretary of transportation, said, "The federal government has greater interest in promoting the efficiency of the common carrier (airline) system of air transportation than it does in promoting private air transportation and, where a choice must be made, the common carrier system will receive preference. . . ."

Max Karant, shooting from behind his barricades at anything that moved, called Boyd a dangerous man who misused his office.

Joseph B. Hartranft, Jr., AOPA president, testified that the AOPA's members "account for the ownership of about 70 percent" of the active General Aviation fleet. In brief, he supported a uniform excise tax on all aviation fuels used by all aircraft operators, a tax on air cargo waybills, and abolishment of airline ticket taxes.

Bill Piper, Jr.'s ad hoc committee presented its case. Before House and Senate committees and subcommittees he testified that General Aviation supported a higher tax on fuel provided that the money reaped from "user" charges be put into a "designated account" for both airport and airways improvement.

"The airport," he said, "is simply that portion of the airway that happens to be on the ground."

General Aviation airports, he said, had not benefitted much from the federal aid airport program, though two-thirds of the nation's airports, privately owned, as well as three thousand publicly owned, derived their day-to-day revenue wholly from fees and taxes paid by nonairline operations.

"General Aviation," said he, "is today making a direct and indirect contribution to the gross national product of from $6 billion to $9 billion which will grow by 1980 to from $16 billion to $24 billion. . . ."

He pointed out that about 90 percent of the airlines' passengers were enplaned at fewer than 150 stops.

What General Aviation wanted from any user taxes enacted, he emphasized, was "improved airways—perhaps they should be termed multi-lane, superhighways of the air—in order to bring to bear on the economy and into the nation's air transportation system additional tens, even hundreds of thousands, of aircraft."

The Airport and Airway Development Act of 1970 was adopted in separate bills by the Senate and the House, differences between the respective measures resolved, and sent to the president, who signed it. For General Aviation aircraft only it provided a federal tax of seven cents a gallon on fuel, to replace an existing tax of four cents, and a $25 annual aircraft registration fee on aircraft of 2,500 pounds maximum weight, plus two cents a pound on piston-powered planes and three and one-half on jets over that weight. For the airlines the bill provided an 8 percent (instead of the then current 5) ticket tax on domestic flights, a $3 head tax on outbound international passengers, and a 5 percent air cargo tax. A five-year program called for an annual expenditure of not less than $280 million for airports, $250 million for airways facilities and equipment, and $50 million for research and development.

In December 1969 the Utility Aircraft Council had cut its hawser to the Aerospace Industries Association to become the General Aviation Manufacturers Association (GAMA). On signature of the airport/airways bill, Joseph Geuting said it "will pump $15 billion into the national air transportation system over the next ten years." It was, he said, the greatest step forward for aviation and the traveling public in the recent history of the industry. Dwane Wallace, GAMA chairman, said that helping fill the seats of the commercial airlines' giant jets was one of General Aviation's main roles.

Thunder from the storm over the "crowded skies"—the airlines vs. General Aviation—still reverberated. For AOPA, alone unsanctified, Karant said the new law expressed its purposes in "loose cliches and platitudes." He added, "We want to know where all the money that it generates is going. The user charges are far in excess of what they should be because the entire proposed system will be built for the commercial airlines. In its complexity, it's useless to General Aviation. The General Aviation industry has been hoodwinked."

Whatever the validity of his arguments, the first six months of the recession year of 1970 were gloomy for General Aviation Manufacturers Association. While Detroit's business was off 12 percent and that of pleasure boating 5 percent, General Aviation suffered a cut of 50 percent.

Whatever the future held, it would take years to undo the evils to flying that decades of neglect had incurred.

The Raid

ON THE MORNING OF THURSDAY, January 23, 1969, Herbert J. Siegel, president of Chris-Craft Industries, a Delaware corporation, telephoned William T. Piper, Jr., president of the Piper Aircraft Corporation, with an announcement: Piper Aircraft was targeted for takeover.

"He told me," Bill, Jr., related later, " 'We have 200,500 of your shares and intend to tender for up to 300,000 at sixty-five dollars a share.' "

Chris-Craft was one of the world's biggest manufacturers of pleasure boats. It also dealt in plastic and latex forms, carpets, yarns and related products, organic chemicals, and the insecticide, DDT. Through subsidiaries, it owned and operated television stations in Los Angeles, Minneapolis–Saint Paul, and Portland, Oregon.

To say that the president of the aircraft company was surprised by Siegel's call was understating the case. On his own testimony, he and his family had never seriously considered combining with any other company, let alone yielding their financial control to someone else after almost four decades of independence.

In retrospect they recognized that the U.S. business climate was encouraging the acquisition of healthy companies by "conglomerates," highly diversified holding companies. It was strictly legal so long as the conglomerates adhered to the rules of the Securities and Exchange Commission and did not offend the antitrust division of the Justice Department. Such takeovers, some friendly, some against spirited opposition, were going on all the time. Newspaper financial pages regularly devoted a column to acquisitions. At that very moment one of Akron's oldest rubber companies was fighting an attempt to absorb it.

Piper Aircraft was ripe for a raid. Its sales for the fiscal year ended September 30, 1968, had been $96,724,000, a 20 percent increase over the previous year. (In 1969 they jumped to $106 million.) Net income per share of common stock was $2.36, an increase of 29 percent. Net income as a percent of sales was four, and that too was up by 0.3 percent. Working capital stood at almost $33 million. But the key figure in the annual report was the ratio of current assets to liabilities. That was 4.6 to 1.

While Piper Aircraft common shares had traded as high as $72.25 on the New York Stock Exchange in the eight months prior to Siegel's telephone call, a generally softening economy had reduced that sharply, along with the prices of hundreds of other stocks. In January Piper hovered around $50. In terms of the current market, it was a fairly low price-to-earnings ratio. The company's balance sheet contained no "water"—inventories and total assets were valued conservatively. The company followed a policy of accelerating its depreciation of the physical plant. If need be, it could borrow a considerable wad of money. Its credit was largely unused. Piper was a juicy morsel.

Within the aircraft manufacturing community, it stood out as a valuable operation. While it had lagged behind Beech and Cessna in dollar volume of aircraft sales since and including the year 1959, it was far ahead of them in earnings per share for five of those years. In 1964, for example, Piper's were $4.15 compared with Cessna's $2.27 and Beech's $1.21. In 1966 Piper, at $4.23, was ten cents ahead of Cessna and $1.19 ahead of Beech. Piper was second to Cessna in the number of aircraft delivered during the ten-year period but considerably ahead of Beech. There was a significance in the source of Piper's income: Beech and Cessna leaned heavily on Washington, D.C., for aircraft orders; Piper did not. In 1967 Beech's military orders accounted for four out of each ten of its aircraft sales dollars, Cessna's for three out of ten. Piper's were less than one in a hundred. Military contracts were an iffy source of income. They depended on the state of world affairs, the mood of the current White House administration, and the temper of Congress.

The arithmetic of the Chris-Craft takeover was simple.

When Piper went public in 1938 the number of common shares issued was 88,000. By 1940 that had become 136,000, and a four-for-one split in September 1944 brought the total to 670,000. By the time 100,000 shares had been issued to Consolidated-Vultee for the Stinson purchase, the number outstanding on December 1, 1948, was 845,000. Stock dividends and sales in the next sixteen years raised the outstanding shares to 1,620,000. The exercise of options raised that to 1,638,350 on September 30, 1968, at the close of the fiscal year.

One thousand dollars invested in Piper stock prior to May 4, 1944, now had a paper value of $118,500. Convair, anxious to unload its 100,000 shares in the dark days before the Tri-Pacer began pouring money into the till, sold its equity for approximately $300,000. As of the autumn of 1968, Convair would have had an equity of

$2,400,000 in Piper if it had held on. Many individual investors had let fortunes slip their grasp, among them Ted Weld, the former Piper vice president, and Gordon Curtis, Mr. Piper's old friend and confidant. Like Convair, they had sold their stock. Weld would have been a millionaire, Curtis that several times over.

Chris-Craft needed just over 50 percent of the issued Piper stock for absolute control, a bit more than 819,000 shares. That did pose a problem for Siegel. The Piper family owned approximately 30 percent of the common. One of the basic rules of the conglomerates' company acquisition by the process of buying shares on the open market was to tackle only such concerns as had their stock ownership thinly distributed. In such circumstances, a relatively small percentage of the stock would assure nominal control.

Six days before Siegel's telephone call to Bill, Jr., the *Value Line Newsletter,* an investors' service, told its customers that Piper stock had an "excellent" three-to-five-year appreciation potential. But it warned that Piper's relative market performance in the coming year would be below par. It observed that three investment trusts held 188,300 Piper shares at the end of the latest reporting period.

In its issue of September 1968 *Dun's Review,* the financial periodical, carried an article by "Anonymous," described in a footnote as a "veteran who has manned the barricades in many a takeover war." Titled "The Anatomy of a Raid," the article could have been a blueprint for Chris-Craft's assault on Piper. It related the story of a raid on an imaginary company that had treasured its assets, did not conduct a systematic search for potential corporate marriage partners, and failed to entertain the idea of acquiring some smaller companies. It did not have much authorized but unissued stock to dilute the holdings of a conglomerate bent on a raid.

The typical raider (said *Dun's*) offered the stockholders of a company targeted for takeover a one-for-one share trade at a handsome premium. He offered sweeteners to shareholders—a gift of subordinated (that is, unsecured) debentures, promises to pay, carrying 6 percent interest, plus a gift of warrants to buy his own stock. The practices of the U.S. Internal Revenue Service made raiding attractive. If the victim company was paying $1.90 per share (for example) in dividends, the raider—unlike the ordinary private stockholder, who paid a much higher rate—would pay only fourteen cents of the $1.90 in taxes. This was because of the corporate tax rate and the intracompany regulation of the IRS. The IRS excluded 85 percent of the dividend from taxation. So the raider netted $1.76 on each share acquired. Half of his interest payments on the debentures were a write-off against business expenses. If the interest was $3.00 he paid only $1.50. This, subtracted from his net on the dividend per share, left him with a profit of twenty-six cents per share. To the raider the warrants were gravy. To exercise them the stockholder had to put additional money into his company. In Wall Street, warrants were known as "funny money" and "Castro's pesos" after Cuba's Fidel.

But the raider's biggest prize was the target company's assets. Selling some of those provided him with more cash.

Fortune magazine for February 1969, in an article by Gilbert Burck that had been prepared months before Siegel's call to Bill, Jr., warned of the current business mood in stock acquisitions: "Some of their [the conglomerates'] sharpest critics, significantly are conservative multimarket managers like President Roy Ash of Litton Industries and President G. William Miller of Textron. . . . Both have denounced 'arithmetic mergers' and 'mergers by numbers,' or combinations in which sound planning for internal growth is subordinated to the mere piling up of assets. . . .

"The targets of this aggression are some of the most upright, prudent, powerful, and self-assured corporations in the land."

Fortune hardly explained the consternation in Lock Haven on January 23. Who in the world would have supposed that anyone could have designs on the Piper Aircraft Corporation, least of all the members of the Piper family in their mountain-girt little community in mid-Pennsylvania?

For the moment, Chris-Craft's Siegel didn't quite follow the procedure outlined in *Dun's Review*.

The *Wall Street Journal* of January 31 carried a full-page advertisement by Chris-Craft offering to purchase up to three hundred thousand Piper shares at sixty-five dollars. The offer would expire at twelve noon eastern standard time on Monday, February 3, "unless extended." Brokers would get a commission of one dollar a share. Half the advertisement was addressed to Piper stockholders and reproduced a letter of transmittal to be used "in submitting your shares of common stock to Chris-Craft Industries, Inc." The tender included no sweeteners—as yet—beyond the handsome price. The Chris-Craft advertisement stated somewhat anomalously that the company was making the purchases "for investment with a view to control of Piper, but it does not presently have any specific plan or proposal to liquidate Piper, to acquire control of Piper, to sell its assets or to merge with any other companies or to make any major change in its business or corporate structure."

Piper common closed on the New York Stock Exchange on the day before Siegel's telephone call at 52½. On the twenty-third it closed at 60½.

Conscious of what the effect of all this might be on the morale of company personnel and the field force, Bill, Jr., on the day after

Siegel's call, addressed a letter to employes, dealers, and distributors reciting the content of the Chris-Craft message. Management, he wanted to make clear, knew what was going on. Simultaneously, a notice was issued to the financial wires: "It has not been Piper Aircraft's policy in the past to consider merger offers. The tender offer . . . was made without notice to, or discussion with, Piper's management. Piper's management is studying the offer and will advise Piper's shareholders as to management's evaluation and recommendation as soon as possible. Piper's management urges that no shareholder act upon the offer before receiving management's recommendation."

The next day a telegram was drafted to be sent to all Piper shareholders: "The board of directors . . . strongly urges you not to tender your Piper shares to Chris-Craft Industries, Inc., in response to its tender offer of sixty-five dollars per share. A letter containing important information is being mailed to all Piper shareholders. The [Chris-Craft] offer remains open until February 3, and we urge you not to act hastily." It was signed by W. T. Piper, Jr.

The tone of the letter, under date of January 27, was predictable: "Your board of directors has carefully studied this offer and is convinced that it is inadequate and not in the best interests of Piper's shareholders. Accordingly, your board unanimously urges that it be rejected. Not one member of your board of directors or management will tender his shares. Obviously, if Chris-Craft is suddenly willing to offer you sixty-five dollars per share for your shares, Chris-Craft must believe that Piper stock is worth substantially more than it is offering. . . ."

The next day another letter was mailed to shareholders, urging them to send proxies to the present board of directors "regardless of the number of shares you may own."

On January 29 Bill, Jr., took action after extended conversations with members of the directorate, his father, and brothers. If Chris-Craft's present and prospective Piper holdings could be diluted—assuming that the tender offer would harvest in the area of three hundred thousand shares—it might make it too expensive to attain absolute control. He was not, then, entertaining any idea of disposing of any family-owned stock as a battle strategem. He had a weapon for the dilution—three hundred thousand stockholder-authorized but unissued shares of common. Piper Aircraft had a friend in Grumman, on Long Island. Bill, Jr., approached L. G. Evans, Grumman's president, with a proposal that he, Evans, buy the three hundred thousand shares at sixty-five dollars. When Chris-Craft heard about this, it pointed out that the price was the same that Piper had termed inadequate only two days before. Evans signed an agreement to buy. Then he telephoned Chris-Craft.

"Lou Evans," the magazine *Business Week* quoted C. Leonard Gordon, a Chris-Craft vice president, as saying, "told us he had a deal to buy three hundred thousand shares of Piper, and asked whether we were interested in selling out."

Siegel had no intention of selling out. He promptly filed suit to vacate a Piper-Grumman deal on the ground that it violated the antitrust laws. Both Grumman and Piper manufactured aircraft. Chris-Craft did not. A number of conditions that were not acceptable to the New York Stock Exchange led Grumman and Piper to cancel the deal.

Meantime Siegel had had a resounding success with his tender offer. On February 4 Chris-Craft announced that it now owned 545,000 shares. The additional shares had cost about $22,400,000. The acquisition of 300,000 more would give Chris-Craft 51 percent of the outstanding Piper stock. On February 27 the company filed with the Securities and Exchange Commission a registration statement covering another tender offer, this time for the requisite number of shares, or more, on an exchange basis.

On the same day that Chris-Craft announced its prize of 545,000 shares, Piper's annual meeting of shareholders was called to order in Lock Haven. The current slate of eight friendly directors was nominated for reelection. So were four officers of Chris-Craft—Gordon, Siegel, J. J. Rochlis, and Lawrence R. Barnett, another vice president. To permit counting stockholders' proxies, the meeting was recessed to February 10. Fighting for time, Piper's president obtained additional recesses until March 25. The *Wall Street Journal* reported that Piper was challenging a substantial number of Chris-Craft proxies.

In the intervening weeks Piper again moved to dilute Chris-Craft's holdings. It negotiated with the United States Concrete Pipe Company for outright ownership of its properties in exchange for 320,000 shares of Piper stock. U.S. Concrete Pipe manufactured both concrete pipe and vitrified clay pipe at eight plants in the east and north-central states and at two others in Florida. In calendar 1968 its sales were $18,920,000 and its operating income after taxes $935,000, equivalent to $2.92 for each of the proffered Piper shares. Piper also moved to acquire 99 percent of Southply, Incorporated, a manufacturer of plywood, in Natchitoches, Louisiana, specializing in southern pine exterior grade construction sheathing. An exchange deal covered 149,199 shares of Piper common. The acquisition agreement guaranteed to Piper that Southply would have net earnings of $900,000 before taxes in calendar 1969.

On March 25 the election judges submitted their report to the reconvened annual meeting. They awarded Chris-Craft valid proxies for only 365,601 shares. W. T. Piper, Sr., Howard Piper, Tony Piper, and Bill, Jr., were announced as directors for the coming year, plus Pool and Jamouneau. Gordon and Rochlis assumed seats on the board, half the number Chris-Craft had nominated. The inclusion of W. T. Piper, Sr., was a courtesy to the founder of the company and patriarch of the clan. He promptly resigned as a director and chairman and was named to those posts emeritus. Both Mr. Piper and Jamouneau, company secretary, bawled without shame as the resignation was offered and approved. They had worked together for thirty-five years. Bill, Jr., assumed the chair pro tem.

Now the Pipers made another move. The directorate was expanded from eight to nine, giving Chris-Craft not a quarter of the votes but only 22-odd percent of them. Places eight and nine on the board were awarded Putnam B. McDowell, a vice president and director of the Pittsburgh Coke and Chemical Company, and Wesley C. Adams, an officer of the Hillman Land Company, also of Pittsburgh. It so happened that the U.S. Concrete Pipe Company was a subsidiary of Pittsburgh Coke, and the Hillman Land Company owned 61.5 percent of Pittsburgh Coke's stock.

At an organizational meeting following adjournment, Bill, Jr., was reelected president and made chairman, and Tony was reelected a vice president. Pool and Jamouneau retained their posts as treasurer and secretary. To nail down family administrative control, Howard Piper was made executive vice president and chief operating officer.

If Chris-Craft had won round one in the free-for-all for control of Piper, round two had gone to an embattled industrial family on the bank of the Susquehanna's West Branch.

The distress in the affairs of Piper and Chris-Craft was compounded, no doubt, by a consistent underestimation of each other's stubbornness. In terms of personalities this came down to a test of wills between Siegel and the Pipers. If Piper could not remain fiercely independent—if it must submit to deflowering—it wanted the act performed by someone with affection. Siegel was not the man.

Chris-Craft lost no time challenging the U.S. Concrete-Southply acquisitions. It stated that they could not comply with regulations of the New York Stock Exchange, that the deal diluted its Piper holdings, and that Piper actually sought a delisting of its stock to escape the exchange rules.

The New York Stock Exchange did indeed on Thursday, April 3, announce that its listing agreement with Piper had been violated by the issuance of 469,199 shares to conclude the deals without stockholder approval. The exchange board of governors voted to suspend trading in Piper common effective at the opening of the market on the succeeding Monday and authorized the filing of an application with the SEC to delist the stock. The financial wires reported that Piper officials had no comment.

The battle was being taken over by the lawyers, the money managers, the propagandists adroit at finding chinks in the armor of the opposition, and by the professionals trained in the art of punching and counterpunching in intercorporate fisticuffs under the rules set forth by law.

While its tender offer was under review by the SEC, Chris-Craft on April 7 was told by that body to stop acquiring Piper shares on the open market. *Business Week* reported, ". . . Chris-Craft held 33 percent of Piper stock, and believed . . . that if it could not buy Piper shares on the open market, neither could Piper or its allies."

At mid-month Piper rescinded its agreements on the acquisitions of U.S. Concrete and Southply. The company said it would "move promptly" to obtain the lifting of the suspension in the trading of its stock on the exchange. McDowell and Adams would resign from the directorate. Piper denied that the rescission was due directly to the Chris-Craft takeover attempt. "Since the agreements were executed," it stated, "various problems not related to Chris-Craft's current attempt to obtain control had become apparent. . . ." Chris-Craft had no comment.

On Friday, April 18, the stock exchange board of governors voted to resume trading in Piper stock at the opening the following Monday. During the ten trading days since April 7 the stock's high and low on the Philadelphia-Baltimore-Washington exchange were 69½ and 64¼.

Two stock-dilution maneuvers had failed. Pending before the SEC was a Chris-Craft proposal for another tender offer that, if successful, would give the Delaware conglomerate a solid majority of the shares in the Piper Aircraft Corporation. The only avenue of escape from that appeared to be absorption by another company. On May 8 Piper and its founding family surrendered to exigency. Their press release read:

"The Bangor Punta Corp. and the Piper family have reached an agreement whereby Bangor Punta will acquire the Piper family's more than 500,000-share interest in the Piper Aircraft Corp. . . .

"Bangor Punta has agreed to file a registration statement with the Securities and Exchange Commission covering a proposed exchange offer for any and all the remaining outstanding shares of Piper Aircraft for a package of Bangor Punta securities to be valued in the judgment of the First Boston Corp. [a leading New York financial house] at not less than $80 per Piper share. . . .

"Mr. [W. T.] Piper [Jr.] said that in view of Bangor Punta's long-standing policy of maintaining autonomy in the management of its operating companies and the similarity of operating philosophy between the two companies, he and the Piper family would strongly support the merger and would recommend it to all shareholders. . . .

"Sales of the combined companies will reach $450 million in fiscal 1969 with approximately $180 million, or 40 percent, in the aircraft, recreational, and leisure-time fields."

Except for an implied administrative control, the Piper family was relinquishing its empire, subject to approval by the SEC.

What was Bangor Punta? Like many another holding company, it was unknown outside financial circles, but there it was big. *Fortune* magazine listed it at 326th among the country's leading 500 corporations. Diversified companies constituted no less than 390 of the magazine's 500. Bangor Punta's manufactories turned out sailboats, houseboats, campers, motor homes, lifesaving resuscitators, traffic control devices, law enforcement equipment (chemical Mace, handguns, tear gas, gas masks, tear gas grenade launchers), emergency power units, marine power generators, and total energy and environmental control systems. It manufactured almost all the alcohol breath-testing equipment sold to U.S. police departments. It produced cottonseed oil from 58,000 acres of land it owned in California's San Joaquin Valley and from 6,000 in Arizona. It leased 47,500 additional acres for this purpose. It owned Metcalf and Eddy, a Boston-based consulting and engineering firm. It provided business management services.

Piper had chosen a marriage partner of considerable girth.

The name Bangor Punta derived from two of the company's early acquisitions, the Bangor and Aroostook Railroad, in Maine, and the Punta Alegre Sugar Corporation in Cuba, later expropriated by Fidel Castro.

The question, What was Bangor Punta? more properly could have been put, *Who* is Bangor Punta? The magazine *Metalworking News* said that the power behind the company was Nicolas M. Salgo, fifty-five, a naturalized Hungarian who had bootstrapped his way to the chairmanship.

In a space of only nine years, Salgo had put together a multi-industry corporation that was about to wind up its fiscal year with revenues of $334 million. A Wall Street acquaintance described the feat as "a classic demonstration of managerial acumen." Salgo was graduated from Hungary's Pazmany University with a law degree in 1936.

When Lloyd's of London opened its doors to non-Commonwealth members for the first time, Salgo was one of only seven Americans admitted.

Bangor Punta's annual report for the fiscal year ended September 28, 1968, had carried a foreword by Salgo: "We believe that growth is an absolute necessity. We cannot expect full commitment from our people unless we provide them with the potential for both human and economic growth. A company in a stationary status, without growth, cannot satisfy human aspirations."

The report quoted the "Boston Consulting Group": "Conglomerates are the normal and natural business form for efficiently channeling investment into the most productive uses. If nature takes its course, then conglomerates will become the dominant form of business organization, particularly in the United States."

President and chief executive officer of Bangor Punta was David W. Wallace. An engineering graduate of Yale, he was awarded a doctor of jurisprudence degree by the Harvard Law School in 1951. He went up fast. On the boards of several other corporations, Wallace was named to his Bangor Punta posts in May 1967.

So much for the bare bones of biography. What the administrative personnel of Piper Aircraft not privy to what was transpiring between Lock Haven and Greenwich, Connecticut—seat of Bangor Punta—wanted to know was the temperature and pulse rate of the Salgo interests. How did they operate their divisions? A study of BP by the Harvard Business School in 1968 supplied a clue.

It quoted Wallace as saying, "We must avoid like a plague having centralized headquarters. These divisions of ours are operated in most instances by the entrepreneurs who founded them and operated them successfully for many years."

Men working on East Bald Eagle Street who had been on tenterhooks since January drove out to the country club for a highball in celebration.

Insofar as Chris-Craft was concerned, they were premature.

Only a day elapsed between the Piper press release on Bangor Punta and a blast by Chris-Craft in Washington, the precincts of the SEC, complaining that the announcement was a clear "gun jump" —offering shares to the public without first filing with the SEC. The SEC, said Chris-Craft, should call Piper to an accounting.

On May 14 Bangor Punta negotiated the purchase of 120,000 Piper shares as a prelude to the filing of a prospectus with the SEC for the acquisition of a majority of the stock. This, said Arthur L. Liman, a Chris-Craft attorney, was the crowning indignity. Leonard Gordon, the Chris-Craft vice president, explained: "We were offered those shares, but we had been told by the SEC that neither we nor anybody else bidding for Piper could buy them." He added, "The SEC goofed, they forgot to tell them [Bangor Punta]."

The SEC acted. It issued a voluntary consent decree barring Bangor Punta from buying any more Piper stock. But the fat was already in the fire.

On May 21 Chris-Craft published its tender offer, duly sanctioned by the SEC. It would exchange its preferred stock, $2 convertible series of 1969 (convertible between August 1, 1969, and June 1, 1979); warrants to purchase Chris-Craft common at $25 and $10 cash for a minimum of 80,000 and up to 300,000 (and at Chris-Craft's option, up to an additional 100,000) shares of Piper Aircraft common in the ratio of one share of Chris-Craft convertible preferred, plus two warrants for one share of Piper common. Tendering Piper shareholders would also receive the regular quarterly 35-cent Piper dividend payable in June 1969 and interest at $5.36 annually for each share tendered. The exchange offer expired at 5 P.M. New York time, June 5 "unless extended."

Within hours of the Chris-Craft tender Piper had a flyer in the mails to its stockholders headed: "DO NOT TENDER YOUR PIPER AIRCRAFT STOCK TO CHRIS-CRAFT." The flyer stated that Chris-Craft's offer was "objectively evaluated" to be worth seventy-two to seventy-three dollars a Piper share, though the stock was selling at seventy-seven dollars.

"Why get involved with a financial 'house of cards' like Chris-Craft?" asked Piper's management. While Chris-Craft's debt-equity ratio was one to three, its per share earnings had decreased from 1967 to 1968. "Intangible" assets accounted for almost a quarter of its total assets. "Piper's low debt position," continued the flyer, "would offer Chris-Craft the ideal outlet to further its acquisition path via additional debt, more preferred or convertible 'paper' . . . the usual conglomerate route now being reviewed by Congress as being unsound for the economy."

Piper's management described Bangor Punta as a bigger, financially stronger corporation, with a proven growth and profit record:

	BANGOR PUNTA	CHRIS-CRAFT
1968 sales	$259 million	$74 million
% change	up 61	up 3
Earnings per share	$2.61	$1.89
Current assets	$168 million	$46 million
Working capital	$120 million	$30 million

"Bangor Punta," concluded the flyer, "has agreed to offer Piper shareholders securities conservatively valued by the First Boston Corp. at $80 per share . . . more than 10 percent above the value of the Chris-Craft offer. Bangor Punta has a larger share of Piper stock than Chris-Craft and the support of the Piper management which is vehemently opposed to Chris-Craft's take-over efforts."

The Piper family's shares were on the scale. Herbert J. Siegel's curt telephone call to W. T. Piper, Jr., on January 23 had started quite a fire.

Chris-Craft netted only 98,000 Piper shares in its second tender offer. It had sunk some $35 million into Piper stock, plus the securities issued to obtain the final block, and with approximately 650,000 shares it was still far from its goal. As for the warrants to purchase Chris-Craft common at $25, that stock had closed on May 16 at 21 7/8 and on May 27 at 20 1/4.

"Our stock," said Gordon after his comment had been laundered for publication, "fell out of bed and our tender offer fell on its behind."

Eight days after the Chris-Craft tender, Bangor Punta filed with the SEC a registration statement covering its proposed exchange offers to Piper stockholders. There would be two separate packages of securities: (1) For Piper shareholders other than "certain members of the Piper family," Bangor Punta would exchange one share of its own common, 3.25 of its existing warrants to purchase BP common at fifty-five dollars per share, and fifteen dollars principal amount of a new 5½ percent convertible subordinated debenture due in 1994 for each share of Piper stock. (2) For "certain members" of the Piper family, BP would exchange one share of its common, 2.2 warrants, and the debentures. If successful in obtaining 50 percent or more of the Piper stock, and if in the opinion of the First Boston Corporation, the value of the BP securities delivered to the family under the exchange offer was less than eighty dollars, then BP would promptly pay the Piper family in cash or securities the difference between the value of the package offered the family and eighty dollars. The offers were subject to approval by BP stockholders and the SEC.

In mid-July Chris-Craft's Gordon and Rochlis wrote Piper shareholders that Bill, Jr., "fails to disclose that he and his family have entered into a private agreement with Bangor Punta which provides them with a lucrative personal financial incentive for promoting the Bangor Punta offer over the Chris-Craft offer."

It made no difference. The First Boston Corporation was in the act of issuing a prospectus for Bangor Punta. The deal had been upped. Bangor Punta now was offering 1.2 of its common shares for each Piper share, warrants good for the purchase of 3.5 BP shares, and thirty-one dollars principal amount of debentures carrying a return of 8.25 percent. The terms offered the Piper family were unchanged. Its shares aggregated 501,090.

Chris-Craft raised its own ante, and again it made no difference. Bangor Punta's offer, effective July 18, lasted only six days and netted

105,000 Piper shares. By purchase on the open market of 101,564 more, BP now claimed 45 percent of the outstanding stock, Chris-Craft 40 percent. Everyone was profiting except the principal protagonists. While Bangor Punta had given out a package of securities for most of its Piper stock, it had had to pay seventy-six dollars a share for the 120,000 it had negotiated before the SEC put a stop order on open-market buying. Nor was BP through. The deal with the Pipers calling for payment of an "incentive" amounting to eighty dollars a share if BP gained outright majority ownership of the company could put BP on the hook for $15 million if the stock dropped to, say, fifty dollars. The stock didn't drop. By the time that BP announced on September 10 that it had succeeded in laying its hands on 50.7 percent of the Piper common, it was being traded in over-the-counter transactions as high as eighty-two dollars—in a securities market that had been on a toboggan for months.

Piper by then had been delisted by the New York Stock Exchange. At the close of trading on Friday, August 1, only 319,468 Piper Aircraft Corporation shares were in the "float"—free for bidding by any buyer. The exchange rules required 400,000.

How BP got its hands on the last block of stock to achieve a majority holding was explained perhaps in a book titled, *"Do You Sincerely Want to Be Rich?"* published in 1971. Detailing the collapse of Investors Overseas Services (IOS), a multibillion dollar firm headquartered in Europe and captained by Bernard Cornfeld, the authors wrote:

"Sometimes the chieftains of IOS pulled better deals out of the conglomerate whirl—as when Cornfeld caused the purchase of a block of Piper Aircraft shares. . . . Cornfeld heard a whisper that a take-over battle for Piper was impending. . . . This turned into one of the bitterest of all take-over battles, which reached a climax when Cornfeld flew dramatically to a meeting in Nassau and gave Bangor Punta the victory by selling them the block of Piper shares he controlled."

Insofar as ownership was concerned, the Pipers actually turned over their empire to the embattled behemoths, the conglomerates, on August 12. On that date the company announced the election of five new directors: Nicolas M. Salgo, W. Gordon Robertson, David W. Wallace, and John E. Flick, all officers and directors of Bangor Punta, and Lawrence R. Barnett, an officer and director of Chris-Craft. Howard and Thomas Francis Piper resigned from the board, along with Walter C. Jamouneau and Charles W. Pool. The fifth new director filled a vacancy open since April. Two other officers and directors of Chris-Craft, Rochlis and Gordon, remained as board members. Nicolas Salgo took over the chair. Jamouneau was elected a vice president.

Of the Piper boys, Howard and Bill, Jr., remained as part of the administration, the latter as a board member, president, and chief executive officer. Tony divorced himself completely from the company, moving to Texas to manage some of the family properties.

Thus ended the saga of Mr. Piper and the cubs who had come from his loins as independent aircraft manufacturers. The paper value of stock that had changed hands in the fight for control was close to $100 million. That was an awful lot of scratch to have been run up by a man who had begun his investment in the business four decades before—through the back door—with $400.

A Monarch Passes

AT EIGHTY-EIGHT MR. PIPER WAS
feeling his years. He shuffled rather than walked. His eyesight was
suffering, and his hearing. Tony Piper, ever in attendance on him
prior to the consummation of the company's absorption, had rigged
up earphones, a microphone, and an amplifier so that visitors could
talk to him without raising their voices. Sometimes Mr. Piper napped
in the big chair at his desk. Age notwithstanding, he showed up like
clockwork in his office five days a week and sometimes on Saturdays.
He browsed through his mail and talked with Tony or Bill, Jr., or
Pug. Now and then a company photographer would drop by and
ask if he would mind having his picture taken with a visiting guest
of the company. He enjoyed that, making a mouth as though he
didn't. He had read an article by a famous surgeon in the *Reader's
Digest* recommending jogging to strengthen the heart muscles. So,
summer and winter, he shuffle-jogged, hatless, to and from his home
on East Water Street, abutting the airport. He timed himself with a
stopwatch over the course of a mile and a half. It took him a half
hour, give or take a few seconds.

"I'm not very fast," he said, grimacing.

He was an inveterate gardener.

By spells he was morose. It showed not on his face, only in his
conversation. This was not the kind of a world he had been born
into. The disk harrow had preceded him by only three years, and
he was fourteen before Marconi succeeded in generating a radio
signal. Big business, big labor, big government, big spending, big
deficits, and what he looked upon as a creeping socialism in the
politics and economics of the times escaped his understanding. All
of it offended his sense of prudence.

He had erected an empire with his own hands from the clay
and straw of his own bricks. Now everyone was beating a path to
Washington, D.C., asking for handouts of prefabs. He had faced
his crises without whimpering for help and survived. The prototype
of what the new-day, long-haired social scientists called the classic,

233

unrepentant reactionary, he had no truck with left-leaning public office holders.

"A bad actor, that fellow," he would remark.

Current welfare riots, student violence, and crime in the streets of the big cities outraged his sense of discipline and orderliness.

The fight over control of his company had caused his cup of disillusionment to overflow.

He had been an obscure oil man in an obscure Pennsylvania town. By dint of persistence, imagination, persuasion—and a reasonable percentage of good guesses, necessary to any business—he had left his mark on the American scene. The name Piper was known throughout the world. His retailers sold his products in ninety-one foreign countries, and 400-odd dealers in the United States emblazoned his name on their offices and hangars. From stick-and-rag contraptions that flew seventy miles an hour, he had graduated to all-metal machines with almost four times that speed. From his factories in four decades had come more than 86,000 airplanes.

What was, essentially, an esoteric but romantic business had thrown him and his sons into the company of the mighty in politics, industry, and entertainment.

He had had his share of honors. Alderson-Broaddus College in Philippi, West Virginia, and Lycoming College in Williamsport, Pennsylvania, endowed him with honorary degrees. The National Aeronautic Association named him the Elder Statesman of Aviation, and the OX–5 Club, an exclusive fraternity of pioneer airmen, pronounced him Mr. Pennsylvania Aviation of All Time. The National Business Aircraft Association gave him its annual Award for Meritorious Service to Aviation "in recognition of his vision and determination which have brought the realm of flight to untold thousands of pilots and passengers the world over, and in tribute to his dynamic leadership of Piper Aircraft Corporation—producers of more civil aircraft than any other airframe manufacturer in the world." He was cited for outstanding service to flying by the Aviation Council of his state. The 99ers, an organization of women fliers, gave him the Amelia Earhart Award, named for the tousle-headed flier who disappeared on her transpacific flight in 1937. The town of Quehanna officially changed its name to Piper. The auditorium in the Fort Lauderdale High School, for which he donated the land, was named for him. So was a high school in a Fort Lauderdale suburb. His children and grandchildren contributed to an auditorium at the Harvard Graduate School of Design, and that too bore his name.

He had earned his plaudits. At a time when private flying was

HONORS SHOWERED UPON HIM
Mr. Piper and Aircraft Distributors and Manufacturers Association trophy.

reserved to men with money and to adventurers in goggles and silk scarves, he produced airplanes within the means of shoe store clerks and youngsters who pumped gas at filling stations. To hundreds of thousands of men and women he supplied the ecstasy of slipping the bonds of earth and becoming one with the flight of eagles. Thousands who fought the nation's wars and carried on the nation's commerce on wings first felt the tug of wind on stick and rudder in the cockpit of a Piper airplane. He recognized and filled a need for executive-type aircraft priced for a business community that measured personal income in five figures. He piloted his own airplane up and down the land preaching the gospel of flight.

"Bridges are expensive," he said. "I can fly from here to Saint Louis without crossing a single bridge. Did you ever see anything as inefficient as a passenger train—all those thousands of tons just to haul a few people?"

He was devoted to Lock Haven, Clinton County, and Vero Beach. "If you're going to operate in a town," he said, "you've got to contribute to it."

His payroll, sixteen million dollars a year, comprised more than two-fifths of that of Clinton County's industries. He spearheaded a drive to build a new Lock Haven hospital and for years was chairman of its board of governors. To the YMCA he donated a swimming pool in memory of his grandson Dan. He established a foundation to handle his charities, most often unpublicized, and to provide college scholarships for the sons and daughters of his employes in both Pennsylvania and Florida. Running as high as fifteen hundred dollars a year for four years, the scholarships were awarded through college entrance examinations prepared by an independent agency in Princeton, New Jersey.

He was rich in family ties. His sons and two daughters—Mary, Mrs. John S. Bolles of San Francisco, and Elizabeth, Mrs. Thomas Harford of Spring Lake, New Jersey—had given him fifteen grandchildren and five great-grandchildren.

"I've always hoped to lead the Harvard Parade," he said on several occasions. This was an honor reserved to the school's oldest living graduate at commencement. "I guess I'm too young."

On November 19, 1969, Mr. Piper entered the hospital he had helped to build, with a circulatory ailment.

At 9 P.M. of the following January 15, one week after his eighty-ninth birthday, his son Bill returned home from a daily visit to his bedside.

"I don't think Dad's going to make it through the night," he somberly told his wife Pud.

At 10:30 the telephone rang. Bill, Jr., answered. Mr. Piper had died at 10:20. In thirty years of marriage Pud Piper had never seen her husband so shaken. That the entire family had been alerted was no insurance against the shock. Wordlessly, Bill handed the receiver to his wife and walked to a window overlooking the icy West Branch. He stared for minutes before recovering his voice.

Howard Piper was incredulous. His father was indestructible.

They notified Tony, in Texas.

On the third floor of the modernistic Piper administration building, Grace O'Donnell, supervising secretary to all the Pipers, could still hear the echo of the old man's plaint: "They don't give me enough to do!" The first office to the left as one emerged from the executive elevator into the big, soft-lighted reception room had no occupant now. Paneled in walnut, carpeted with a thick green pile, it was curiously free of the self-adulatory, inscribed pictures common on the office walls of captains of industry. The big desk with its barometer-thermometer, calendar, and push-button telephone sat, clear of papers, catty-corner to eight huge windows, four of which looked out on the airport. There was a casual table. Chairs scattered about had held conferees on decisions that shaped the company and now were vacant.

Over all of it a silence had descended. A spirit, robust in its day, was gone. A monarch, in his medium, had departed.

Into Lock Haven four days later flew the movers and shakers of aviation to do homage to the memory of the man who had contributed so much to the third great revolution in U.S. transportation. They greeted each other with those faint smiles that men assume at funerals in recognition of their own mortality.

In the hundred-year-old, brick Trinity United Methodist Church, white painted, on West Main Street, the casket was draped with an American flag as a token of Mr. Piper's military service. Atop it rested a J-3 Cub fashioned in flowers.

"Mr. Piper," said the Reverend J. Carl Williams in tribute, "was a mixture of conservative and dreamer. You are as young as your hope and as old as your despair."

Outside, six Piper airplanes in V echelons of threes droned over the city. The widow had requested it.

The active pallbearers were six men who had accompanied Mr. Piper from Bradford when he moved the factory to Lock Haven in 1937.

In bitter cold the funeral cortege turned from West Main onto North Fairview and thence to Highland Cemetery on the flank of a hill. The cars slipped and skidded and stalled in deep snow on the rutted dirt roads. Their passengers dismounted and, with collars turned up against the wind, tramped to the gravesite. The family plot, containing the remains of the first Mrs. Piper and grandson Dan, was shielded by evergreens. It looked out on the city of Lock Haven and in the distance, on the airport, the factory, and the blue-hued administration building. The minister said a prayer of commitment.

The Vermont granite tombstone read:

Father
W. T. PIPER
1881–1970
Capt. U.S.A. W.W. I

Tony Piper had a more appropriate epitaph:
"My father did all that he wanted to do in his lifetime—except lead the Harvard Parade. I'm sure that if he had everything to do over again, he wouldn't choose to change anything, including his mistakes."

Cable Address

ONCE AGAIN IT WAS SPRING ON THE West Branch of the Susquehanna. Mist, like smoke, curled over the river at dawn. Members of the Lock Haven Boat Club were scouring their craft for the new season. The display windows of Bud's Recreation Center and the Draucher Sport Center on Main Street were loaded with fishing tackle. For several years now it had not been unpleasant to gaze from Lock Haven across the river to the high, steep north bank—the separately incorporated community of Lockport, over there, had removed from the bluff what may have been the only two-story outhouse in all America.

The boisterous West Branch had been tethered. Four earth-fill holding dams upsteam from Lock Haven had been built by the Commonwealth of Pennsylvania and the Army Corps of Engineers to skim off 4.2 feet of floodwater, and that would take care of most of the torrents from the mountain defiles.*

The summer theater in nearby Mill Hall was painting its scenery and props. Greening trees marched in file along the crests of the enfolding hills.

Becky Gross was talking of retiring. She had had her days of newspaper "scoops," and had been commended by the Associated Press Managing Editors Association for her coverage of a multiple murder story when the dateline "Lock Haven" hit page one all over the country. A berserk employe of a paper mill ventilated an even dozen persons, good and true, with shotgun slugs, to be gunned down himself by the police.

A new, posh motel had gone up on the bank of the river behind the ageless Fallon.

Otherwise, little had changed in the hometown of Mr. Piper's

---

* In June 1972 Lock Haven experienced the worst flood in its history as rains from the remnants of a Caribbean-born hurricane swelled the West Branch. Damage to the Piper plant and the loss in ruined aircraft ran to millions of dollars. Water was five feet deep in the administration building—built on stilts to escape the ravages of the river—and rose over the reception desk in the Fallon Hotel downtown.

239

manufacturing complex. The Rotary Club, meeting on Tuesdays in the Fallon dining room, knew in advance what would be on the menu: baked meat loaf or baked ham or fried chicken or roast beef. Mr. Piper had always attended. It was the one day that he ate lunch. He had had a weight problem.

A barkeep in the Fallon saloon, the Duke of Riansares Room, liked to reminisce on the good old days of Prince Farrington, the bootlegger, and Nell Bowes, the brothel proprietor. The hotel's guests sat on the front porch and wondered about the red building across the street housing the William Marshall Crawford post of the American Legion. It was almost eyeless. The windows had been bricked over. A block to the east, patrons of the Locks Restaurant built on the site of old Fort Reed wondered whether the artist who painted the murals in the main dining room had ever painted circus posters. They needn't have. He had.

A green hitching post, a relic of the days of high-stepping bays and tasseled carriages with brass lamps, still stood on West Main Street. A Hudson sales sign still hung on Grove Street, though the last of that brand of automobile had been manufactured in 1957. The cops killed a red fox on West Church Street. Teenagers—complaining like those in Kankakee, Bakersfield, and Austin that there was nothing to do in the lousy town—dropped coins in the jukeboxes at the Texas Restaurant and munched sandwiches. Then they drove out to Highland Cemetery or to Castanea Road near the Hammermill paper plant or to darkish Farrandsville Road, across the river, to park and pursue their romances. Trailer trucks barked their way through the center of town on Route 220 past the Soldiers and Sailors Monument at 2 A.M. to awaken everybody for blocks around. Owners of television sets paid $4.50 a month to have the picture and sound piped in, a service made necessary by Lock Haven's mountain barriers. Pud Piper explained to friends that she bought that fawn-colored rug in the family room of the new house because of her husband's fawn-colored, sixty-pound English bull, Tom. Tom shed.

On East Bald Eagle Street, behind the ivy-grown walls of the onetime silk mill, drop hammers and riveting guns fashioned the newest generations of Piper Aircraft Corporation flying machines. Piper airplanes growled off the Lock Haven airstrip, now renamed the W. T. Piper Memorial Airport.

For a score of years Howard Piper and his brothers had labored, by deft engineering and sophisticated design, to live down the image created by the name of their first airplane.

Yet throughout the world the corporation's cable address remained, "CUB, U.S.A."

Mr. Piper had always rather liked that.

Bibliography

BOOKS

Aircraft Year Book. Philadelphia: Aeronautical Chamber of Commerce, 1928.

Allen, C. B., and Lauren D. Lyman. *Wonder Book of the Air.* Philadelphia: John C. Winston Co., 1936.

Bain, Donald. *The Case against Private Aviation.* New York: Cowles Book Co., 1969.

Cleveland, Reginald M., and Leslie E. Neville. *The Coming Air Age.* New York: McGraw-Hill, Whittlesey House, 1944.

FAA Statistical Handbook of Aviation. Philadelphia: John C. Winston Co., 1970.

Ford, Corey. *Donovan of OSS.* Boston: Little, Brown & Co., 1970.

Griswold, Wesley S. *A Work of Giants.* New York: McGraw-Hill Book Co., 1962.

Johnston, S. Paul. *Horizons Unlimited.* New York: Duell, Sloan & Pearce, 1941.

————. *Wings after War.* New York: Duell, Sloan & Pearce, 1944.

Lundberg, Ferdinand. *The Rich and the Super-Rich.* New York: Lyle Stuart, 1968.

Miller, Isabel Winner. *Old Town.* Annie Halenbake Ross Library, Lock Haven, Pa., 1966.

Munson, Kenneth. *Private Aircraft.* New York: Macmillan Co., 1967.

Piper, W. T., with D. J. Duffin. *Private Flying.* New York: Pitman Publ., 1949.

Politella, Dario. *Operation Grasshopper.* Wichita, Kansas: Robert R. Longo Co., 1958.

Raw, Charles; Bruce Page; and Godfrey Hodgson. *Do You Sincerely Want to Be Rich?* New York: Viking Press, 1971.

Rolfe, Douglas; Alexis Dawydoff; and William Winter. *Airplanes of the World.* New York: Simon & Schuster, 1962.

Shirer, William L. *Rise and Fall of the Third Reich.* New York: Simon & Schuster, 1960.

Statesman's Year Book. London: Macmillan Co., 1942.

Strickland, Patricia. *The Putt-Putt Air Force.* U.S. Dept. of Transportation, Federal Aviation Administration, 1971.

Ten Eyck, Andrew. *Jeeps in the Sky.* New York: Commonwealth Books, 1946.

Wagner, William, in collaboration with Lee Dye. *Ryan the Aviator.* New York: McGraw-Hill Book Co., 1971.

Works Progress Administration. *Picture of Clinton County.* Lock Haven, Pa.: Clinton County Commissioners, 1942.

PERIODICALS

Aero Digest, news items 1928–41; *Air Facts,* Apr. 1965; *Air Force Historian,* July 1963; *American Aviation,* Feb. 3, 1969; *AOPA Pilot,* May 1, 1964; *Army Aviation Digest,* series, June 1962 through Feb. 1963; *Aviation News,* Mar. 13, 1944; *Aviation Week and Space Technology,* Feb. 3, 1969; *Business Week,* Feb. 8, 1969; *Collier's,* June 14, 1941; *Dun's Review,* Sept. 1968; *Field Artillery Journal,* May 1944; *Flight,* Dec. 1969, Jan. 1970; *Flying Aces,* June 1944; *Flying and Popular Aviation,* Nov. 1941; *Fortune,* June 1940, Feb. 1946, Feb. 1969; *Liberty,* Oct. 14, 1944; *Life,* Oct. 29, 1945; *New Yorker,* June 17, 1944; *Park East,* Mar. 1944; *Popular Mechanics,* June 1961; *Popular Science,* Aug. 1952; *Saturday Evening Post,* Apr. 1, 1944; *Time,* Sept. 16, 1943; *Value Line Newsletter,* Jan. 17, 1969.

NEWSPAPERS AND PRESS SERVICES

Army Times, Associated Press, *Baltimore Evening News, Bartlesville* (Okla.) *Enterprise, Beatrice* (Neb.) *Times, Bradford Era, Chicago Daily News, Chicago Times, Columbus* (Ga.) *Enquirer, Harrisburg Telegraph,* Hearst Consolidated Publications, *Indianapolis Times, Lock Haven Express, Louisville Times, Los Angeles Express, Los Angeles News, Los Angeles Times, Memphis Press-Scimitar, Newsday* (L.I.), *New York Mirror, New York Times, New York World-Telegram, Norfolk Ledger-Dispatch, Omaha World-Herald, Palm Beach Times, PM* (N.Y.), *Rochester* (N.Y.) *Democrat and Chronicle, Sedalia* (Mo.) *Capital, Stars and Stripes, Toronto Daily News, Tulsa World,* United Press, *Vero Beach Press, Wall Street Journal, Washington Star, White Plains Reporter-Dispatch, Yank.*

Acknowledgments

THE CHIEF CONTRIBUTOR TO THE research for this story was, appropriately, its chief character, the late William T. Piper, Sr. Intermittently for weeks he tape-recorded his reminiscences. He was by turns bemused by recollections of incidents in his career, generous in judgments of his adversaries—he had little time for animosities—and brimming with belief in the innate goodness of the human heart. In conversation he was a merchant of basic moral values—honesty and integrity. He indulged in no self-praise and no self-pity. Discussion of his private life was off limits.

His sons supplied countless facets of his personality. William T. Piper, Jr., was the moving spirit behind the book. He wanted it to be a monument to his father, and the research on it was begun eighteen months before Mr. Piper's death. No prohibitions were placed on the author by him or by his brothers, Thomas F. and Howard. Less can be said of their willingness to talk about themselves. Material on the men who came from the loins of the family patriarch had to be elicited from other sources. Thomas F. Piper was the second most important source of information on his father and the company he founded. It was he who unearthed the Cub's enshrinement in the U.S. Army archives and information on its entry into combat in World War II.

Walter C. Jamouneau was an especially rich source of company history, and, like Jacob W. Miller, a master of the anecdote. Both instantly grasped the nature of the material the author was seeking. Others in the immediate or past corporate family who played archeologist in musty files included William D. Strohmeier, Charles W. Pool, and Findley Estlick.

Special votes of appreciation are due others for their collaboration in the assembly of material:

The late John E. P. Morgan, who supplied all the narrative on the battle to gain acceptance of the lightplane by the military.

Gordon M. Curtis, the chief source of information on the financial aspects of the Piper operation for the first seventeen years of the company's existence.

Jean Ross Howard, who produced long-lost copies of valuable correspondence in the 1940–42 period.

Rebecca Gross, who supplied the background on the community of Lock Haven and opened to the author the dusty files of the *Lock Haven Express*.

And Mrs. Harold H. Strickland, who supplied typewritten copies of her manuscript, *The Putt-Putt Air Force* (the story of the Civilian Pilot Training program and the War Training Service), a full year before her own book appeared in print.

The author also wishes to express his appreciation to the following persons listed alphabetically but not necessarily in the order of importance of their research and/or other contributions: Alfred B. Bennett, Madelyn Blesh, Wilfred M. Boucher, Carlton Bucher, Thomas J. Dolan, Norman D. Dunn, Devon Alan Francis, Carl Friedlander, John H. Glenn, Jr., Arthur Godfrey, Rensselaer Havens, the late Beverly Howard, Max Karant, William K. Kershner, Kenneth T. Kress, Robert A. Lovett, Ralph McClarren, Martin Mann, Mrs. David L. McKee, Lee B. Morey, Mike Murphy, John W. Oswalt, Mrs. William T. Piper, Jr., George D. Rodgers, Robert E. Rogge, David Scott, Michael J. Strok, William Van Dusen, William Wagner, Fred E. Weick, and Theodore V. Weld.

These organizations generously supplied additional material: U.S. Army Aviation Center, plus its Aviation School, Military History Branch, and Personnel Record Center; Army Corps of Engineers; Bureau of the Census; Bangor Punta Corporation; Purdue University; National Aeronautics and Space Administration; Aerospace Industries Association; General Aviation Manufacturers Association; National Business Aircraft Association; National Air Transportation Conferences; Aircraft Owners and Pilots Association; Interstate Commerce Commission; Department of Commerce; Smithsonian Institution; Post Office Department; Civil Aeronautics Board; Federal Aviation Administration; National Transportation Safety Board; Friedlich, Fearon and Strohmeier; Harvard University Archives; Rockefeller Family Archives; Beech Aircraft Corporation; and Cessna Aircraft Company.

Index

247

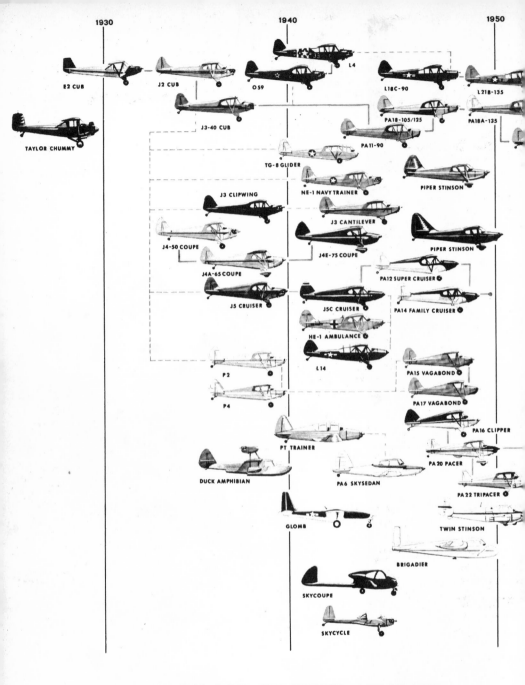

GENEALOGY OF PIPER AIRCRAFT

THE AIRCRAFT SHOWN REPRESENT THE COMPLETE LINE
OF AIRPLANES BUILT BY PIPER AIRCRAFT CORPORATION
AND THE PREDECESSOR COMPANY, TAYLOR BROTHER
AIRCRAFT CORPORATION. INCLUDED ARE EXPERIMENTAL
PRODUCTION AIRCRAFT.

PRODUCTION ———————   ROOT LINE - - - -